PLUTARCH
AND HIS TIMES

AMS PRESS
NEW YORK

PLUTARCH
and his times

By

R. H. BARROW

1967

INDIANA UNIVERSITY PRESS

BLOOMINGTON & LONDON

Library of Congress Cataloging in Publication Data

Barrow, Reginald Haynes, 1893-
    Plutarch and his times.

    Reprint of the 1967 ed. published by Indiana
University Press, Bloomington.
    Includes bibliogarphical references and index.
    1. Plutarchus—Biography. 2. Plutarchus—
Contemporary Rome. 3. Rome—Civilization.
I. Title.
[PA4382.B3   1979]   938'.007'2024 [B]   76-6599 √
ISBN 0-404-15276-7

Contents

CONTENTS

Preface

LITTLE has been written about Plutarch in England; on the Continent he has fared better. This book is an attempt to provide something in English till the big work appears which undoubtedly ought to be written. References have been kept to a minimum and none is made to the older books and articles, chiefly in German, now accessible only in large libraries. But enough references have been given, it is hoped, to enable a reader to carry study of Plutarch a stage further, if he wishes.

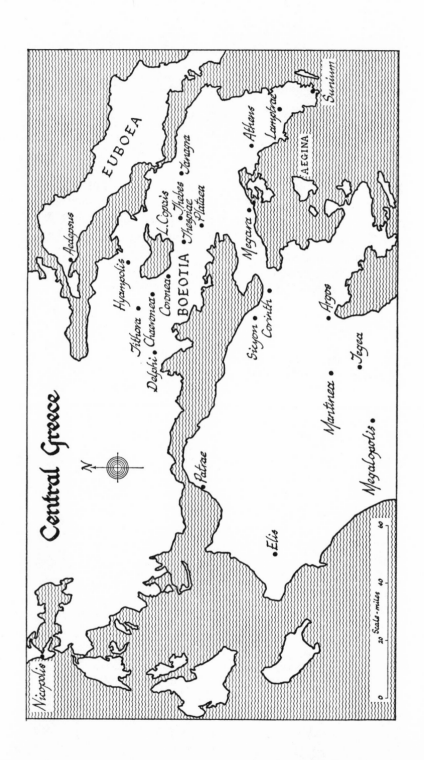

Central Greece

N

Scale·miles
0   20   40   60

Nicopolis

EUBOEA

Aedapsus

Hyampolis
Tithora
Delphi   Chaeronea
Coronea   L.Copais
BOEOTIA   Thebes   Tanagra
Thespiae
Plataea

Athens
Lampptrae
Sunium

AEGINA

Megara

Sicyon
Corinth

Argos

Tegea

Mantinea

Elis

Megalopolis

Patrae

Plutarch's Family

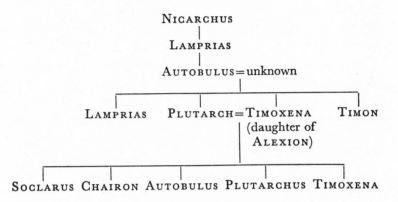

NICARCHUS
|
LAMPRIAS
|
AUTOBULUS = unknown
|
LAMPRIAS   PLUTARCH = TIMOXENA   TIMON
(daughter of
ALEXION)
|
SOCLARUS   CHAIRON   AUTOBULUS   PLUTARCHUS   TIMOXENA

Sextus of Chaeronea, Stoic philosopher and tutor of Marcus Aurelius, was the son of one of Plutarch's brothers (see S. H. A. *Marc. Ant.* 3. 2, Apul. *Met.* 1. 2. and Suidas Σέξτος, ἀδελφιδοῦς. The passage of Apuleius does not mean that Apuleius was descended from Plutarch, merely that Plutarch was well known).

Some Dates

Plutarch b. *c.* 47
        d. after 120
Seneca *c.* 5 B.C.–A.D. 65
Pliny 60–112
Tacitus 55–120
Quintilian 35–95
Suetonius 69–140
    (*Vitae c.* 121)
Aulus Gellius fl. 140
Apuleius fl. 155
Aristides d. 189
Dio Chrysostom b. *c.* 40
        d. after 112

Emperors Claudius 41–54
Nero 54–68
Galba ⎫
Otho ⎬ 68–69
Vitellius ⎭
Vespasian 69–79
Nerva 96–98
Trajan 98–117
Hadrian 117–138
Antonius Pius 138–161
Marcus Aurelius 161–180

Date of birth. The only evidence is in *de E*
  a. Ch. 1, 'when Nero was in Greece', probably A.D. 67,
  b. Ch. 7, Plutarch was at the Academy studying mathematics.
  c. Ch. 17, Plutarch was 'a young man'.
If the age of twenty is taken to satisfy *b.* and *c.*, Plutarch was born in A.D. 47.

Date of death. *a.* The inscription to Hadrian at Delphi (p. 12) is probably to be dated early in the Emperor's reign, *c.* A.D. 120. *b.* The notice in Eusebius (p. 49) refers to A.D. 119. There is no other real evidence, hence 'after A.D. 120' is all that can be said.

Foreword

THE works of Plutarch fall into two main divisions, the *Parallel Lives* and the *Moralia*; in size they stand in the relation of about six to seven. About three-quarters of the whole is devoted to the Lives of Greeks and to philosophy approached from the Greek point of view; the rest is concerned with Lives of Romans and enquiries into Roman matters. The specifically Roman works are, besides the Roman Lives, *On the fortune of the Romans* and *Roman Questions*. If the works listed in the so-called Lamprias catalogue* were extant, we should have a complete series of the Lives of the Emperors from Augustus to Vitellius and also a Life of Scipio. But there would also be much more to put under the head of *Moralia*, and the proportion of Roman writings would be reduced.

The *Moralia* is a loose title used to embrace the sixty or so writings, other than the *Lives*, which are extant. And the title needs to be loose, for the works are extremely varied. Very roughly, they fall into categories, but a work may easily be classified under a different heading by a different reader, and the same book may contain matter of varied nature. If some categories are suggested here and some of the works are given as instances, it must be understood that the classification is tentative and the instances cited are few. Under 'Religion' might be put *On superstition*, *On Isis and Osiris*, *On the Genius of Socrates*, and the three Pythian Dialogues and the treatise *About those whom the Gods delay in punishing*; under 'Philosophy' in the strict sense *Platonic Questions*, *Against Colotes* in which Epicurean and Stoic doctrines are attacked, *On Stoic Contradictions*. On ethical themes, which include also matters concerned with education, we have *How the young should listen to poetry*, *How to distinguish between the flatterer and the friend*, treatises *On Tranquillity* and *On freedom from Anger*, *On being over-busy*, *Precepts for the married*, *On exile*, *On*

* See Appendix A.

xiii

progress in virtue. Writings on political subjects are not many; the chief are *Political Precepts* and *Should an old man engage in politics?* Psychology is directly or indirectly treated in most of the works, but we have fragments of a treatise *On the soul.* The best known scientific work is *On the face appearing on the circle of the Moon,* though it includes much besides; but we have also the *Natural Questions,* and some treatises on animals, notably *On the question whether brute animals possess reason.* The *Moralia* as a whole are so full of quotations, which are often discussed, that literary criticism runs through them all; but special treatments of two themes are presented in *On Herodotus' spite* and *A comparison of Aristophanes and Menander.* There are essays, written probably in Plutarch's youth, which may have been written as contributions to an academic debate, *On the Fortune of the Romans* and *On Alexander's Fortune.* Of antiquarian interest are the *Roman Questions* and the *Greek Questions.* The *Table Talks,* of course, defy classification.

The chronology of the works is notoriously difficult; few bear any indication of date. Occasionally one writing can be placed in relation to another. Speaking generally, it may be said that certainly the *Lives,* and much of the *Moralia,* fall into the latter period of Plutarch's life: thus, since he was born about A.D. 47 and died soon after A.D. 120, they were written in the reign of Trajan. On the other hand there are some which seem to have been written when he was a young man; some bear signs of being unfinished and may have been published by his family.

Plutarch wrote in Greek; he appears therefore in histories of Greek literature or of Greek philosophy and religion. He is treated as one of the late witnesses to the vitality of Greek letters, as a lover of all things Greek, as a Hellene born out of due time. By the historian of Greece and Rome he is treated as a secondary 'source', preserving some useful information but essentially a compiler with little historical sense of his own. But in fact he was born into the Roman Empire and lived through the last half of the first century A.D. and part of the second. He was a Roman citizen, living in a Roman province, travelling in Roman provinces, spending periods of time in the Rome of the Emperors, and counting among his numerous friends many Romans, some of distinction. He may have loved his native Boeotia with an ardent patriotism; he may have been heir to Greek learning and thought; but the world in which he lived was now Greco-Roman, and he could not fail to be influenced by ideas which were Roman. He is imperfectly understood if he is not seen in the environment of the Roman Empire. And equally the Empire is not understood unless it is seen to be such as to enable a Plutarch to be such as he was.

The time has gone when it was thought right to describe the early Empire as a night of wickedness in order that the light of the Gospel might appear to shine more brightly, or when the times were reconstructed largely from a reading of Tacitus and Suetonius and Juvenal. Popular imagination may still follow the spotlight turned on the capital city by film and novel, and think the worst. Perhaps it too will change. For the whole field has been surveyed again; the old familiar writers, Latin and Greek, have been re-assessed, and less familiar writers have been read with care and their significance has been better understood. It is now clear that there probably has not been any age in which interest in religion and philosophy and science, psychology and ethics, theoretical and practical, was so widespread and so earnest. Every aspect of religious experience was explored; the emotions were analysed; science and pseudo-science were eagerly pursued; natural history and exploration exercised their fascination; the springs of conduct were examined and ideals were formulated. Popular teachers were never so active or so ardently sought. There was a great spiritual upsurge, and aspiration expressed itself in much moral endeavour and practical goodness. Of all this there is evidence abundant and convincing, and Plutarch himself is a part of that evidence.

CHAPTER 1

The Greek Mainland

'I AM not going to say anything about this Greece of to-day which for a long time now has been brought to abject ruin by its own policies.' We could wish that Cicero had described in detail the Greece of his day, for he would thus have filled a serious gap in our knowledge.

He goes on to say that the Greece which had such a glorious past, with its wealth, its empire, its prestige, collapsed through one single malady–its uncontrollable freedom and the licence of its assemblies. 'Whenever those ignorant men met in the theatre –inexperienced and untrained in every respect–and sat down there, they committed themselves to useless wars, they put trouble-makers in charge of their state and turned out of the city anyone who had served it well.'[1]

No doubt that was the Roman view of the political life of Greece, and, as far as it goes, it is not unfair. In one respect the statement does not apply to Greece after the Roman occupation in 146 B.C., for the city-states lost their power to wage those petty wars which divided and weakened the country, and which make up a large part of its history. Whatever disservices Rome may have done to Greece, at any rate this was a great service, as Plutarch himself saw.

Cicero's judgment is expressed in political terms; nowadays we are as much concerned with a country's economic life. And since, as will be seen, there is so little politics of any moment in Greece during the age of Plutarch, the economic conditions become of even greater interest. But no ancient writer ever wrote an economic history; for this age, as for all ancient history, scanty references have to be pieced together to give some general outline of conditions of work and trade, industry and wealth, and that outline is often only tentative.

First we may look at Greece from the Roman administrative point of view.

In 27 B.C., the year in which Augustus reorganised the provinces of the Empire, Achaea meant the whole of Greece, part of Epirus, the Ionian Islands, the Cyclades and a few more islands. From the date of the Roman occupation in 146 B.C. till 27 B.C. Achaea had been part of the province of Macedonia; it now became a separate province, and was assigned by Augustus to the Senate. It was governed by a propraetor, but he was given the title of proconsul: to put it another way, he was a proconsul who had achieved praetorian rank in the ladder of promotion. He had a *legatus* who was subordinate to him. Since it was a 'senatorial' province, as opposed to a province administered by a governor nominated by the Emperor, its governor had no troops under his command, and no army was stationed within its boundaries. In A.D. 15 Tiberius made it an imperial province under the jurisdiction of the *legatus* of the northern province of Moesia. So it remained till A.D. 44 when Claudius, as part of his show of respect for the Senate, restored the Augustan arrangement.

The next change was made by Nero. At the end of his progress through Greece, on 28 November A.D. 67, Nero himself came to the front of the stage of the theatre at Corinth and made the only speech of his of which we have record. He announced that he was going to give Hellas an unexpected gift, '. . . save that there is nothing that cannot be expected from my generosity. . . . All you Greeks who now live in Achaea and the land till now called the Peloponnese, receive your freedom together with exemption from tribute, freedom which not even in your most prosperous days did you all enjoy; for you were slaves either to foreigners or to yourselves. . . .' The stone on which the speech was recorded was found built into the wall of a church at the village of Acraephiae in Boeotia, on the east of Lake Copais; Plutarch's native town, Chaeronea, was on the west. The speech is followed by a decree about as long, passed by the Magistrates and Councillors and People.

Forasmuch as the Lord of the whole world Nero, mighty Emperor
... the new Sun which has shed its light on the Greeks ... the one
and only liberator of the Greeks from the beginning of time ... has
restored us to our ancient possession of autonomy and freedom, adding to his great and unexpected gift also exemption from tribute, now
therefore it is resolved ... that statues should be set up to Zeus our
liberator, Nero, and the Goddess Augusta (Messalina).[2]

No doubt other Greek states expressed their thanks in similar
decrees, which, if they survived, would demonstrate, as this
decree does, that local pride could still be stirred.

The Roman government was generous of the gift of freedom
to individual cities, as we shall see later. To make a whole province independent was unexampled. From the point of view of
defence a free Greece would not matter much; the loss of taxes
was more serious; above all it was an ill-advised step because it
was a bad precedent and success was impossible. Cicero could
have told Nero what would happen. The states fell to quarrel-
ling among themselves, and party-strife broke out again. And so
Vespasian, remarking that Greece had forgotten what liberty
meant, promptly revoked Nero's 'generous gift', and the province of Achaea reverted to its senatorial status in A.D. 74.

Greece never forgot Nero. Nor did Plutarch. At the end of
one of the dialogues he tells a 'myth', a story told in the Platonic
manner, describing the world to come and giving details about
reincarnation. The souls in Hades are being battered into new
shapes of animals suitable for the lives they had led. Nero amid
much torment, including red hot nails, was being turned into
a viper which lives in the womb of its mother and feeds on her.
'Suddenly a great light shone out, and a voice came from the
light commanding that he should be turned into some gentler
animal, an animal which sings round swamps and meres; for he
had been punished enough for his sins, and the gods owed him
some return because, of all his subjects, he had given liberty to
that best and most god-loving of all nations, Greece.' So Nero's
gift to the Greeks, together with the voice which won him
prizes at Greek festivals, secured for him a remission of sentence
– to croak as a frog in the marshes.[3]

If Greece was not to be free, the Romans had always been generous in granting the status of 'free' city to individual townships. Some forty cities enjoyed 'freedom', some famous, some obscure. A 'free' city was not subject to Roman officials, and very often was exempt from taxes paid to the Roman government. In its internal affairs it was independent, though on occasion a neighbouring Roman governor was bound to interfere in the interests of order. The finance of these 'free' cities often fell into confusion; thus Trajan was compelled to send financial administrators (*correctores*) to Athens and to Sparta to put matters right.

All the land was assigned to cities, though of course individuals owned most of it; there were no imperial estates (like crown lands), though some quarries were under Roman control. At first regional leagues and associations of cities were frowned upon; but they were soon tolerated, and indeed a revised version of the old Achaean League came into being and included most of Greece; it had no political power, but it kept a record office, organised the cult of the Emperor and gave a sense of self-importance. Hadrian went further and created a vast synhedrion or gathering of all Greeks, including Greeks in any part of the world. All townships and villages enjoyed their own constitutions; assemblies and officials still bore the local names handed down from earlier centuries; Rome imposed no common type of local government. Any one familiar with early institutions of Sparta – the *phylae, obae, Apella, gerousia*, ephors, the system of education of boys – will find them still operating in the age of Plutarch. The Emperors sometimes paid cities the compliment of holding their offices; for example, Titus and Hadrian were archons at Delphi.

A few new towns were established. To celebrate the victory at Actium A.D. 31 Augustus founded Nicopolis there; he gathered together the inhabitants of the surrounding countryside, gave the new town the status of a 'colony', and made it into a thriving centre of industry; for two generations it was probably the most prosperous town in Greece, with Corinth and Patrae as rivals. Patrae too was given a new foundation; soldiers from the tenth and twelfth legions were settled there to form a colony, and as an industrial town and a port this ancient city became important, as it still is to-day. The rebuilding of Corinth, begun by Julius Caesar in 44 B.C., was continued by Augustus; it too became a colony and the centre of the administration of Achaea. Its restoration would have surprised Servius Sulpicius who in 45 B.C., only the year before the rebuilding, wrote to Cicero that in his voyage from Asia he had skirted Greece–'As I sailed across from Aegina to Megara, I began to look at the places roundabout; behind me was Aegina, before me Megara, on the right Piraeus, on the left Corinth: they were once flourishing towns, now they lie in ruins, flattened.'[4]

Greece has always been a poor land–the poorest, probably, of all the Mediterranean lands. In the centuries before the Roman occupation she had never kept herself alive from her own resources: she could not produce enough grain. Hence she depended on her export of oil, wine and manufactured articles. The seasons were not always kind to her, and so her produce was very variable. Her inhabitants did their best by their wars to make things no easier. An olive-tree does not come into full bearing for many years: when one state raided the territory of another and cut down its olive groves, there resulted a capital loss which was felt for a long time. Many districts grew enough vines to supply their own needs; others managed to produce a surplus of wine for export, though they had to compete with some of the Greek islands which were famous for their vintages. Greek craftsmen were pre-eminent; the wares they produced spread all over the Mediterranean and beyond. Silver mines and quarries increased the revenues of certain favoured places or individuals. Temples and public buildings might rise in their magnificence in the richest cities, but housing lagged far behind, and the standard of living was not high.

This precarious economy deteriorated in the centuries immediately preceding and following the birth of Christ. The population decreased; many cities languished and finally were left empty; areas of the countryside became desolate and the ports handled only a fraction of their earlier trade. There is

5

plenty of evidence; it cannot be discussed here, but later a little must be said about the nature of certain accounts which profess to describe the condition of the Greek mainland in the first and second centuries of our era. In the meantime what was the reason for the progressive depopulation?

It is easy to point to the havoc brought about by the wars waged in Greece by the Romans without going back to wars waged by the Macedonians and the Greeks themselves. The plunder carried off by Mummius in 146 B.C. is notorious, and for years afterwards works of art were carried off by individuals to supply the insatiable demands of Italy. The civil wars were fought to great extent in Greece; it was not merely the scenes of battle that were laid waste; towns and villages had to support the rival armies as they gathered or reorganised or lay inactive during the winter. Plutarch's *Lives* provide some of the evidence for the hardships which Greece suffered; but one episode was handed down by his family.

My great grandfather [says Plutarch] used to tell us that all the citizens were forced to carry on their shoulders to the sea-coast at Anticyra a specified measure of grain; they were hurried along by the lash of the whip. Only once did they carry these burdens; a second time when the grain was measured and they were about to lift it, the news came of Antony's defeat and saved the city. Immediately Antony's agents and soldiers fled and the citizens distributed the grain among themselves.[5]

But in fact the plight of Greece began long before the Roman occupation and indeed was taken over by them with the country. It began with the Empire of Alexander. This is a theme which cannot be developed here. It must be enough to put the matter shortly thus. Alexander took as his ideal the fusion of Greek and Asiatic cultures into one magnificent civilisation combining the assets of both. The measures which he took to this end are well enough known. All over the Eastern Mediterranean towns prospered as never before; seventy new cities are said to have been founded by him. Everything Greek was in urgent demand—craftsmen and artists, teachers of everything, doctors, philosophers, all who could contribute to the establishment of a new

6

civilisation. A tremendous 'dispersion' of Greeks took place, who forsook a stagnant Greece for new opportunities in places pulsing with life and new aspirations. And, of course, traders went too. But trade was no longer what it was; new patterns of commerce traced themselves. As new sources of supply were tapped and crafts and industry established themselves in new places, the trade-routes altered. The mainland of Greece found itself outside the main currents of commerce, and the produce and goods on which it had depended in the past were supplied from other quarters.

Virtually the same processes continued in the centuries that followed. The growth of Rome, whose policy it was to develop cities, her increasing admiration of Greek learning and literature and art, her need of skilled craftsmen, architects, doctors, bankers, accountants, musicians, entertainers–all these influences tended to draw to the west Greeks from the Eastern Mediterranean; some came from the mainland of Greece, many from the Greco-Oriental cities of Asia Minor, Syria and Egypt. Meantime it was part of the Roman achievement to develop the western provinces; industries throve in Gaul and Spain and Africa. The natural resources of these countries were developed and their communications improved. And so the patterns of trade were again altered. Commerce flourished between East and West; the products of one province were available to the rest. But Greece, in the midst of a prosperous world, had little to offer and so could receive little. The stream of inter-provincial trade flowed past her; in comparison with the rest of the Empire she was in a backwater where she had little to do but to contemplate her past. Her art and her literature were held in due veneration by Emperors, notably Claudius, Nero, Trajan and Hadrian and became a necessary part of higher education. The one thing Greek for which the Roman world had nothing but disdain was contemporary Greek character; to the Roman mind it was irresponsible, unscrupulous, unreliable and selfish.

Towards the end of the first century of our era there was the beginning of a mild revival in Greece. Earlier Emperors had taken some steps to help her economy, but Trajan and Hadrian

7

did most for her. Unfortunately the measures which they took could do no more than provide palliatives; in a highly competitive world the land of Greece could not compete with success.

But life went on, and not much more can be said. Athens now had little commerce; she sold marble and oil; she manufactured statues, almost on mass production lines, for export. She had her institutions for the teaching of literature and philosophy, and she had her antiquities; students and the tourist trade became very important to her. Arcadia seems to have been tolerably prosperous, for the towns of Megalopolis, Mantinea, Tegea, all famous names in Greek history, are shown by inscriptions to have had a fairly active life. Boeotia, of course, was still unhealthy. We hear of a rich Boeotian, Epaminondas, who earned the regard of his neighbours by his benefactions. He organised festivals and gave prizes to artists competing in them; he went on an embassy to Rome to congratulate Caligula on his accession. For this kind of service he received fulsome praise, recorded in an inscription. His most valuable service receives little recognition, his reopening of drains to lower the level of Lake Copais.[6] It was reserved for Hadrian to undertake more extensive work of reclamation. Thebes seems to have been in decay, while Tanagra and Thespiae held their own. The new foundations of Nicopolis and Patrae achieved success as ports, and in particular Nicopolis built up a thriving industry in textiles.

The inscriptions make it clear that even in the mainland of Greece there were rich men: for in little country towns we read of benefactions which required considerable sums of money. There were few who could show the wealth of Opromoas, of Rhodiapolis, who spent untold sums on the cities of Lycia. But Athens had Herodes Atticus, and Sparta her Eurycles. Herodes was born about twenty years before Plutarch died, so that his benefactions, which extended far beyond Attica, fall rather later than the period with which we are concerned. But it was his grandfather who laid the foundations of the great family fortune, and we have no idea of the means by which it was amassed. Elsewhere in the Empire in Plutarch's time a man who wanted to become very rich quickly went in for commerce and transport, chiefly maritime; as he made surplus money he started an industry in a favourable situation, or he lent at high interest or he bought land, again with a shrewd eye for site and area. In Greece, however, the opportunities for such enterprise and investment existed only here and there and on a small scale. In default of evidence we can only assume that men like Plutarch, of independent means yet of means large enough for them to travel, to entertain and undertake public services, derived their income from their lands. Yet he makes no mention of land, crops and produce, labour or tenants, income or expenditure. He takes all for granted, and leaves us in ignorance.

This brief sketch of the economy of Greece must finish with a word of warning. The easiest way to give a picture of Greece would be to copy out the statements of Strabo, Dio Chrysostom and Pausanias, together with a few sentences from Plutarch himself. But it would be a picture inconsistent with the assessment which can be gathered from inscriptions and from incidental evidence in the literature. Strabo, of Amasia in Pontus, c. 64 B.C.–A.D. 21, knew very little about Greece at first hand; he went to Corinth, Argos, Athens, Megara; he saw Argos, but did not know that the remains of Mycenae existed. He probably visited these places en route for Rome. There is no evidence that he went to Arcadia; yet he describes this region as having no inhabitants, though inscriptions show that the towns there still flourished. Dio Chrysostom, of Prusa in Bithynia, roughly contemporary with Plutarch, draws a sorry picture of Euboea in the treatise *Euboicos*. But most of it reads like romance, and we know that it was partly propaganda; for Dio was a close friend of Trajan and he preached, apart from sermons to him about kingship, the need to bring back the small landowner if it was wished to restore economic health–a policy which was not new to the Romans and was pursued especially by the Antonines. Pausanias, of Lydia, fl. c. A.D. 150, had travelled extensively in Greece; he describes in much valuable detail the antiquities, with much mythological and historical commentary. Occasionally he makes observations about physical features, and notes points about trade and produce. For instance, it is he who tells

9

us that at Patrae there were twice as many women as men, and accounts for this unusual proportion by noting that the women worked in textile factories, making up into hats and cloth the *byssus* of Elis, a kind of flax.

These men were Greeks from Asia Minor. It is true of Dio, and it may be true of the others, that he took pleasure in exalting the wealth and prosperity of the Asiatic cities, though he had a poor opinion of the ways in which they used their wealth; he likes therefore to write down the condition of the mainland and many of his disparaging judgments are to be taken with considerable reservations. Moreover, for the first time they were seeing the Greece from which so much of their own Greco-Roman civilisation had sprung; they had been nurtured on its literature and art. They came; the monuments and temples and antiquities, with their richness of legend and association, did not disappoint them, certainly not Pausanias; but they may well have expected to see towns as prosperous and as bustling with citizens and traders as their own, to see a countryside as fertile and as rich. Instead, they found a life which was placid and unenterprising, without sign of what we now call expansion or productivity, a life turned inwards upon itself and its past. The contrast between expectation and reality may well have been too much for them; they may well have described the emptiness of Greece in terms which were exaggerated.

In one point, however, they could not have exaggerated, consciously or unconsciously – the complete sterility of literature. There were plenty of learned, and well-educated, men in the Greek mainland; we shall meet many of them. For three centuries before the age of Plutarch Greece produced in no field of literature any notable work which has survived, and, what is more, we do not hear that any such work was written. Plutarch himself is the sole exception. Outside Greece in all quarters of the world books in every field of literature were written in Greek, some of which are extant; the names of Diodorus Siculus, Dionysius of Halicarnassus, Strabo, Philo, Josephus, Dio, Aristides, Pausanias are familiar enough. Besides such writers we know also the names of scores of learned men who are stated by later writers to have written during these years, though we know extremely little about them; to find any from the mainland is not easy. Exception cannot be made for Epictetus, the lecturer on religion and ethics at Nicopolis at the turn of the first century A.D.; for the *Discourses*, which we have, were compiled by Arrian who was his pupil; he came to Rome from Bithynia and was later governor of Cappadocia. But it can be made for some letters, the letters of St. Paul to the Romans and to the Thessalonians, written in Corinth.[7]

CHAPTER 2

Plutarch at Home

SOMETIME about A.D. 126 the Emperor Hadrian visited Delphi to meet the Amphictyonic Council, an assembly which after a history of several hundred years was now gathered together chiefly to venerate its own past. Perhaps some six years earlier, soon after Hadrian's accession, a statue was dedicated by the Council to the Emperor, and on its base a Greek inscription recorded that Mestrius Plutarchus was the priest who officiated at the time.[1]

Mestrius is an Italian name, found most commonly in inscriptions in Northern Italy round the town of Brixia, about forty-five miles east of Milan. How did it come about that a man who belonged to a family long established at Chaeronea in Central Greece, about twenty miles east of Delphi, acquired an Italian 'family' name and handed it on to his heirs, as other inscriptions show?[2]

It is a reasonable inference that he gained this name, and with it Roman citizenship, because he was recommended to the Emperor Trajan as a man deserving honour by his close friend L. Mestrius Florus. Of Florus more hereafter; at the moment it is important to draw attention to two points. The friendship of a leading and influential Greek with a Roman who combined official position with an interest in learning and philosophy, a friendship which induced one of the proudest Greeks of his time to accept Roman citizenship and his Roman friend's gentile name, is slight but significant evidence of the ties which united distant parts of the Empire and drew together traditions of widely different character. None the less it is equally significant that the sole evidence of Plutarch's Roman citizenship is the inscription set up at Delphi; it marks a public and a Roman occasion when the Roman name would be in place. Plutarch himself does not record in his writings either his Roman name or his citizenship. He admires Rome in all sincerity, as his works on Roman history and antiquities show; but he is above all a Greek, proud of the achievements of the Greek intellect, and it is as a Greek that he wishes to write and as a Greek that he wishes to be known – Plutarch, the son of Autobulus of Chaeronea, for many years[3] priest at Delphi, sometime archon eponymus and telearch of Chaeronea, a small city to which he gave his devotion 'that it might not become smaller'.

If Chaeronea was a small place, it enjoyed fame as the scene of three significant battles, for it lay in a plain in which troops could manoeuvre. In the first battle, 447 B.C., Athens lost all hope of supremacy over Thebes and Boeotia and her land empire thus failed; in 338 B.C. Philip of Macedon defeated the Athenians and Thebans and the independence of the Greek city-states perished. None the less to honour the bravery of the Thebans who fell in the battle a monument was dedicated, a gigantic lion in bronze. In the third battle Sulla defeated the generals of Mithridates and Greece was claimed by Rome. Chaeronea had also its legends; under the name of Arne it was thought to have contributed to the 'assembly of ships' bound for Troy; the sceptre of Agamemnon, made by Hephaestus, was preserved and venerated there, and other legends are recorded by Pausanias.

But for the present purpose the legends and battles are of less importance than the dinner-parties held at Plutarch's father's house and at Plutarch's own house. For these parties were the occasion, and in part the excuse, for discussions and conversations and debates on a wide variety of topics, and Plutarch made notes of what was said and later wrote them up in nine books of *Table Talks*. It is very largely from them that we gain a knowledge of his family and friends and their interests and can form an impression of the rich intellectual life, the kindliness and good humour of his circle.

About half of the *Table Talks* took place in Chaeronea, others in the house of friends when Plutarch attended the Isthmian games at Corinth, the Pythian at Delphi, the Olympian at Elis.

One occurred at the baths at Aedepsus, another at Patrae with Sosius Senecio as host, and another at Rome with Sulla as host. The preface to the first of the nine books explains that Sosius Senecio had suggested to Plutarch that he should gather together the essential parts of conversations 'at table' and 'over the wine'; this he has now done following the example of Plato and Xenophon and Aristotle and others; to bury in oblivion such conversations is to defeat the object of fellowship, which is to make friendships. And so he sends to Sosius a first instalment of three books and he will soon send the rest if these are not thought 'unworthy of the Muses'. And in the preface to the second book Plutarch explains that his readers must not expect any special order in the conversations; they are written just as he remembered them and therefore they are written 'at random'.

From the *Table Talks* and other writings of Plutarch we learn over a hundred names of his relations, friends and acquaintances, men and women. Some of these people are sketched for us in considerable detail; their characters and attainments and interests can be gathered; others are less clear. Most of them naturally bear Greek names, but sixteen have Roman names, and some of these play a very prominent part in the dialogues. Many of the Greeks we know from other sources than Plutarch, but of many too we know nothing. Of the sixteen Romans all but five are known to us. There is no reason to doubt that all the names, Greek and Roman, stand for real people. They are not literary creations, lay figures of Plutarch's art; for his works were published as they were written; his friends would expect a reasonably accurate portrait of themselves and they certainly would not wish to be put into invented dialogues and be made to converse with figments. In short, though the exact words of the conversations cannot be guaranteed, we should assume that the characters and the substance of what they say are true to life.

It is partly because the dialogues are records for friends that they suffer from a most annoying defect, from our point of view; at many points where we would welcome definiteness they are vague. But this vagueness may be thought to confirm their essential truth; for friends reading them would be expected to know the background and to take much for granted. As for Plutarch himself, he was a tantalisingly modest man and he effaces everything personal from his narrative or refers to his activities in the most general and casual way.

For example, we know on Plutarch's statement that his father was a little slow in expressing himself, though, when the meaning of a certain adjective applied to horses was under review, he leapt in readily with an opinion, for 'he always kept the best horses'. In another passage he gives way to Plutarch as a better philosopher, but maintains eloquently, with allusions to Homer and Aemilius Paulus, his own view about the proper arrangements to be made for guests at dinner. Again, he raises a problem about wine for discussion by 'the young men who were philosophising with us', but himself offered no solution. In book three he shows himself a critic of pseudo-Aristotle on another matter relating to wine and adds to a somewhat idle discussion a facetious mythological supplement. A pleasant touch is given elsewhere in an anecdote;

I remember [says Plutarch] that when I was sent as a young man to the proconsul my colleague had to wait behind me on the journey for some reason and I had to carry through the business alone. On my return I was on the point of giving an account of my mission when my father got up from his seat and privately bade me say, not 'I went', but 'we went', not 'I said', but 'we said' and so to associate my colleague with me in my report. Behaviour of this kind [adds Plutarch] is not only courteous and polite but also leaves one's reputation immune from jealous criticism.[4]

But, though we are given this much information about Plutarch's father, we are never told his name. It is a reasonable, but not certain, inference from a passage in another treatise that it was Autobulus.[5] And of course Plutarch does not tell what business took him to Corinth or in what capacity he went.

The family seems to have been long established in Chaeronea, though it was not one of those which could trace their origins back to mythical times. His great grandfather Nicarchus remembered the battle of Actium. His grandfather Lamprias takes a lively part in the *Table Talks*; he was 'imaginative and full of good stories'. He had been a friend of the physician Philotas, of Amphissa; he had heard Philotas describe the extravagance at the court of Cleopatra and Antony in Alexandria, where he had studied medicine.[6]

Plutarch tells us little about his education. He was taught by Ammonius at the Academy at Athens, though we also hear of Plutarch and his brother and other young men meeting Ammonius at Delphi. Who Ammonius was is uncertain; he has generally been thought to be Ammonius of Lamptrae, and this identification would fit well with what we know of him; for he wrote a work *On Altars and Sacrifices*; he speaks mainly on religious matters in the *Table Talks*, indeed Plutarch's interest in religious matters of every kind may be derived from him. On the other hand, Plutarch does not refer to his teacher's famous book, as perhaps a conscientious pupil should do, and there is some reason for thinking Ammonius of Lamptrae to have lived rather earlier.

All the *Table Talks* in which Ammonius took part occurred in Athens; he does not seem ever to have gone to Chaeronea. It is clear that Plutarch owed him a great deal—an early introduction to mathematics which he passionately liked and a training in Platonic philosophy. From whom Plutarch received his very thorough and extensive knowledge of Greek literature we do not know, but, as it was the foundation of education, it must have run through all his studies. That he had a very retentive memory is shown by the frequency of his quotations and his inexhaustible store of incidents to illustrate his theme of the moment.

Plutarch's father must have had a large house, roomy enough to hold many guests; he was no doubt of independent means, living on the revenues of his estate. Round about were neighbours in similar circumstances and of similar interests. On his death Plutarch inherited.

Plutarch tells us nothing about his house. Nor would it be right to assume that it resembled the villas of Pompeii. But an author of the time of Augustus[7] has left us a short description of the 'Greek' house of a well-to-do man: it is not clear whether he is speaking of his own times or the Alexandrian age, of a house in the town or in the country: but its main features may well be true of Plutarch's house.

You approach through a narrow passage: on the left are the stables, on the right the porter's quarters. The passage leads to a quadrangle, open to the sky, round which run cloisters: doors give access to women's bedrooms and store-rooms. The cloister which faces south is recessed so as to form an ante-room, whence a door leads to the main hall where the women live. A passage from the right-hand side of the quadrangle leads to another and more splendid quadrangle, surrounded by cloisters with ceilings of stucco or plaster or panelling. Through doorways of suitable dignity the dining-rooms, large and small, men's bedrooms, libraries and perhaps a picture-gallery. Off these buildings are wings or suites provided for guests: they are approachable from outside without going through the quadrangle. These suites contain dining-rooms, bedrooms and store-rooms. When visitors arrived, they would be invited to dine with the family on the first night of their stay: thereafter they would look after themselves, drawing upon the supply of country produce – poultry, eggs, vegetables, fruit – with which the lady of the house would keep the store-rooms supplied. But in the evening they would come into the main dining-room of their host for dessert and talk. Outside, the house would show little but blank walls built with perhaps a lower course of masonry and the upper course of brick: the aim was to keep the house cool: light entered chiefly from the quadrangle. The farm buildings would be separate.

So we are to imagine the guests in Plutarch's house spending their time as they wished – perhaps hunting or fishing, walking with their host, reading a book borrowed from his library in preparation for the evening's discussion, or making ready for to-morrow's journey to Delphi. Thus, says our author, the head of a family staying as a visitor 'does not feel away from home when he enjoys private generosity'. He has the freedom of his own house. And over the whole establishment stretched the kindly influence of Plutarch as host and the care and forethought of Timoxena, his wife, and her servants.

Of the servants we hear nothing from Plutarch. But perhaps in parenthesis a story recorded by Aulus Gellius may be quoted. Plutarch had a good-for-nothing and impertinent slave who had read enough and had listened to enough discussions to have gained a smattering of philosophy. He was guilty of some misdemeanour and Plutarch ordered him to be stripped and flogged with a strap. At the first blows the slave protested that he had done nothing wrong; as the flogging went on he changed his tune; Plutarch was not behaving as a philosopher should; it was a disgrace to give way to anger; he had often discoursed on the evils of anger, indeed he had written a treatise on the subject, 'a very fine treatise, too'; its sentiments scarcely corresponded to the complete abandonment to temper displayed by Plutarch now. Then in a slow and gentle voice Plutarch replied.

You think I am angry. From my face and voice and colour and words would you gather I was angry? My eyes do not blaze, my speech is not confused, I am not shouting; I am not foaming at the mouth or purple in the face. I am saying nothing to be ashamed of or to regret; I am not trembling with rage or throwing myself about in a paroxysm. In case you do not know it, those are the symptoms of fits of temper.

Then he turned to the one who was doing the flogging and said; 'While he and I are discussing things, you just carry on.'[8]

This house became in time a kind of unofficial academy of letters, unorganised, informal and dependent entirely on the personality of its host and leader. Hints gathered here and there from Plutarch's writings suggest that it began in a small way—neighbours coming in for dinner and lingering over their wine to discuss a literary or scientific or ethical problem; Plutarch and his brothers, Lamprias and Timon, as they grew older, were allowed to be present at such gatherings and later to take a part; when the brothers returned on vacation from Athens they brought their friends home with them. The sons of neighbours joined the group; fathers brought their sons and sons their fathers, as the attractions of these informal discussions became known. As Plutarch grew older, he became the leader; he gave a lecture, threw the matter open to discussion and later put the results into written shape. Roman friends were welcome and indeed took a leading part. The activities of this centre of learning and fellowship were described by Plutarch as *scholē* and *diatribē*, terms which suggest something voluntary and spontaneous, and the ultimate issue, though not the professed motive, was a way of life. The affiliation of the gatherings is indicated if it is noted that the birthdays of Socrates and Plato were observed as 'feast days'.[9] To use modern ideas, it seems that we are to think of a combination of elements taken from 'a university extension lecture', a reading party, a literary club, a discussion circle, a house-party, while Plutarch himself must have been something like the highly cultivated 'squire-parson' found here and there in the eighteenth century.

To the success of these gatherings a good hostess, if only behind the scenes, might have contributed much. But Plutarch does not explicitly say anything about his wife's part. Indeed we know little of her. Her name was Timoxena; when her four-year-old daughter named after her died, Plutarch, who was at Tanagra at the time, wrote her a letter of comfort. It is a moving piece of writing, which might be summarised thus: Plutarch had heard with what restraint and dignity she had taken her loss; the blow had been heavy; the child was a sweet child, gentle to all, even to her dolls. Before her death we had no cause for complaint against fortune; we must try to join up this moment with then; otherwise we shall be in danger of making her birth a cause of complaint. Her memory we must treasure because her life gave us such delight. The child herself is spared all pain and suffers no loss. Do not believe that death is extinction. You and I have shared in the teaching of the mysteries and we know that the soul is immortal; it is of divine parentage and has a divine destiny. A short imprisonment in the body is a blessing; this child had no time to grow to love its cage, as captive birds sometimes do. The worst misery of old age is not grey hairs nor physical weakness, but ensnarement in the things of the world and a forgetfulness of what is divine. Those whom the gods summon back are saved from long wanderings.

From the praise which Plutarch gives his wife in this letter it is clear that she was a devoted mother, with a strong sense of order and good manners, modesty and simplicity. She appears again in the *Marriage Precepts*[10] where Plutarch advises his correspondents to read and commit to memory his wife's letter (an essay) addressed to Aristylla, a young friend of hers; the theme was love of adornment, and, if it bore any resemblance to Plutarch's following remarks, it advised adorning the character rather than the body and enjoying all the fruits of education and philosophy. Did Timoxena write it, or Timoxena with Plutarch's help?

There were four sons of the marriage. The eldest son, Soclarus, and another son died before their young sister; the two others, Plutarchus and Autobulus, apparently survived their father. The family left traces of itself for two hundred or more years, partly at Chaeronea, partly elsewhere.[11]

If the works of Plutarch were published for the first time to-day, popular curiosity would demand a portrait on the dust-cover. There is no evidence from which to offer even a sketch. Neither in the *Moralia* nor in a digression in the *Lives* is there any hint of Plutarch's appearance, nor has any head been preserved as traditionally of Plutarch. But for those who desired something tradition preserved a link which was better than nothing. When William Martin Leake, formerly Lieut.-Colonel of the Artillery and a Fellow of the Royal Society, visited Chaeronea, then Kápurna, shortly before 1853, he found in the ancient church of Panaghía an 'antique chair of marble called by the learned' the throne of Plutarch. And eighteen years later Hermann Hettner reported seeing this same throne of Plutarch, and noted how the smallest town liked to be well thought of as a lover of art and literature. But now this link has parted, for enquiry suggests that the chair no longer exists. We must be content with his works.[12]

CHAPTER 3

Talkers and Topics

THE strict title of the *Table Talks* is *Symposiaca Problemata*, matters talked about at a symposium; the Latin translation is *Quaestiones Convivales*.

'Symposium' is not easy to translate; it is not what is now meant by 'drinking party'; it is much closer to 'dessert', though dessert somewhat prolonged. A few guests would be invited to dinner; on arrival their shoes would be removed for them, and their feet washed. They would recline on low couches, propping themselves on one elbow, with the other hand free. A low table was set before each guest or each pair of guests. The meal was simple; it was of such character that it needed no implements; the fingers, with bread for soaking up sauces, were enough. The first course over, the tables were removed, and others, with sweets, cakes and fruit, were brought. At some point in this dessert a libation of unmixed wine was poured – a 'good health' said as a kind of Grace; then wine was mixed with water, and poured, generally into three bowls, and from them offering was made to the Olympian gods, to the Heroes and to Zeus Sōter. At elaborate dinner-parties this ceremonial might be accompanied by a flute-player, who might then play at intervals later.

It was when the second set of tables were brought in that the dessert began, and the guests stayed on their couches drinking and talking. In the *Table Talks* some of these points emerge clearly; often it is said, 'when the tables were removed, so and so asked . . . '. One *Talk* considers the arrangement of the couches and the places of honour, another the character of the good 'president of the party', another the use of flowers and garlands, another whether flute-girls should play at dessert.[1]

There is no sign of excessive drinking; the conversations are admirably conducted, often with great earnestness; but humour and personal touches abound, and good humour never fails.

The importance of the *Table Talks* rests not on their subject-matter, which, as will be seen, is often trivial, but upon the picture which they give of the society in which Plutarch moved, the texture of social life, and the ease and frequency of movement of people from place to place.

We know of a round hundred of Plutarch's friends. Some are names, some are living figures. Their callings are varied— musician, grammarian, rhetor, Syrian prince, doctor (at least eight), officer, philosophers owing allegiance to Stoicism, Platonism, Epicureanism, Cynicism, Aristotelianism, mathematician, schoolmaster, sophist. The *Talks* take place at Athens, Eleusis, Corinth, Delphi, Elis, Aedepsus in the north-east corner of Euboea, Hyampolis in Phocis, Thermopylae, Patrae and Rome. The conversations recorded in the ninth book all took place in Athens at the time of the Festival of the Muses, to whom, as Plutarch says, it is fitting to dedicate a ninth book. Many of the members appear at more than one place, for example Protogenes is present at Athens, Chaeronea, Corinth, and the participants in the longer dialogues which are not *Table Talks* are mostly to be found in one or more *Table Talk*. Some of the parties were given at the time of the Games at Elis, Corinth and Delphi and it is clear that some people attended them all. No less clear is the variety of places from which Plutarch's friends were drawn; we know of two or three from Chaeronea itself, others from Athens. The rest come from Syria, Soli, Prusias, Sardes, Pergamum, in Asia Minor; in Greece from Sunium, Megara, Sparta, Thessaly, Macedonia, Thespiae, Thebes, Sicyon, Tithora, Coronea and Nicopolis; one man came from Arelate in South Gaul and the Roman members came from Rome and Africa. Demetrius, who came from Tarsus, had spent some time in Yorkshire, and drew upon the experience of his travels to illuminate a point under discussion.

It is, of course, a commonplace that under the Empire travel was easy, safe and frequent. The evidence of inscriptions confirms and illustrates what was already familiar in general terms in the literature. But here is evidence of a slightly different kind; for here numbers of people are gathered together, and we can infer something of their lives and interests. The making of a livelihood does not seem to have borne so hardly upon them that they could not take many days off to attend festivals and celebrations.

Of Plutarch's friends from Chaeronea, Aristion, Nigros, Philinus and Soclarus, the two last are the most important. Of Aristion it is enough to say that he seems to be interested in food and wine; in one talk he argues, against Nigros, in favour of straining wine and shows much learning in the process; in another he explains why it is that a fowl can be served up a month later without signs of being overkept if it has been hung from a figtree. The subject arose because the party praised his cook.

Philinus was present at the party given in Rome to celebrate Plutarch's second visit there. It is probable that Philinus actually travelled with Plutarch. He was a vegetarian, which means that he was a Pythagorean. The subjects of discussion were: (a) the command of Pythagoras that on a person's rising from his bed he should 'tumble' the blankets and (b) that a swallow should never be allowed to enter a house or build under the eaves. Philinus went with Plutarch to Hyampolis, where they were entertained by Philon, a doctor; the meal was most elaborate, but it caused a long disquisition by Philinus on the virtues of a simple, uniform diet. In another *Talk* he becomes involved in a philological argument, in another, at the table of Florus, on the physiological effect of eating salt. He seems to have visited Egypt (with Plutarch?), for in the dialogue *On intelligence in animals* he is said to have returned with a story that he had seen a tame crocodile sleeping on a stool in an old woman's bedroom.[2]

The most interesting resident of Chaeronea was perhaps Soclarus. He seems to have been a family friend. He appears in talks which took place at his house, or rather in his garden on the banks of the river Cephisus, in Plutarch's house, and at some place where Mestrius Florus was host. Now on the 24th October, A.D. 118, a Lucius Mestrius Soclarus, of Chaeronea, had his name recorded as a witness at a law-suit concerning some farms. The inscription was found at Daulis, which is seven or eight miles from Chaeronea. Thus both Plutarch and his friend Soclarus, both of Chaeronea, took their names as Roman citizens from the same man, L. Mestrius Florus. Plutarch is careful to distinguish this Soclarus from another, who came from Tithora, at the foot of Mount Parnassus; he too occurs in inscriptions which inform us that the family took the name Flavius. Plutarch's friend was T. Flavius Soclarus, archon at Delphi, A.D. 98/99. It is not a wholly imaginary conjecture that Plutarch called his eldest son Soclarus, who died before reaching manhood, after one of these two Soclari, or possibly after both.[3]

Seven friends take part in the dialogue *On the failure of the oracles*; Plutarch is not one of them, but his brother Lamprias is. The discussion took place at Delphi; it was started by Cleombrotus, a Spartan, and Demetrius, of Tarsus, takes a good part in it. Here is Plutarch's introduction.

By chance two holy men came to us from opposite ends of the globe and met at Delphi, Demetrius the grammarian, returning home to Tarsus from Britain, and Cleombrotus, the Spartan. Cleombrotus had wandered about a great deal in Egypt and roundabout the country of the Troglodytes, and he had sailed far up the Red Sea, not by way of trade, but because he loved seeing things and learning about things. He had sufficient private means and attached no importance to having more than was sufficient; so he used his leisure thus and gathered together his enquiries as the raw material of a philosophy which was to result in a theology, as he called it.

Demetrius is no less interesting. The argument had reached the subject of evil daemons, and:

Demetrius said that many of the islands round Britain were deserted and widely scattered and some of them bore the names of daemons and heroes; he himself, on the instructions of the Emperor, had sailed on a voyage of investigation and observation and gone to the nearest of the deserted islands, which had a few inhabitants who were all regarded as sacred and were left unharmed by the Britons. Very soon after he had arrived, there was an atmospheric disturbance, many signs in the sky; powerful winds crashed together and

24

flaming masses fell. When it all stopped, the islanders told him that one of the 'mightier ones' had faded from existence. Just as a lamp, so they said, when alight has no objectionable effect but when put out is very unpleasant to many people, so it is with great souls; alive, they are comfortable and without pain, but their extinction and death often cause winds and hurricanes, such as you see now, and they often infect the air with pestilential influences. They said there was one island in which Cronus was held prisoner, guarded as he lay asleep by Briareus; for sleep had been invented as a means of chaining him, and he was surrounded by many daemons as servants and attendants.[4]

Now in 1860 two bronze plates were found in York, one dedicated to Ocean and Tethys, one to 'the gods of the imperial praetorium' by a certain Demetrius. This man, who makes a dedication to the gods of the imperial praetorium, has very reasonably been identified with Plutarch's friend who undertook exploration 'on the instructions of the Emperor'. Unfortunately the date of the meeting described in the treatise cannot be established with certainty; if it is A.D. 83/84, as has been plausibly suggested, Demetrius was in Britain during the governorship of Agricola to whom no doubt he was recommended by the Emperor Domitian. But the important point to note is that Plutarch is drawing on his acquaintance with a real person and giving us a detail, which was by no means essential, but which happens to connect with a chance find in York. It may reasonably be assumed, therefore, that other minute and unimportant details of characterisation are correct. Thus, when Aristion is said to 'shout in his usual way', or Apollonides is represented as 'credulous and hasty in judgment', when Lamprias gave 'the traditional account' and Ammonius 'smiled knowing that Lamprias was capable of improvising a traditional view', we are to put together these innumerable touches and build up a portrait which may be accepted as true.[5]

Another who appears in the *Table Talks*–though only in one– is Favorinus. He was a close friend of Hadrian. In the *Table Talk* Plutarch explains that Favorinus, who was a most ardent admirer of Aristotle, on this occasion brought out 'an ancient and smoke-begrimed argument of Democritus and began to clean it and polish it'. Here again is a small detail which it would be pointless to invent. The impression which Plutarch made on Favorinus must have been considerable; for, according to the physician Galen, Favorinus wrote a dialogue called 'Plutarch' in which the philosopher of Chaeronea was no doubt represented as the greatest authority on Platonic questions. In another dialogue addressed 'To Epictetus' he makes Onesimus, a slave belonging to Plutarch, discourse with Epictetus, the lame philosopher, who when exiled from Rome by Domitian opened a lecture-room in Nicopolis. It is interesting to see Plutarch at any rate connected remotely with Epictetus; though very different in temperament, they had a great deal in common, but there is no evidence that they ever met.

Another prominent member of the discussions is Theon; his main interest was clearly literature, as is shown in the valuable contribution which he makes. He is vividly portrayed and stands out as a real person, though we know little or nothing about him from other sources. He seems to have been a close friend of the family, for we are told that Plutarch's wife Timoxena was of much assistance to his sister when she was in trouble and needed comfort.

These men—Philinus, Soclarus, Cleombrotus, Demetrius, Favorinus—have been considered at some length because it is possible to say something about them; their characters or experiences are described in Plutarch or we have independent knowledge of them. For dozens more names it would be possible to write, from Plutarch's own evidence, short notes, of the following kind: 'Sospis, a rhetor: interested in Homeric questions; appears to be a distinguished man, e.g. he was twice *agonothetes* at the Isthmian Games; hence he was a Corinthian.' Or again, 'Apollonides, described as an officer: in *On the face on the moon* there is an Apollonides who, to illustrate his point, chooses an analogy taken from "tactics"; hence we assume identity; also shows interest in mathematics; in each dialogue Sextius Sulla is also present; was Apollonides a friend or colleague of Sulla?'[6] But such notes would soon become tedious unless the conversations were also read in full. Anyone who does not read the conversations, whether the short *Table Talks* or the longer conversations, must take it for granted that the members of these groups are educated men, professing a variety of callings, versed in philosophy (which is a broad term in this context), literature, medicine and so on, many of them distinguished in their own field and all of them supremely interested in things of the mind and on the best of terms with one another. Yet why do they appear to discuss such trivial things?

For example, the meal was over, the wine was on the table and Xenocles, of Delphi, teased Plutarch's brother Lamprias about his large Boeotian appetite. So Plutarch comes to his brother's rescue, and explains that not everyone accepted the view of Epicurus (and Xenocles was inclined to Epicureanism) that the removal of pain was pleasure; and recommended Lamprias to support Aristotle who said that everyone was hungrier in the autumn. But Plutarch could not remember the reason given by Aristotle. So the party proceeds to consider the problem afresh.

'Why are clothes better washed in water which can be drunk than in sea-water?' 'Why does the letter A come first?' 'Why do we not believe in dreams which we dream in the autumn?' 'Why does meat suspended from a fig-tree get tender quickly?' 'On people who give large dinner-parties.' 'Why does Homer always put boxing, wrestling and running in this order?'[7]

It is not quite fair merely to quote the initial theme of a dialogue. The problem posed, which often arises from an episode or a chance remark at the party, gives rise to other questions; it is seldom long before the disputants are plunged into philosophical, or mathematical or literary or scientific arguments; they may be ruthlessly brought back to the point, only to leave it again. In short, the *Table Talks* are interesting for their incidental matter, seldom for the original question or its answer. A Greek of Plutarch's day would perhaps think it very odd to see educated men spending time on a crossword puzzle. Imagine three or four well-read men doing a difficult crossword together; soon there would be discussion; some literary allusion would need to be explained; the derivation of a word might be relevant and would need to be discussed; by-paths would be pursued till at last someone would interrupt with 'You know, we are supposed to be doing this crossword'. On looking back, the gathering might agree that an interesting and instructive hour had been spent. The original question of a *Table Talk* corresponds to the clues of the puzzle; what follows may well be worth while.

No woman took part in the *Table Talks*. If women and children had meals with the man of the household, and with his guests–and a passage in one of the *Table Talks* show that it happened–they would retire when the tables were cleared for the wine.[8] Nor do women take part in other dialogues. But two are honoured with dedications. The more important of them is Clea. Of her we learn that, when she lost a dearly loved relation Leontis, well-known for her goodness, Plutarch had a talk with her to offer her consolation and followed up with an (extant) treatise *On the Virtues of women*; in this he demonstrated by historical examples that 'goodness in a man and a woman were one and the same thing'. To Clea was dedicated also the important essay *On and Isis Osiris*. From this we learn that she was the chief of the Thyiades, or women devotees of Dionysus, at Delphi. Moreover, she was 'dedicated by her father and mother to the sacred rites of Osiris', and so she was well able to recognise the truth of Plutarch's contention that Osiris and Dionysus were in fact the same god. An earlier passage shows that she was priestess of Isis, and that the essay was dedicated to her because 'all sensible people pray the gods to give them all the knowledge about themselves that the human mind can take in'. Presumably Clea took in Plutarch's very considerable learning. If the essay is due to Plutarch's regard for her, she ought to be remembered, for it is the fullest account of an ancient religion by a contemporary that we have. A good deal of the matter is no doubt derived from other writers, but it has been well worked over by Plutarch and it is very probable that much was contributed and explained by Ammonius, and by others whom Plutarch met in Alexandria.

Eurydice was the young bride to whom, with her husband

Pollianus, the *Marriage Precepts* were addressed. Both of them, apparently, have been instructed by Plutarch in philosophy, and he sends them the gist of his teaching conveniently summarised into 'similes' – anecdotes, sayings, parallels from every source – and so more 'easily committed to memory'. This, he says, was his wedding present!

Of Aristylla all that is known has already been said on p. 20.

CHAPTER 4

Delphi: the Pythian Dialogues

TWENTY miles or so west of Chaeronea is Delphi. Two spurs
from the range of Parnassus fork out towards the sea, and thus
enclose a horse-shoe. The ground slopes down from the embrac-
ing hills in terraces; on the highest was built the temple to Pythian Apollo; below was the town and the countless temples,
shrines, statues and dedications of all kinds. From the precipi-
tous cliffs fell the stream of Castalia, with whose waters all
enquirers were purified; it eventually flowed into the river
Pleistus which ran along the open side of the horse-shoe. The
Sacred Way provided the approach and it was lined with buildings and statues. Very many features of the place are noticed by
Plutarch; for in some dialogues we find the company moves
along from building to building, statue to statue, conversing as
they go. With the help of Pausanias and the French excavations
few sites can be reconstructed in such detail.

The advent of the Roman Empire brought no revival to the
oracle. The early Emperors virtually ignored it. Nero was the
first to take an interest. In return for an answer which pleased
him he bestowed on it the sum of 100,000 sesterces (later recovered by a thrifty Galba); but the oracle fell under his displeasure
for an answer which he stupidly failed to understand correctly.
He is said to have taken away five hundred statues from the
place, though Pliny records that in his time there were still three
thousand remaining. Titus became a chief magistrate, and
Domitian assisted in the restoration of the temple. But it was
under Hadrian that some revival took place. He himself visited
the oracle, put a question which he might well have improved
upon, and received a very definite answer.[1] The greatest benefactions were made by Herodes Atticus, who restored buildings

and statues, spending great sums of money in the process. But that was just after Plutarch's time.

Delphi seems to have become almost a second home to Plutarch. There is no evidence that he possessed a house or land there. We find him there when he was a young man in company with Ammonius and his brother Lamprias 'about the time of Nero's visit' to Greece, *i.e.* A.D. 67. All his life he was anxious that the prestige of Delphi should be restored, and it seems that this passion was aroused from his earliest days; he devoted himself to the purpose with an ardour which secured for him especial recognition. For we discover that he became one of its two priests; 'Euthydemus my colleague-priest' is the incidental way in which he lets drop information which we could wish he had amplified. We can guess a little more, for when he was an old man he says, 'You know that I have served Pythian Apollo at many Pythian festivals; but you would not say to me "Plutarch, you have sacrificed enough, and taken part in procession and chorus; now that you are old it is time you laid aside your crown and relinquished interest in the oracle, giving your advanced years as the reason".' The Pythian Games were held every four years, in the third year of each Olympiad; if then we knew how to interpret Plutarch's 'many', we should know how long he held a priesthood – perhaps we can guess twenty or twenty-four years. But besides being priest, he also served as 'manager' of the Games in Hadrian's reign, that is after A.D. 117, and, if another passage is to be interpreted as referring to himself, he was an agonothetes (director of the Games), Boeotarch and a proedros of the Amphictyonic Council, which met at Delphi.[2]

That Plutarch's devotion to the oracle met with some recognition may be inferred from another passage in another dialogue,[3] which is supposed to have taken place at Delphi. After an argument about the nature of inspiration Theon finishes a long speech with a passionate defence of the present prosperity and prestige of the oracle. The oracle, he says, strives after truth; its good faith is beyond question; many buildings have recently been added, many which were in ruins have been restored; new trees have been planted; the beauty of the temples and halls and fountains has never been so great in the last thousand years. After drought, poverty, abandonment we now have splendour and prestige.

Now, though I am well pleased with what I may have contributed to this end by my enthusiasm and my services, together with Polycrates and Petraeus, I am well pleased too with him who has been a leader to us in this policy, who has been responsible for most of the thought and the planning. But it is not possible that changes of such nature and such extent could have been achieved in so short a time by merely human management, I mean without a god being present here and aiding the oracle with his divinity.

The natural view of this passage is that Theon had rendered services to Delphi of which he is proud, that, knowing Plutarch's modesty, he pays tribute to Plutarch without making mention of him by name, that he acknowledges the aid of Apollo in restoring the fame of Delphi.[4]

In a dialogue called *On the E at Delphi* Plutarch writes a short dedication to Sarapion, a poet living at Athens who wrote verse on scientific subjects. Presents of money are less valuable, he explains, than presents of literature; it is nice to give such presents and to demand a return in kind. 'And so I send you and my friends in Athens some of our Pythian dialogues, a first instalment; I admit I expect from you some dialogues, more and better than those I send, since you have the advantages of a great city with plenty of books round you and discussions of all kinds.'

It has generally been assumed that three dialogues still extant are some of those sent to Sarapion. They are (1) *On the E at Delphi*, (2) *Why the priestess does not now give oracles in verse*, (3) *On the failure of the oracles*. All these dialogues took place in Delphi and relate to matters connected with the oracle. These were not the only dialogues that took place at Delphi. Their long titles make it convenient to refer to them by number.

In the fore-temple were inscribed brief aphorisms, all conveying precepts of practical wisdom. Plato tells us of three, 'Know thyself', 'Nothing too much', 'Go bail and rue it'.[5] From Plutarch only do we learn of the inscription of the letter E, pronounced eh and therefore of the same sound-value as ei which as a word in Greek has two or three meanings. When the god enjoined that this letter should be inscribed, what was his reason? This question, as Plutarch explains in his opening chapter, was recently raised by his sons who fell into conversation with some strangers at Delphi; he had not felt it fair to put them off, though in fact he had always avoided the problem in his teaching of pupils. So they sat down near the temple and discussed the matter. What was said then reminded him of a similar conversation which had occurred at the same place years ago, about A.D. 66, when he was a young man and Ammonius and others were present to give their help. This early conversation he then sets out in full as he remembered it. The company included Ammonius, a Platonist, Theon and Nicander, a priest of the temple, and the discussion ranged into fields of logic, metaphysics and mathematics, whither we cannot follow. It is enough to say that seven different solutions to the problem were propounded and discussed.

The second dialogue is also narrated. Basilocles has been waiting for his friend Philinus outside the temple. When at last he appears, Basilocles asks why he has been so long. His friend explains that the party which he was showing round the temple included a young visitor, Diogenianus, from Pergamum, and he had been very intelligent and inquisitive. Basilocles asks Philinus to repeat to him the conversation, since the rest of the party has left. This he does. The members of the party were Philinus, Theon, Sarapion, Boethus a geometrician, Diogenianus and two guides from the temple. At first the party had to listen to the lectures of the guides, who paid no attention to entreaties to cut short their eloquence and to skip most of the inscriptions. At last Diogenianus set the ball rolling by asking about the tint of a bronze statue which caught his eye. This led to a discussion of the effect of olive oil on metal; thence to the properties of the air at Delphi, and in the process views expressed by Aristotle and by Homer had been quoted. Diogenianus now notices an inscription and asks why the oracles are written in such bad verse. This subject is discussed in the light of a theory of inspiration, till Diogenianus is moved to protest against treating a serious subject with levity. Meantime the party went on till they came to a statue of Hiero. Again the conversation ranged wide – about providence and chance, about vague general prophecies which might come true by luck and prophecies expressed in specific terms; again Diogenianus asked a question about a Corinthian brazen bowl; more philosophical discussion followed. Meantime the guides were utterly confused by the talk which was far out of their reach till finally Diogenianus reminded the company of his original question and they all sat down to consider it. And there we may leave them.

In the third dialogue, too, a party makes its way among the treasures of Delphi. They are Lamprias, Cleombrotus, Didymus a Cynic, Philippus a historian, Demetrius of Tarsus, Ammonius, and Heracleon a young man. The date may be A.D. 83/84. The dialogue is dedicated to a Roman friend, Terentius Priscus. It would be difficult in a short space to give any indication of the range of this dialogue; but it may be said that it is of very great interest as giving the views of the rival schools of philosophy at this time on a variety of topics. It contains a discussion of the nature and influence of 'daemons', besides many anecdotes about oracles, a highly mathematical interpretation of the nature of the universe, a description of the depopulation of Greece and especially Boeotia, 'where in a whole day's journey you would scarcely find a single man looking after his flocks', and the highly interesting experiences of Demetrius in Britain.* The dialogue closes with a consideration of the 'inspiration' of the Pythian priestess.

But the efforts of Plutarch and his fellow-priests and friends gave the oracle only a short and tenuous existence. Hadrian, as we have seen, helped considerably, but within a century Delphi had lapsed into silence. Indeed it virtually capitulated of its own will; for when the Niceans asked whether it was desirable that they should go on making sacrifices at Delphi, as the oracle had enjoined, the answer, in hexameter verse, was that it was impossible to revive the oracle so that it would speak; length of time

* See page 24.

had dimmed its powers; a silence which would not prophesy had clamped down upon it; none the less they were to continue their sacrifices to the honour of Apollo (and no doubt to the profit of the priests).[6] But Delphi's rest was disturbed again; for Julian in his attempt to restore all things pagan tried to revive also the oracle. He sent Oribasius with a question which we do not know. But the answer, unlike most, is unequivocal. 'Tell the Emperor, the splendidly-wrought hall has fallen to the ground; Apollo has not a hut, no prophetic laurel, no speaking fountain. The water of speech is cut off.'* Plutarch, fortunately, had long been dead and was spared much sorrow; but surely he would have noted with satisfaction that the dying words of the oracle were in hexameters. The oracle was dead; but it was not buried till A.D. 390, by Theodosius.[7]

* Or, if a drought or earthquake can be assumed, 'Even the chatter of (falling) water has been silenced'.

CHAPTER 5

Plutarch Abroad

HOWEVER much Plutarch loved his home and his native town, he travelled widely. Athens, of course, he knew well; indeed it is to his descriptions of it that we owe some of our knowledge of its topography. As a citizen, of the tribe of Leontis, he must have spent much time there, and it is possible that he might have become the Director of the Academy if he had not been devoted to Chaeronea.[1] He went to Delphi and Elis for the religious festivals, and we know that he stayed at Thespiae, Helicon, Tanagra, Sparta, Aedepsus (in Euboea), Patrae, Hyampolis, Plataea, Thermopylae and Chalcis. His travels took him further afield; he delivered a lecture[2] at either Sardes or Ephesus, and his *On Exile* strongly suggests a visit to Sardes. He went to Alexandria while still young, for when he returned his grandfather Lamprias was present at the celebrations held to receive him. He tells us of the visit to Alexandria in his own typical way '. . . at the dinner which my friends gave me when I returned from Alexandria'; and, though he has many occasions in the *Lives* to speak of Alexandria, he never states, or even hints, that he had ever been there. And so his purpose in going there is obscure; it is possible that Ammonius suggested the visit, or Plutarch may have wished to follow in the footsteps of his master, Plato, who according to his biographers spent some time in Egypt. At any rate Plutarch put his time to good use; for his treatise *On Isis and Osiris*, based almost certainly on his own enquiries, is invaluable for the study of Egyptian religion.

Among his father's Roman friends Plutarch must have met Romans, but his first meeting with them officially was when he was sent to transact business on behalf of his township with the proconsul of Achaea. He says he was a young man at the time; if he was born in A.D. 47 he must have been under twenty at the time of the visit, since in A.D. 67 Greece ceased for a time to be governed by proconsuls. If he had gone some dozen years earlier, he would have been interviewed by Gallio and might have set eyes on St. Paul.

What the business was is unknown; but there was ample scope, for the cities—especially the 'free' cities such as Athens, Delphi, Tanagra—gave constant trouble to Roman administrators by their quarrels and complaints about each other. It might have been a boundary dispute, such as C. Avidius Nigrinus was sent to settle much later between Delphi and her neighbours;[3] he came as an official arbiter when perhaps Plutarch was priest at Delphi, and the two became friends. We shall meet him later.

Plutarch visited Rome and Italy more than once. His journeys by sea seem to have made an impression on him. Metaphors taken from ships, the sea and its tides, storms, sea-faring life are familiar enough in Greek literature. But such metaphors seem to be especially common in all Plutarch's writings and to be worked out in considerable detail. Yet we may have here only a trick of style. Of the route by which he travelled we have no hint.

The evidence about these visits is scanty, trivial and inconclusive. But it is worth while to give it in some detail, partly to show the casual and incidental way in which Plutarch refers to events which must have been of great significance to him, partly to indicate in one field the kind of method which has to be used to establish anything at all about Plutarch's life.

'When I was in Rome and when I was staying at various places in Italy I had not time to occupy myself seriously with the Latin language, partly because of public business, partly because of the large numbers who came to me as a philosopher; and so it was late, in fact well into middle age, when I began to read Latin literature.'[4] He went to Rome, therefore, to do business on behalf of Greek cities and to lecture or to take part in philosophical discussions. Further, anything that he wrote as a young man on Roman matters had not been derived direct from Latin writers.

In Rome he witnessed a trick done by a performing dog; 'it moved considerably all the spectators and the Emperor too (for Vespasian then an old man was present in the theatre of Marcellus).'[5] The important part of the statement, it may be noted as typical, is in a parenthesis. Vespasian died in A.D. 79 at the age of 69. Thus Plutarch was in Rome before A.D. 79, when the Emperor was old; when can an Emperor be considered to be old?

Again, when Plutarch was giving a lecture in Rome he had Arulenus Rusticus as a member of the audience; in the middle of the lecture 'a soldier came in with a despatch from the Emperor. I stopped and gave time for him to read it, but he refused and did not break the seal till I had finished and the gathering had dispersed.'[6] We are not told who the Emperor was, but Arulenus was a well-known Stoic philosopher whom Domitian put to death in A.D. 93 or 94. There is a possibility that he was consul in A.D. 92; and, if it might be conjectured that a despatch so urgent as to interrupt a lecture was sent by the Emperor to the Chief Magistrate, we should thus have Plutarch in Rome in A.D. 92.

The last passage to be quoted may perhaps be thought to confirm this date. In a digression on the successive rebuildings of the temple of Jupiter on the Capitol Plutarch says that the fourth temple was built by Domitian to replace the temple built by Vespasian and burnt down soon after his death. Plutarch had himself seen in Greece the columns of Pentelic marble destined for the rebuilding and had admired their proportions. But at Rome they had been recut and polished. The account clearly implies that Plutarch had himself seen them in position, for he says that they had been made too slender and tapering. And he adds that the costliness of the temple appears insignificant when compared with even one gallery, or hall, or bath of the Palace of Domitian.[7] If, then, Plutarch had made this comparison for himself, he was in Rome some time in or after the early nineties A.D., for Domitian's Palace was built then.

There are other passages in which Plutarch records things which he had seen in Rome, but none helps in determining

38

dates. Thus, we are left with the meagre information that he visited Rome in the late seventies and in the early nineties. That there were two visits is attested by a passage in which he refers to himself as 'having arrived in Rome after an interval of time'; it is very probable that there were other visits.

Nor do we learn much about the visit to northern Italy, whither he went, for at least part of the time, with L. Mestrius Florus, one of his closest friends, who, as has been seen, was probably responsible for Plutarch's Roman citizenship. His family came from Brixia or roundabout; he himself had unwillingly joined the cause of Otho and had been present at the defeat at Bedriacum in A.D. 69. He showed Plutarch the field of battle and pointed out a temple in which the dead had been piled to the roof. It is interesting that Plutarch's account of the battle of Bedriacum may have been derived from one who took part in it, and it is especially useful since Tacitus' narrative is by no means without difficulties.

He went also to Brixellum where he saw Otho's grave and to Ravenna where he notes a statue of Marius.

How long Plutarch's visits to Rome and to Italy lasted we have no means of knowing; we can only imagine from the kind of things he did that they probably lasted a few months.

Apart from the 'public business', Plutarch spent his time in Rome in lecturing, in talks with friends and admirers, in reading and consulting libraries. A lecture involved discussion afterwards with a group and with individuals who came to him for counsel and advice. For it is clear that by the time of his second visit to Rome his fame was considerable, if so well-known a philosopher as Arulenus Rusticus attended, and his audiences were not small, as he himself says. His subjects probably fell within the field of practical morality and behaviour rather than of abstract philosophy, and these were interests which were of special appeal to Romans. To make a guess at the kind of subject we may employ a method which clearly can give no certain results. Many of Plutarch's essays are dedicated to individuals— indeed some are written by request. If then we consider the titles of those essays and dialogues which are dedicated to

Romans, we may gain some indication of the kind of subjects treated in lectures. For it is reasonable to think that the interest of a friend may have been aroused by a lecture which Plutarch later 'wrote up' and sent to him, or that an essay may have been written specially to help an enquirer who had discussed with him some point arising from a lecture. It is not likely that lectures and *Table Talks* were unrelated, at any rate in Rome.

To C. Avidius Nigrinus, who has already been met, and to Avidius Quietus, his brother, Plutarch addressed an essay *On brotherly love*, to Quietus, perhaps the proconsul of Asia of A.D. 125/126, an ambitious dialogue, *About those whom the gods delay in punishing*, which raises difficult problems of divine providence and justice and vindication of right, and ends with a Platonic myth. To Cornelius Pulcher was addressed an essay *On turning the enmity of others to one's own good;* he held some office 'in which you can be of great service to the public while preserving the best of relations towards those with whom you have personal dealings'.[8] Lucius, whom we cannot identify, was present at the dinner-party which Sulla gave in Rome to welcome Plutarch on his second (?) visit to Rome; he was a Pythagorean and on that occasion maintained that Pythagoras originally came from Etruria, and he produced evidence for his belief.

A treatise *On tranquillity* was sent to Paccius; it was written specially at his request, in a hurry—all the same it is as full of quotations as any other work—and it seems to have been written in response to a need, as help in some time of anxiety and worry; in short, Plutarch was being asked for counsel as a spiritual adviser. We do not know which Paccius it was, merely that he was a senator. In a dialogue entitled *On the control of anger* Fundanus and Sulla are the only speakers. Fundanus is probably to be identified with C. Minicius Fundanus, consul A.D. 107. It is not known that he held any official position in Achaea, and it may be presumed that Plutarch came to know him in Rome. On the other hand, Saturninus, to whom *Against Colotes* was dedicated, is probably L. Herennius who was proconsul of Achaea in A.D. 98–99 and *consul suffectus* in A.D. 100. This treatise deals with Epicureanism; for Colotes of Lampsacus was a fanatical admirer of Epicurus and had written a work which in a rather superficial way attempted to show that any theory of knowledge other than the empiricism of Epicurus could afford no sure foundation for practical life. Plutarch and some friends had read this work together and Plutarch offers his criticism. Saturninus is described as 'a lover of all that is fine, a lover of antiquity who found a royal pleasure in storing up in his memory and having at his fingertips the teachings of the ancients'.

The most distinguished of Plutarch's Roman friends was Sosius Senecio, himself a friend of Trajan and consul in A.D. 99, 102, 107. An essay *On consciousness of progress in virtue* was addressed to him; he took part in *Table Talks* at Patrae and Athens, indeed it was he who suggested to Plutarch the idea of writing up these *Talks*. The subjects of the *Talks* in which he appears are: a discussion on 'love and poetry' in which he contributes a dictum of Theophrastus that sorrow, pleasure and 'divine possession' are the motive forces; elsewhere he takes part in a discussion on whether the egg or the hen came first and maintains that the whole must come before the part; elsewhere Plutarch refers to his disapproval of the Epicurean doctrine of the dependence of the soul on the body. More important, it was to Senecio that Plutarch dedicated the *Parallel Lives*. He probably held a high command in the Dacian Wars, but we know of no office in Achaea. We shall meet him again more than once.[9]

There remains one other Roman friend, Sextus Sulla, of whom something can be said, and four others, of whom little more than the names need to be recorded, Terentius Priscus, Aufidius Modestus, Bestia, Moderatus. Sextus Sulla of Carthage gave a dinner-party in Rome to welcome Plutarch on his second (?) visit to Rome. The scene of the dialogue *On the control of anger* is Rome, with Sulla and Fundanus as the speakers. Sulla says he has been staying with Fundanus for five months. Whether Sulla ever went to Chaeronea is unknown; neither the dialogue *On the face on the moon* nor the *Table Talks* in which he appears give any indication of place.[10] The *Table Talks* show him interested in medical matters, while on the topic of the hen and the egg he observes that nothing less than the nature of the cosmos is here involved; in the dialogue on the Moon he contributes an interesting tradition concerning a religious survival in the islands west of Britain; he was clearly well-informed on daemonology and similar matters. To Terentius Priscus was addressed an important dialogue *On the failure of the oracles*. But it is not easy to discover who he was.[11]

These samples do little justice to the full range of subjects about which Plutarch talks with his Roman friends. But, even so, certain things are worth noticing. Even among these few Romans we have evidence of Platonism, Aristotelianism, Pythagoreanism, Stoicism. It is clear that to some of them at least Plutarch acts as guide and counsellor; he is a close friend of many, and some he sees not only at Rome but also in Chaeronea and elsewhere in Greece. Among them there is no historian, and no political subject is discussed, though many of them held public posts of importance and Plutarch himself regarded public life as providing the fullest opportunity for the exercise of moral qualities. The reasons are, perhaps, to be found partly in the character of the times; in the reign of Domitian political discussions could be interpreted in the worst light. But the main reason is that Plutarch himself is not really interested in political theory or in the problems of organisation or administration, but in the qualities of mind and character of men as men, as citizens, and, if the call should come, as holders of office; and he seems to be unable to think outside the range of offices which might be held in a city-state. The Empire as such did not interest him.*

* See further chapter 10.

CHAPTER 6

Plutarch, Roman Literary Society and the Emperor

PLUTARCH then made some mark in Rome. People thronged to his lectures; he was invited to the houses of his Roman friends and there no doubt made new friends. If only we knew how often he went to Rome, in what years and how long he stayed, we might find some answer to problems which force themselves on our attention. Let it be assumed that Plutarch visited Rome in the late seventies and the early nineties. In the late seventies he was little over thirty years old and his fame lay in front of him; in the early nineties he had a number of Roman friends and a reputation high enough to attract large audiences. Why is it then that no contemporary Roman makes mention of Plutarch? Was he merely on the fringe of learned circles in Rome? Was he merely one of those visiting Greek philosophers who for the last two centuries had carried Greek learning to the capital? Were educated Romans at this time less interested in philosophy than they had been a generation earlier? Was there even an antipathy to philosophy, and, when in A.D. 93 Domitian expelled philosophers from Rome, was this act more than a merely personal dislike or suspicion? And is it possible that Plutarch himself came under this order of expulsion and departed with Mestrius Florus to north Italy? Finally, if answers to these questions were to be found, would they be found in the nature of educated society at this time or would Plutarch's own character be part of the solution?

The problem becomes more puzzling when it is recalled that four of Plutarch's most distinguished friends–Senecio, Fundanus, Nigrinus and his brother–were also friends of Pliny the Younger. We have two letters from Pliny to Senecio; in one[1] he

asks him to give a tribuneship to the nephew of a friend whom
they both had in common; in the other he complains that people
do not attend 'recitations' as regularly or as conscientiously as
in his parents' day; he himself makes a point of hearing his
friends recite and indeed he has often stayed up in Rome for the
purpose: 'there is practically no one who likes letters who does
not like men.' Why then did Senecio not interest Pliny in Plutarch? It is true that often Pliny speaks rather slightingly of
philosophy; yet he bestows the most lavish and genuine praise
on Euphrates. If ever liberal studies flourished in Rome, he says,
they flourish now; there are many distinguished instances, I will
name one only, the philosopher Euphrates. He had met him
first in Syria and had learned to admire him greatly. He describes his appearance, manner and character at length; he himself is far too busy to profit from studying with him, though he
does complain to him occasionally about being so absorbed in
public affairs and receives reassurance that devotion to duty and
to the cause of justice is in itself no mean part of philosophy.
Pliny says he is not convinced that it would not be better for
him to spend his whole day listening to so saintly a man; but if
he cannot, there is no reason to withhold good from his friends
and he urges his friend Clemens to come to Rome earlier than
he intended, indeed to come specially to hear this remarkable
teacher. Most of Pliny's description of Euphrates would apply
to Plutarch himself; Euphrates is a Platonist, sociable, kindly,
well-mannered, affecting none of the gloom of the typical philosopher; his teaching is subtle, comprehensive, sublime; he chastises vices rather than people, his purpose is to help people to
mend themselves rather than to condemn them. Perhaps Pliny
was so firm an admirer of Euphrates that it would have been
useless for Senecio to suggest that he might hear Plutarch.[2]

During the nineties there existed in Rome a circle of writers
whose works have come down to us. Quintilian, who might have
had something in common with Plutarch, gave up his official
post as Professor of Rhetoric about A.D. 90 and had undertaken
the task of teaching Domitian's great-nephews. He too knew
Pliny. Martial's friends included Lucan, Frontinus, Juvenal,

Valerius Flaccus, Pliny, Silius Italicus and Statius. Tacitus, another of Pliny's friends, returned to Rome about A.D. 94. Yet, as far as their writings are concerned, there was no contact between Plutarch and any of them. Nor is there any firm evidence that Plutarch knew Dio Chrysostom who was driven from Rome by Domitian but returned under Nerva; as a philosopher and a staunch Hellenist he has perhaps the closest affinity to Plutarch of all the writers of whom mention has been made.*

It has been suggested earlier that Plutarch's silence about contemporary Romans, other than his own friends, might arise from something in his own nature. His interest is in philosophy, psychology, ethics, religion, and it is from this point of view mainly that he studies Roman history and antiquities. But he sets no value on Roman philosophy; he never speaks of Lucretius or Cicero or Seneca as philosophers. It is true that Roman philosophy was largely Stoical in outlook, and Plutarch professed himself an opponent of Stoicism, though in fact much of his teaching was not out of tune with it. It would seem that he felt that Roman philosophy had nothing to teach educated Greeks. Was Plutarch's indifference to Roman philosophy well known and did it account for many Romans' indifference to him? Plutarch's Roman friends would then be men who were anxious to put themselves under the guidance of a Greek philosopher, a Platonist rather than a Stoic, and were interested in more speculative matters–metaphysics, physics, comparative religion, superstition, religious rite–than Roman moral philosophy cared to pursue.

But, if Plutarch has given no evidence that he came in contact with the Roman writers of his day and if they for their part are silent about him, there persisted, as though to compensate, a most curious tradition that he knew the Emperor Trajan well enough to receive high distinction from him and to offer him advice, even instruction. For this tradition we have three pieces of evidence; the first may well be true, the second is doubtful, the third is patently false, but, true or false, they are of historical value.

* See page 136.

The first is contained in the tenth century Lexicon which goes under the name Suidas.[3] There it is said that 'when Trajan gave to him (Plutarch) the honours which belong to consuls, he enacted that none of those who held office in Illyria should carry out any policy which was outside his (Plutarch's) approval'.

There is nothing inherently improbable in the idea that Plutarch might have known Trajan; his friend Senecio was a close friend of Trajan; Plutarch himself had written a treatise on the theme that a philosopher had a special duty to talk with rulers. Nor is it impossible that Trajan should bestow the *ornamenta consularia*—for presumably that is meant by the Greek text —on a distinguished person, no doubt at the suggestion of Senecio; but the award does imply that Plutarch had won a considerable reputation at Rome. There are however difficulties in the last part of the notice in Suidas. It seems odd that the Governor of Illyricum should be required to refer to Plutarch if he wished to act in Achaea, for in Plutarch's time Achaea was governed by an independent proconsul of its own. If, however, it is remembered that under Diocletian Achaea became part of the prefecture of Illyricum, it is at any rate intelligible that the writer of this passage should have substituted Illyria, which he himself knew as the administrative unit, for Achaea, which he had forgotten was a separate province in Plutarch's day; he meant really 'officials in Achaea'. Again, it seems odd that Trajan should have given orders that the proconsul and his officials should be limited to acts which had Plutarch's approval, if that is the meaning of the passage. But it would be quite intelligible if Trajan, having invested Plutarch with the 'ornaments' of consular rank, should advise his proconsul to consult with a distinguished and learned citizen of Athens on matters of cult and observance, local rivalries and ambitions, Delphi and the Academy and the like; this would be the field in which the advice of Plutarch would be invaluable, and a wise proconsul would gladly accept help when the local traditions and sentiments of a very touchy people were involved.[4]

The second piece of evidence is the letter of dedication

addressed to Trajan which precedes the work *The sayings of kings and generals*. This work contains over five hundred anecdotes generally culminating in a saying; it stretches in time from the Kings of Persia and Egypt, through Greek generals to the tyrants of Syracuse and finishes with twenty Roman names, from M. Curius to Augustus. Whether this is a genuine work from Plutarch's pen has been much disputed; if spurious, the dedication is likely to be spurious; if genuine, the dedication may none the less be spurious. It reads as follows:

Plutarch sends many greetings to the Emperor Trajan. Great Emperor, Caesar Trajan, the King of the Persians, Artaxerxes, who thought it no less a kingly and humane thing to do to receive with graciousness and eagerness small gifts than to give large gifts, was riding along the road one day when an ordinary worker in the fields scooped up some water from the river in both his hands and offered it as a gift, for he had no other. Artaxerxes gladly received it with a smile, for he measured the kindness not by the usefulness of the gift but by the eagerness of the giver. In Sparta Lycurgus appointed sacrifices of the most inexpensive kind; his purpose was that the Spartans should be able to honour the gods readily and easily, using things already to hand. In such spirit make acceptance from me too, when I offer you humble gifts, presents of friendship, the common first-fruits of philosophy – accept from an eager giver these notes and see if they help you to understand the moral qualities and principles which belong to rulers, which become apparent rather in what they say than in what they do. And yet the collection of the most illustrious teachers and lawgivers and sole rulers among the Romans and Greeks includes also lives. But in their actions there is as a rule an element of chance, whereas the utterances and assertions made at the moment of action or of emotion, or of a chance happening give the means of studying quite clearly, as in mirrors, the mental make-up of each individual. When people were surprised that, though what Seiramnes the Persian said was always shrewd, his deeds were not successful, he replied that he himself controlled his words, but chance, together with the King, controlled his actions. Now there (*i.e. in the Lives*) the utterances of the men, with the deeds set beside them, await a devoted reader, but a reader with leisure. But here (*i.e. in the following work*) their words are collected by themselves, like samples and seeds of the lives, and I do not think the opportunity will be a burden to you; you will get briefly a close sight of many men who became worthy of memory.[5]

47

On the whole it is reasonable to believe that this dedication has been attached to a treatise (whether genuine or not does not matter) by someone other than Plutarch who tried to make it look authentic, but did not succeed. But it is no less reasonable to hold that the author would not invent the whole situation, for the dedication would not have seemed plausible if it did not rest upon some basis of truth. It must be taken, therefore, to attest at least a belief that Plutarch and Trajan were in some degree acquainted.

That this belief became a tradition is shown by the third piece of evidence. It comes from the fifth book of the *Policraticus*, a medley of information and reflection on statecraft, written by John of Salisbury at the end of the twelfth century. More than once John speaks of the *Institutio Traiani*, which seems to have meant to him an essay, written by Plutarch, to educate or instruct Trajan in the principles of government. He quotes it, in the fifth book, first *in extenso*, as far as we can judge, and later makes incidental references to it; he gives it in Latin. Such treatises were common indeed about A.D. 100. Dio Chrysostom wrote four essays *On kingship* which are extant. They were addressed to Trajan and they dealt with the character of the ideal ruler and offered advice on the principles of government which he should observe. Under Plutarch's name we have works with the titles *To an untrained ruler, Political Precepts* a fragment, *On Monarchy, Democracy, Oligarchy, Should an old man take part in political life?* and *A philosopher has a special duty to converse with rulers.* It is not unthinkable that Plutarch could have written a treatise on government and addressed it to Trajan, but it could not have contained a great deal that John of Salisbury supposes it did.[6]

Briefly, there are four things which the writer strives to impress on the rulers of a state; reverence for God, veneration for themselves, discipline on the part of officials and holders of authority, love and protective care shown by their subjects. The ruler then declares that above all God must be held in honour; next, that he himself must be venerated; after that, he strives that the discipline of his whole house shall be permeated by the

48

influence of its controller, and finally that his subjects, one and all, shall rejoice in the safety of the head of those set over them. Also he makes use of the strategy and tactics of the great men (at this point John adds, 'but if these were cited individually, they would be tiresome to the reader and would depart in great measure from our sincere beliefs'.)

There are elements in this passage which recall the essays on the ideal ruler of which mention has been made.* The classes of society specified in the passage bear some resemblance to those of Plato's *Republic*, priests, administrators (civil, judicial, military), agricultural workers and artisans. But the most striking feature is the subordination of the secular to the religious power; the tone and indeed the wording recall the struggle between Church and State, Pope and Emperor of the early middle ages. Whether the basis is some document written in Greek in the East Roman Empire, whether John of Salisbury could have translated such a document into Latin or whether he received it in a Latin version, whether in its original form it bore the name of Plutarch—questions of this kind are probably unanswerable, and certainly not here. The important points are the association of Plutarch with Trajan and the high reputation of Plutarch which invited the attachment of his name to a document of this kind.

Such, then, is the evidence. Opinions will vary about its cogency. Clearly there is something in these three passages which cannot be explained away entirely, and it is not unreasonable to suppose that at least the acquaintance of Plutarch and Trajan must be accepted as a fact.

But there is more; curiously enough, Plutarch is said by the historian Eusebius (*c.* A.D. 260–340) to have been known to Hadrian. Under the year A.D. 119 he notes, 'Plutarch of Chaeronea, the philosopher, was appointed when he was an old man to be in charge of (epitropeuein) Greece'. If this notice refers to some real fact, whatever exactly it may be, it is important as establishing that Plutarch was still alive in A.D. 119. But, as usual, the meaning is not clear; *epitropos* is the Greek for *procurator*,

* See also pages 138 ff.

but Achaea was governed by a proconsul. It is true that Hadrian appointed *correctores civitatium liberarum*—that is, officials to put the accounts of the free cities of Greece into order—but the Greek equivalent for *corrector* is *diorthotes*; nor is Plutarch likely to have been appointed to carry out such a task, for he would be a Greek examining the affairs of Greek cities, which would be inappropriate; and at the age of seventy or so he would scarcely be able to carry out such exacting work. Perhaps Eusebius is referring to the position which Suidas says Trajan gave Plutarch, but then he is wrong as regards date and Emperor, which is unusual.

Finally, it must not be argued that, because Plutarch says nothing about Trajan or Hadrian or the offices or honours which they may have conferred on him, the tradition is to be rejected entirely. As has been seen, he says nothing about the business which took him to Corinth or to Italy, nor about his Roman citizenship. Again, it is possible that he wrote nothing after the award of these honours, for his writings are notoriously difficult to date; perhaps, even, the work entailed prevented him from writing. But nothing can be built on such speculations. How much credence will be given to the tradition, conveyed to us from various quarters at various times, that Plutarch came into touch with the Emperor, will depend largely upon individual interpretation.

CHAPTER 7

The *Lives*

BEFORE writing the *Parallel Lives* Plutarch had written a life of Augustus, no longer extant. Thus he was spared the task of finding a Greek 'parallel'. His first pair of lives was Epaminondas–Scipio, but that too is lost, and unfortunately, for Epaminondas was to him not only the greatest Boeotian, but also the greatest Greek of all time. It was his virtues that gave him this position, and in this estimate we can see the measure by which Plutarch assesses greatness.

Moreover, the life of Epaminondas probably contained an introductory dedication to Sosius Senecio; three references to him in the *Lives* suggest that the work as a whole was dedicated to him, and a fuller and formal dedication in the first life might have elaborated Plutarch's purpose and method in writing them.

The description *Parallel Lives* appears to be Plutarch's own.[1] The life of Theseus, which was not the first to be written, though it stands first in our traditional order, opens with this passage:

You know, Sosius, how in their maps geographers crowd into the margins the parts of the world of which they have no real knowledge and attach notes like 'Beyond here sandy deserts full of wild beasts', and 'Mud and Murk' and 'Scythian frost' and 'Sea of Ice'. I am in the same case; in writing the *Parallel Lives* I have passed through the period which can be reached by reasonable narrative and by investigation which offers a foothold based on reality, and I might very well say about earlier times 'What lies beyond is the realm of marvel and imagination; it is inhabited by poets and story-tellers; it is not trustworthy nor true.' Having published an account of Lycurgus the lawgiver and Numa the King, I thought it reasonable to climb up to

51

Romulus, since I found my narrative had brought me into the neighbourhood of his times. And when I reflected 'Who shall match himself with so great a man? Whom shall I set against him? Who is a trusty adversary to him?' I decided to oppose to him the founder of fair Athens, famed in song, comparing him with the father of invincible and glorious Rome; I hope that in the process of being purified by reason myth will become subservient to our purposes and take on the semblance of the true events. But when myth obstinately slights credibility and will allow no dilution to make it reasonable, we shall need sympathetic readers, willing to accept with indulgence the stories of antiquity.

To compare one statesman, one general with another is not a very original undertaking. It is an elementary exercise which must have been prevalent enough in the schools and 'universities' of Greece. Plutarch himself probably used it in teaching his pupils. It is not a great advance to compare a Greek and Roman general, though on the whole it would be more natural in a Roman, or a Greek living in Italy, than in a Greek devoted to Greek history and literature. What appears to be original is to undertake a whole series of such comparisons. It is probable that Plutarch did not plan such a series; after publishing one or two pairs of lives he was encouraged by his Roman friends to undertake more. The idea was not entirely new. At the end of his series of short lives of 'outstanding generals' Cornelius Nepos, whose work was known to Plutarch, has the following passage: 'it is time for me to put an end to this book and to treat of Roman generals so that, when the achievements of each set of generals have been compared, it will be easier to assess which are to be preferred.' The method seems to invite comparison of Greek and Roman generalship rather than of one individual with another, but doubtless, when the attempt was made, the comparison would be bound to put one individual alongside another.

The manuscripts preserve for us twenty-three pairs of lives. Generally, the Greek was chosen first and a Roman counterpart was found, a procedure natural to a Greek. As regards choice of heroes, and the counterparts assigned to them, Plutarch followed his own interest of the moment; hence he was led

to detect resemblances which, from the standpoint of his purpose in writing, seemed to him to be striking and convincing.
But in the formal assessment of likeness and unlikeness which he
appends to each pair he sometimes seems to find it difficult to
make out his case; to us it is obvious that the original choice was
at fault. Some pairs are happily yoked by historical situation,
character, career, as *e.g.* Demosthenes and Cicero, Agis and
Cleomenes with the Gracchi, Theseus and Romulus; but Pericles and Fabius Maximus have little in common; Aristides and
Cato may turn out on consideration to be a better pair than
would appear. Perhaps from Plutarch's own rather circum-
scribed point of view there was a real link. All depends on his
purpose, which will be examined presently.

In the meantime it is worth noticing that of the Greek *Lives*
ten are of Athenians, three of Spartans, two of Thebans; after
Alexander, the series extends through the Diadochi to the Spartan Kings Agis iv and Cleomenes iii who died in 219 B.C., and
finally to Philopoemen of Megalopolis who died in 182 B.C. On
the Roman side Romulus and Numa represent the kings; in the
early Republic are Poplicola, Coriolanus, Camillus; then come
the names of the second Punic War and a little later—Fabius
Maximus, Marcellus, Scipio Africanus, Cato, Flamininus,
Aemilius Paulus. The remaining lives span the hundred years to
the Battle of Actium and comprise the Gracchi, Marius, Sulla,
Sertorius, Lucullus, Crassus, Pompey, Caesar, Cicero, Cato the
Younger, Brutus and Antonius. Besides the *Parallel Lives* there
are four separate lives—of Artaxerxes and Aratus and Galba
and Otho.

We are left in no doubt about the purpose of the *Lives*.

I am not engaged in writing history, but lives. It is not in the most
conspicuous of a man's acts that good and bad qualities are necessarily best manifested. Some trivial act, a word, a jest often shows up
character far more than engagements, with thousands of dead, or
pitched battles or blockades. Painters get their resemblances of portrait with subject from the face and the parts round the eyes; that is
where character shines out and so they pay little regard to the rest of
the body. In the same way we must be allowed to penetrate into the
manifestations of the soul and by their aid to create a picture of each

individual life, leaving to others all the great exploits and the struggles.*

Again:

The idea of writing lives I owe to others; it is my own resolve to continue in this field and to take up residence there. Using history as a mirror I try by whatever means I can to improve my own life and to model it by the standard of all that is best in those whose lives I write. As a result I feel as though I were conversing and indeed living with them; by means of history I receive each one of them in turn, welcome and entertain them as guests and consider their stature and their qualities and select from their actions the most authoritative and the best with a view to getting to know them. What greater pleasure could one enjoy than this or what more efficacious in improving one's own character. . . ? By spending time on history and by practising writing we prepare ourselves to receive and store in our souls recollection of the best and most famous men, and to drive out and thrust from us whatever mean or corrupt or ignoble influence is exercised on us by those with whom daily life compels association, and to temper and discipline our thoughts and turn them towards the very best ideals of conduct.[2]

And again, however much he may admire the work of a Phidias or an Anacreon, no one for that reason wants to be a Phidias. It does not follow that to admire a work of art is to admire its author, still less to be stimulated to imitation. With virtue it is different.

Virtue, through its expression in acts, at once so affects a man that the moment he admires the things done he emulates the doer. The 'goods' which come from fortune we value in the acquisition and in the enjoyment; the goods which come from virtue we value in the practice; the first we wish to take for ourselves from others, the second we wish to be available to others from us. The beauty of goodness impels us towards itself; it impels us to act; it implants in us an urge to be up and doing; it influences our characters not by inviting us to look at it as in a picture, but in the very narration of a noble act it furnishes us with the necessary disposition of will.[3]

Briefly, then, we are to learn from the noblest examples and

* The first part of this passage is quoted by Boswell to support his own method of biography. *Life of Johnson* i. page 21 (Oxford edn.). Johnson said of his *Lives of the Poets* 'written, I hope, in such a manner as may tend to promote piety' (ii. p. 357).

to form our own characters by constant association with the best, and by our characters to influence others. To help us Plutarch will select the most suitable men to study and will select from their lives the elements which will most edify.

But a difficulty arises, which he faces candidly. The life of a man is compounded of good and evil. To select only the good would be to distort the truth. Yet it is the good which the *Lives* are written to put before us.

The difficulty is resolved as follows. The function of the senses is to receive impressions and to report to the mind. The arts, on the other hand, are so constituted with the help of reason as to select an object suitable to their purposes and to reject the unsuitable; in order to select and to reject they must pass in review all objects. Medicine, to promote health, must take notice of disease, harmony notice of discord; the supreme arts, self-control, goodness, understanding, must consider and judge not only acts which embody them, but also acts which embody their opposites; they do not commend mere innocence which prides itself on inexperience of evil; they give such a state its right names, stupidity and ignorance of what anyone who wishes to live aright should know. And so Plutarch thinks it will be no bad plan to choose one or two men conspicuous alike for their high position and their ill-doing—not, of course, to amuse or divert his readers—and to include them in his collection alongside the lives which provide models of behaviour. As Ismenias used to make his pupils listen to bad players of the flute as well as to good so that they might learn to distinguish, so 'we shall be all the more eager to watch and to imitate the lives of the good if we are not left without a description of what is mean and reprehensible'. And so Plutarch puts together the lives of Demetrius Poliorcetes and Antony the 'autocrat', men who bear eloquent witness to Plato, when he said that great natures produce great vices as well as great virtues.[4]

To this eloquent statement of his purpose—Platonic in its tribute to the compelling power of goodness, once it is seen, Aristotelian in its insistence on the importance of the will—Plutarch adds two corollaries, which reflect his honesty and his kindliness.

55

Lucullus had done the people of Chaeronea a great service by submitting to a court of law a true account of a certain incident for which they, as a township, had been blamed; as a result they were acquitted and in gratitude had erected a statue of him in the market-place. Plutarch still feels gratitude and, since he thinks an image of the character of a man to be a greater honour than an image of his face and person, proposes to include him in his *Lives* and to give a true account of his life. After all Lucullus would not be grateful for a fictitious and counterfeit 'life' in return for a service which consisted in giving true evidence.

It is clear that Plutarch knows that he will have to say a good deal in Lucullus' disfavour; none the less the truth must prevail. But he must preserve a sense of proportion in presenting truth, for there is another side to human frailty which should not be forgotten; and so he proceeds:

We expect that a portrait-painter painting a subject which has beauty and charm but also some small feature less attractive should neither leave it out entirely nor elaborate it to excess, for he would present on the one hand something deformed, on the other hand something which was not a likeness. In the same way it is difficult, perhaps impossible, to exhibit a 'life' which is blameless and pure; and so we must select its good elements and in these we must satisfy truth and present a likeness. The shortcomings and faults which run through a man's conduct owing to individual passion or political necessity we should regard rather as the defects of goodness than the misdeeds of wickedness; these our narrative should not display eagerly or gratuitously; rather it should show restraint out of regard for human nature, which produces nothing of unalloyed nobility, no character beyond the criticism of goodness.

Few authors reveal themselves as unconsciously and as endearingly as Plutarch. In this last passage the charm with which he has captivated readers through the ages is abundantly felt. A service rendered long ago to his beloved Chaeronea 'stretches over the generations' and claims his gratitude; he can make no greater return than to include the benefactor in his *Parallel Lives*. With great delicacy he hints that the 'Life' may contain unattractive features; but truth compels. With a disarming humour he reminds his hero, long since dead, that the service was rendered by telling the truth. And then without condoning human frailty he interprets it with a generosity and insight which reflect his own kindly and reflective nature. It is all beautifully done; here is Plutarch's art, and Plutarch's art is the man himself.

Such is Plutarch's account of his purpose in writing the *Lives*. But modern interpreters are not content: they propose other reasons, not always in agreement.[5] It is maintained that in writing the *Lives* Plutarch wished to explain the Greeks to the Romans, the Romans to the Greeks, to the Romans that the Greeks were not *Graeculi*, but had a distinguished record as statesmen and generals, to the Greeks that the Romans were not barbarians, but in acquiring and maintaining an Empire had shown their high qualities. His purpose, then, was interpretation and reconciliation. To this view others take strong exception; Plutarch, it is held, was a Hellenist who would yield not even equality to any other race. Greek supremacy in literature, art and philosophy was admitted even by the Romans. His task in the *Lives* was to demonstrate the superiority of the Greeks also as statesmen and generals.

Of all this there is nothing in the *Lives*; nor is there any explicit statement in Plutarch's other works; as has been seen, Plutarch's purpose as stated repeatedly by himself is very different. Of course, it is possible to urge that an author may have a primary reason which he states and may also have secondary reasons which he does not state, but which may be read between the lines by his critics and interpreters. As regards Plutarch, the evidence must be found, if found at all, in his selection and presentation of his material in the *Lives* or in his general attitude to Greeks and Romans as far as it can be discovered in his works as a whole.

It has sometimes been urged that in spite of Plutarch's denial that he is writing 'history', he does in fact include much history in his *Lives*. But his avowed purpose in writing the *Lives* does not mean that he should confine himself to the task of gathering together a scrap-book of anecdotes or a collection of 'sayings' illustrating the moral dispositions of his hero. To Plutarch life is activity; a man's actions reveal his character; his actions are initiated by himself or are reactions to the actions of other men. A spotlight on the hero will reveal nothing; the whole stage—scenery and actors—must be lit up if he is to be seen for 'what manner of man he is'. And so the minor part of a life contains strictly moral sidelights on its subject, the major portion is given up to narrative; and, since the hero is a man who has played a big part in the events of his times, campaigns and politics, strategy and state-craft make up most of the narrative. There are times when Plutarch, like the good story-teller he is, is carried away by his story, and a life contains perhaps more of the setting than is strictly necessary. Moreover he is a philosopher, and there are passages of musing, often highly interesting, but not always relevant. None the less he believes that when he includes much 'history' he is true to his purpose. He puts the matter clearly in his life of Nicias. First, he disclaims comparison with Thucydides, who in this part of his narrative has surpassed himself in pathos, kindness and subtlety and is indeed inimitable. But he feels he must run over, even though briefly, the actions of Nicias, which, though described by Thucydides, bring out a character and disposition often concealed by the great sufferings he underwent; for he must not appear negligent. Further, he will gather together much that has escaped other writers; he will get contributions from inscriptions and decrees. But he will not amass merely useless historical material; he will hand on to posterity only what will help to an understanding of his subject's character and disposition.

Indeed there are times when Plutarch almost seems to see his purpose in terms of dramatic writing. In the *Life of Galba*, after two or three sentences summing up the character of the times, he breaks off, reminding himself that a detailed account of events would need a full, systematic history whereas he must confine himself to what the Caesars did and suffered. Again, 'now that the Macedonian drama has been acted through to the end (by Demetrius), watch the Roman drama as it is brought next upon the stage' (with Antony as protagonist). Of Cato the Younger's marriage to Marcia, Plutarch says 'This passage in Cato's life, as though in a tragedy, poses a problem which it is difficult to solve.' If, as Aristotle says, drama is more philosophical than history, Plutarch the philosopher was right to concern himself with men's lives–their characters and their acts–rather than with the details of history.[6]

The theory that Plutarch wishes to demonstrate the superiority of the Greeks over the Romans may be tested by examination of the 'Comparisons' which he attached to eighteen pairs of the *Lives*. Admittedly these Comparisons are artificial, arbitrary in the choice of headings under which comparison is made, superficial in their analysis of the circumstances in which each hero in his pair acted, and sometimes shallow in their estimate of character. They are by no means Plutarch's best work; indeed their ineffectiveness has led some critics to doubt their authenticity, though on insufficient grounds. But they are worth examining. Indeed Plutarch himself virtually invites us in the *Lives* themselves to make comparative assessment paragraph by paragraph under the headings which he has indicated. 'On this score Dion has the greater superiority', 'so that thus far a man would vote for Theseus', 'both may fairly equally be acquitted on this charge', 'their exploits in war were equal and parallel', 'perhaps it will be a reasonable award if we give to the Greek the crown for military experience and generalship, to the Roman the crown for uprightness and goodness'. If such an assessment is undertaken, care must be taken to ask whether in a given paragraph Plutarch himself is summing up in favour of the Greek or the Roman; the competence or the justice of his verdict are irrelevant. On one such assessment the score won by Greek and Roman respectively seems to be about equal; Plutarch is at pains to give each hero his due; indeed he sometimes seems anxious to make the score equal; he is very far from favouring the Greek.

Much time and energy have been expended in attempts to discover whether Plutarch wrote each Life according to a scheme or plan, suggested to him by literary tradition or convention or devised by himself. One answer to this question is to point out that we do not possess the material with which to form any judgment. We have nothing or practically nothing of Greek biography to justify our saying that there was a convention or a tradition, still less more than one. But the best answer is to read the *Lives* themselves; one of their great charms is the varied manner in which their subjects are treated. This manner owes nothing to a preconceived pattern; it seems to determine itself according to the material available and the mood of the author as he writes it. He tells a story as it occurs to him to tell it; sometimes he reflects and ruminates more than at other times; he may on occasion be didactic; sometimes the flow of narrative carries him on and he is content.

In the *Lives*, then, are to be found a historical narrative which provides the setting, the exploits in the State or in the field which illuminate the character of his hero, musings and philosophic reflections which develop the psychology of the characters, a few descriptions of natural scenery, a wealth of small detail which, though perhaps trivial from the historical standpoint, give truth and reality and a kind of intimacy. Above all, the singlemindedness and sincerity of the author stand out; with an earnestness which is free from priggishness and a fervour which does not preach he identifies himself with his heroes and does his best to let us see them as human beings, with human strengths and weaknesses. Of himself he says little: but he stands out in the *Lives* as the greatest and most lovable 'hero' of them all.*

The historian brings many complaints against him. His chronology is woefully weak; geography is largely taken for granted. The social or economic conditions which invite the reforming legislation of a statesman are often imperfectly understood and described; strategy and tactics may be obscure; as with most ancient historians, the development of character is little understood, even though Plutarch is interested in psycho-

---

* In 1823 Edward Schulz wrote of the composer of the Eroica Symphony 'Es wird Sie freuen, zu hören, dass er ein grosser Bewunderer der Alten ist. Homer, besonders seine Odyssée, und Plutarch zieht er allen andern vor.' *Beethoven, Briefe und Gespräche*, herausgegeben von Martin Hürlimann, Zurich, 1946.

logy. None the less the historian and the Roman antiquarian are deeply indebted to Plutarch for much detail that they would not otherwise know, and his testimony, even though it may not be peculiar to him, is always valuable. To examine the value of Plutarch's evidence throughout a single life would need a separate study: here we may take one episode as an example – the Conference at Luca.

The so-called Conference of Luca (56 B.C.) was hastily summoned by Caesar in an attempt to strengthen the fast disintegrating Triumvirate. Domitius and Cato were giving much trouble at Rome. Cicero had already given notice of a motion that the Senate should discuss the legality of the agrarian law of 59 B.C. which gave lands in Campania to Pompey's veterans. Thus Cicero defied the Triumvirate, which was already insecure; for Pompey was unable to control affairs at Rome and Caesar's provincial government would expire in March. Pompey's aid was necessary to prolong Caesar's government. New plans must be made.

The evidence for the Conference is extremely meagre. In a letter[7] of 54 B.C. (June?) Cicero says that Pompey showed no sign of being offended with him, but on his way to Sardinia and Africa had met Caesar at Luca, when Caesar had made many complaints about Cicero, having already been roused to anger about him by Crassus whom he had met at Ravenna. The letter goes on to refer to the guarantee which his brother, Q. Cicero, had given on his behalf that he would not oppose the policy of the triumvirs.[8] And from a letter of 56 B.C. it is clear that Cicero honoured his brother's guarantee, published his 'palinode' (perhaps the speech *de provinciis consularibus*) and withdrew from politics. That is all that Cicero has to say about a Conference which had such momentous consequences for him. He tells us nothing about its decisions, he does not say whether they were made known, he does not speculate about their nature.

And that is all the evidence we have about the Conference of Luca till we come to Plutarch, whose information will be reviewed in a moment. In the meantime we may note that, soon after Plutarch, Suetonius gives us one sentence in which he tells us that Caesar summoned Crassus and Pompey to a town, Luca, in his province and arranged that, to squeeze out Domitius, they should stand for a second consulship and that Caesar's command in Gaul should be renewed for another five years. Appian, a little later still, gives a few details obviously derived from Plutarch.[9]

Plutarch wrote the lives of the three men who took part in this Conference, and so he offers us three separate accounts of it.[10] It does not take very careful examination to reveal that the version in the life of Pompey and the version in the life of Crassus contain different traditions. In one it appears that the terms of agreement were published, at once; in the other the principals 'met secretly'; they 'fell under suspicion' and a 'report' spread. What was the truth? That the terms were broadcast as soon as agreed upon? that they were kept secret until, as event followed event, men guessed that such and such a step had formed part of the agreement of Luca? or was there a leak? And what is the modern historian of this period to do?

As an illustration of Plutarch's method of composing the *Lives*, the three accounts are of great significance. It might have been expected that a writer proposing to write the lives of three men whose careers were interlocked would come to some decision in his own mind about such an event as a conference in which all took part and that he would give in each life the same account. There is no question of each life treating the matter from the point of view of the subject; all three lives are objective.

Clearly, Plutarch did not study the sources of a period of history and as a result of a critical evaluation of the evidence arrive at a version of events which was for him at least definitive. He did not work out for himself a textbook of Roman history to which he fitted his lives. Each life is a separate study, based on sources some of which might be specific to the subject, but dependent also to great extent on Plutarch's own memory of his previous reading. It would be easy to take other historical situations common to more than one life and to point out similarities and discrepancies in treatment. But Plutarch would not mind;

his aim as he himself said was to write not history but lives.

But what Plutarch would mind most emphatically, it is suspected, is the suggestion made by the brothers Langhorne in the life of Plutarch which precedes their translation published in 1770.

Notes in the time of Plutarch were not in use. Had he known the convenience of marginal writing, he would certainly have thrown the greatest part of his digressions into that form. They are, undoubtedly, tedious and disgustful; and all we can do to reconcile ourselves to them is to remember that, in the first place, marginal writing was a thing unknown; and that the benevolent desire of conveying instruction, was the greatest motive with the biographer, for introducing them. This appears, at least, from the nature of them; for they are chiefly disquisitions in natural history and philosophy.

And, in their preface, they say:

We often wished to throw out of the text into the notes those tedious and digressive comments that spoil the beauty and order of his narrative, mortifying the expectation, frequently, when it is most essentially interested, and destroy the natural influence of his story, by turning the attention into a different channel. What, for instance, can be more irksome and impertinent than a long dissertation on a point of natural philosophy starting up at the very crisis of some important action? Every reader of Plutarch must have felt the pain of these unseasonable digressions; but we could not, upon our own pleasure or authority, remove them.*

A writer, still more a talker, may digress because he is incapable of keeping to the point. The narrator of a story of adventure or mystery may interpolate matter not strictly necessary in order to delay action and maintain suspense. A skilful teacher will often put into a digression something which he is particularly anxious to convey to his pupils; for he knows that in this way he will catch their attention. Plutarch digressed out of the sheer exuberance of his interest and the richness of his knowledge. From his narrative he broke away into the two things which interested him above all else—human nature and the behaviour of men on the one hand, on the other nature and her ways. We

* It is the pleasure of some modern translators to remove so-called digressions to the footnotes, though without authority.

may call these interests psychology, ethics, and natural science; to Plutarch it was philosophy. On these things he reflected, and to reflect is to turn back upon the experiences of oneself and of other people, the people whose story he was telling. Moreover, if he himself was interested, he expected his readers to share his interest. And they probably were interested. In those days reading must have been more leisurely than now; books were fewer and their pages could not be flicked over. Readers' interests were more discursive, for the age of specialism had not come. If the writer had time to stray from the high road, so had the reader; and the digressions of Plutarch were no more tedious to his readers than those of Herodotus to his hearers. Plutarch was well aware of his tendency to digress. 'Such digressions,' he says, 'are less likely to meet with condemnation from impatient critics if they are kept within bounds.'[11]

When a Roman army encamped at the foot of Mount Olympus found itself short of water, its general, Aemilius Paulus, inferred from the luxuriant growth of trees on its slopes that there must be water underground and ordered wells to be dug, which were soon filled. Then follows a page of discussion of two rival theories about the origin of such water; are these hidden reservoirs of water waiting to be tapped or is water formed by the sudden liquefaction of vapours inherent in the earth and now released by the boring of a well? 'But of this enough.' Similarly, when a vast concourse of people at the Isthmian Games heard the news of the liberation of Greece and raised a mighty shout, crows flying overhead fell to the ground dead.

Now the cause of this is the disruption of the air. When a large volume of sound is carried up, it parts the air which no longer gives support to birds; they crash down like people walking on nothing. Or it may be that they are pierced by the noise as by an arrow and so fall and perish. Or again a vortex may be caused in the atmosphere which owing to the violence of the disturbance behaves like a whirlpool or eddy in the sea.[12]

The life of Coriolanus offers two more examples. 'Then occurred an event which resembled those frequently described in Homer', though it does not win the credence of most people.

Plutarch does not tell us what it was till after his digression; perhaps this is an instance of the digression as a means of suspend-
ing the interest of the reader.

On the occasion of some great or exceptional action Homer says
and proclaims . . . was it his [*i.e. the hero's*] own thought or did some
God command him? People condemn him on the ground that by
introducing some impossible action or some incredible invention he
invalidates human calculation and will. Homer does nothing of the
kind. Actions which are likely and ordinary and are rationally exe-
cuted he ascribes to our own direct control; for of course he often
says, 'I took counsel with my own great soul.' But actions which are
abnormal and extraordinary, which demand the élan of inspiration
and the state of being beside oneself–on these occasions Homer does
not make God take away the will; rather he stimulates it; he does
not set impulses working in it, but creates images which will induce
impulses. By means of these he does not make an action involuntary,
but rather he provides a starting-point for voluntary action, and in
addition he gives confidence and hope. For either we must get rid
entirely of divine influence on causation and origination in the
sphere of human life or we must accept that the gods do aid and co-
operate with men in the mode which I have described. They do not,
of course, shape the body or change the position of the hands and
feet to get the desired result, but they excite the energies and the will
by offering principles of action and presenting images to the imagination and thoughts to the mind, or else they deflect and inhibit them
in the same way.

All this is a preface to the story of the Roman women suppli-
cating the gods in the temples: Valeria was impelled by a divine
inspiration to persuade Volumnia to head a mission of Roman
matrons to turn the heart of Coriolanus. Only if the reader is in
a hurry will he feel this chapter to be a tedious digression;
Plutarch should not be read in a hurry.[13]

In Chapter 11 there is digression of a different kind. Plutarch
has explained how Coriolanus gained his name, and goes off
into a list of Greek and Roman *cognomina* with their explanation.
He ends up, 'But this really belongs to a different kind of book.'
Exactly: and Plutarch gathered together some of the more
recondite information which he had gained about Roman
things and instead of inserting it as digression in his Roman
lives he gathered it into his *Roman Questions*.[14]

CHAPTER 8

The *Roman Questions*: the *Greek Questions*

WE have already seen that on one occasion when Plutarch was asked by a friend to send him an essay of comfort in time of trouble he immediately consulted his notebooks in search of quotations and thoughts which would suggest the lines of the essay.* It may be taken for granted that in spite of the great powers of memory possessed by ancient scholars Plutarch relied to a great extent on the notes which he made as he read. As he studied his texts of Roman history many matters must have puzzled him; in the Greek field fewer matters would arise to give him pause, for he would be familiar with the explanations put forward by writers and by popular belief. But in dealing with Roman practices he was less at home, and it is more than likely that questions would occur to a learned Greek which would not occur to the ordinary Roman accustomed to take Roman things for granted. Moreover, Plutarch was uniquely fitted to make comparisons between Greek and Roman practice. To us any comparison he made would be of special interest as giving the thoughts of an outside observer.

And so he gathered together some of his reading-notes, and, according to the catalogue of Lamprias, he published three volumes of *Questions*–Roman, Greek, Barbarian. The last volume is lost to us; it probably contained matters which had come to his attention during his visits to Egypt and Asia Minor and in the course of his reading. Some of the notes may have been left unused when he wrote such treatises as *On Isis and Osiris*. That the *Roman Questions* were published we know for certain, for he refers to them in the Life of Romulus, one of the last to be written, and also in the Life of Camillus. It is generally assumed

* See page 40.

that the *Greek Questions* also were published, though their English editor does not believe that they were.[1]

There are one hundred and thirteen *Roman Questions*. They all begin with 'Why?' This question is then followed by others, 'Is it because . . .? or is it because . . .?' Sometimes 'is it because' is amplified with 'as so and so says', and so Plutarch reveals the source of the answer and perhaps of the question. Sometimes the solution propounded appears to be Plutarch's own, always very modestly hazarded, though he never says so. This method of writing has advantages; it is compendious; the point at issue is clearly defined and shortly stated; the rival solutions are put forward tentatively; there is no dogmatic answer; the writer takes no responsibility and the reader is left to make up his own mind.

Most of the *Questions* deal with matters relating to cult, ritual and social habits; philology and the calendar are discussed in about ten each. The Roman authorities whom Plutarch cites are naturally those whom he used in writing the *Lives*—notably Varro,[2] Cato, Cluvius Rufus, Cicero, Antistius Labeo, Livy and Juba, the learned king of Mauretania, who wrote in Greek. But he often uses a vague formula, *e.g.* 'as some say', 'the historians say', 'that is what most Romans say'; and sometimes he rejects a theory with 'popular opinion is wrong' or 'but another theory is much more likely'.

For the study of Roman origins in cult and law and social custom the questions and their answers are of great importance. But their appeal is even wider, for they are of great interest to the student of comparative religion and folk-lore. 'Why do the tribunes not wear the purple edge as other magistrates do?' 'Why are the rods of the lictors carried in bundles with the axes attached to them?' 'Why are the men who carry the rods called lictors?' 'Why was the old coinage stamped on one side with a two-faced head of Janus and on the other with the stern or prow of a ship?' There are many other questions which cite facts or practices of which the origin was quite forgotten; Plutarch does his best to provide it. 'Why did Romulus build the temple of Vulcan outside the city?' Three reasons are offered; the first is mythological, the second is pseudo-historical, the third explains that Rome has always been in danger of fires and so it was decided to honour the god of fire but to make him take up residence outside the city. The priest known as the *flamen Dialis* seems to have interested Plutarch much, for he devotes seven Questions to him; why may he not anoint himself in the open air, or take an oath, or touch meal or yeast or raw flesh or pigs or goats or ivy? and why may he not stand for office?

Plutarch had a great liking for philology, though most of his views are very fanciful. The word *lictor*, he says, is derived from the root *lig-*, to bind, for he was the man who bound malefactors. This derivation the Romans had thought out for themselves, but Plutarch adds the observation that c is a later addition and the word really should be 'litors', that is, 'public servants', from the Greek *lēitoi*. For the word *macellum*, a butcher's shop, he suggests a derivation from *mageiroi*, cooks, and he points out that the letters c and g are related in sound, while people who lisp easily slip from r to l. Or, he asks, 'must we let history solve the puzzle?' And so he relates a story that a robber Macellus was apprehended at Rome and put to death; his property was confiscated and sold and with the proceeds a meat-market was built to which his name clung.[3]

In some of the *Questions* Plutarch gives his own answers. To the question 'Why is it that husbands who have left their wives at home send on a message to say that they are on their way back?' the reply is typically Plutarchean, as any lover of the man will feel:

(*a*) Is it because such action indicates confidence that the wife is not wasting her time; for to arrive suddenly is like setting a trap or spying on her? (*b*) Or are they anxious that the good news of their return shall be brought to wives who are longing for it and eager to offer a welcome? (*c*) Or, preferably, husbands are eager to get news of their wives, wondering whether they will find them safe and longing for them? (*d*) Or is it because when their husbands are away wives are very busy with household duties, and difference of opinion and indeed quarrels with the rest of the household are bound to occur; and so the advance news enables the wife to get free from all this and to give her husband a peaceful and pleasant welcome home?

It would not be unreasonable to suppose that, when Plutarch was in Rome or when his Roman friends were in Chaeronea, he consulted them about questions which puzzled him; perhaps on occasion he consulted them by letter. To some questions no doubt they had ready answers, true or false. But for others they referred him to the 'authorities'; perhaps they even copied out extracts for him. Thus, if Plutarch cites Cicero, say, as a source, he may have been referred to the passage by a Roman. If this supposition is correct, it means that in the *Questions* we may have, in some measure, the kind of answer which an educated Roman would have given, while in addition we have the parallels from Greek lore and learning which only a Greek could give.

The *Roman Questions* should not be underestimated, even though some of their topics appear to be trivial. These *Questions* have themselves given rise to further questions and so they have made their own contribution to the study of Roman origins and of ancient cult and custom.

The *Greek Questions* are very different from the Roman. They ask questions beginning with 'who?' or 'what?' rather than 'why?', and they are about obscure names, technical terms or practices relating to little known cults, many in obscure places in Greece; many would be classed under the description of 'folklore'. The answers are fairly short; they are generally phrased dogmatically, and seldom are alternative solutions presented tentatively, as in the *Roman Questions*. The sources are sometimes cited, and it looks as though Aristotle was drawn upon very considerably. Hence it has been suggested that these questions are the notes which Plutarch made on small and abstruse points as he read the accounts of the various states which Aristotle wrote under the name of *Politeiai*; Plutarch has been at pains to provide fuller information. To the student of Greek cult, and indeed of folk-lore generally, this book is full of interest.

A few of the titles of the chapters will best give an impression of the book. 'Who are the Conipodes and the Artyni at Epidaurus?' 'What is the wooden dog at Locri?' 'What is Palintocia?' 'What is the boys' tomb at Chalcis?' 'Why is a fluteplayer forbidden to enter the shrine of Tenes at Tenedos, and why may not the name of Achilles be uttered therein?' 'Why in Bottiais is it the custom for girls to call out as they dance "Let us go to Athens"?' 'Why does the statue of Zeus Labradensis in Caria carry aloft not a sceptre nor a thunderbolt but a sword?'[4] There is no need to follow Plutarch as he offers the answers.

These two books of Questions are valuable, apart from their intrinsic interest, as providing further illustration, if indeed it is needed, of the kind of mind which Plutarch brought to bear on his studies. No point is too small to claim his attention; no pains must be spared to satisfy a query. Sometimes we may wish that he had asked other questions, or had examined the answers a little more critically; but of his insatiable curiosity and of his tireless industry there can be no doubt.

'Questions' of this kind were not an invention of Plutarch. We know that they were written certainly from the time of Aristotle who made collections of problems, though the book which is extant under the title *Problemata* is not by Aristotle. It was a convenient method of stating shortly problems, or as they were often called *Aporiae*, which the writer did not wish to develop at length. Alternative ways of circumventing the impasse could be suggested and the objections could receive a brief reply. The minutiae so discussed sometimes encountered ridicule, as in the eighty-eighth letter of Seneca. But the method was destined to have a great future in the hands of Neoplatonists and Christians. The Christian scriptures were read with critical interest by an increasing number of people, many trained in the habits of Greek philosophy; the difficulties and inconsistencies which they encountered in their reading were brought to the notice of bishops and teachers who dealt with them in a treatise consisting of answers. Moreover the method presented a ready means of refuting opponents; the hostile case would be presented in the form of doubts and criticisms, which would then be demolished.[5]

Two Greek epigrams were written about Plutarch, one in the sixth century, the other in the eleventh. Neither is very good; the sentiment is better than the execution. The translation aims only at giving the sense.

Chaeronean Plutarch, Italy's mighty sons
In far-famed sculpture set your likeness up.
For you in parallel lives the noblest Greeks
Did yoke to warrior citizens of Rome.
Not even you could write a life to place
In parallel to your own life, because
*There's no-one whom we can compare you with.**

If Thou art minded any pagan soul
From threatened doom to save, O Christ of mine,
Plato and Plutarch save, and please me well.
For each in all his words and all his ways
Clung closely to Thy laws; and if they knew
Thee not as God of all, they stand in need
But of Thy bounty, which it is Thy will
Freely to give to save all men alike.†

* Written by Agathias, A.D. 536–582. He was born in Aeolis and practised as a lawyer in Byzantium. He compiled a *Circle* of epigrams which was later the foundation of the Palatine Anthology; about a hundred of his own epigrams are included. (*Anth. Pal.* 16. 331.)

† Written by John Metropolitan of Euchaita, in Pontus, A.D. 1040, and quoted from *Johannis Metropolitani Euchaitensis versus iambici*, edited by Matthew Bust, of Eton College, printed at Eton in the King's College by John Norton, the King's printer, 1610.

CHAPTER 9

Plutarch as Teacher

THE purpose of the pages which immediately follow is very modest; it is twofold – to give illustrations of the reconciliation of past and present which Plutarch attempted in the field of religion and ethics, and to give some incidental glimpses of the mind and character of the man himself; of the inexhaustible stores of interest accumulated in the *Moralia* no account can be given. Nor must a systematic account of Plutarch's philosophy be expected, because he was not a systematic thinker. It is possible to put together passages under the headings of psychology, religion, ethics and the rest; the result is not satisfactory. The Dialogues as such are ruined and the resulting compilation is fragmentary, often inconsistent, and from it important matters are missing. It is possible to show that he uses (at least) two psychologies; if this inconsistency were explained to him, he would say in all likelihood that it did not matter; for the immediate purpose in hand he had been accurate enough. Nor can we say that, since he was a Platonist, we can fill in the gaps for him from our knowledge of Platonism; for he was indeed an admirer of some aspects of Platonism, but he did not adopt the whole of it. It is often said that he was an eclectic or a syncretist. If these terms mean that he was willing to borrow, if he thought fit, from any system of philosophy, they are applicable; if they mean that he welded borrowed elements into a system of his own, they are incorrect. What he borrowed he fused together in the crucible not of thought but of feeling. If we put to him a problem of religion or ethics, he could tell us what views on it the philosophers had held, and he would give us his own judgment; his judgment would be informed and enlightened by his knowledge of philosophy, but it would spring ultimately from his own right feeling in the matter; it would not be derived from any closely articulated ethical theory which he had worked out for himself. His judgments were the judgments of a good man rather than of a systematic thinker, and probably the same can be said of most of the saints among men. It is much more important to see the man than to formulate for him a philosophy in which he probably would not recognise himself.

i CHAOS AND ORDER

Plutarch lived in an age when there took place a great Hellenic revival, and he himself played an important part in it.

The word 'revival' needs to be used with caution. A civilisation or culture or age does not pass into a state of coma, apparently inanimate for a time, and revive and become active again. A culture takes shape to satisfy the intellectual and spiritual needs of the men of the day; it passes away, as we say, when it fails to satisfy the needs or when the needs are no longer felt. Suppose now that an age arises when those same needs are again felt acutely; whither shall it turn for satisfaction? Then it is that men of knowledge come into their own; they can make available the thoughts and experiences of the past—speculations and creeds, ideals of social and political behaviour, practical standards for the conduct of life; they invite the men of their day to draw upon the resources of the past, to enlarge their experience in the hope of finding means of satisfying their needs. But neither the men nor the circumstances of to-day are the same as those of yesterday, however, similar the needs may be. And so, when new men appropriate the experience of the past, in an environment which is new, they make something new out of it, and a new civilisation may arise, different indeed but still striving to satisfy the fundamental needs of humanity which the men of knowledge realise are much the same.

The men and the circumstances of the Greco-Roman world of the Empire were not the same as those of classical Greece. The Romans were now the dominant power; they admired Greek learning and were ready to learn, but they believed too in the value of their own experience of many centuries. Foreign peoples had been brought within the orbit of civilisation and they were now being educated. Over all there was peace and security. But human nature remained much the same; its needs, though expressed in different terms, craved for satisfaction. Men like Plutarch, and Plutarch pre-eminently, felt themselves charged with a mission to make known the ideals and achievements and experience of the past, believing sincerely that in them the men of their day would find satisfaction as they sought new springs of inspiration for their lives and new standards of thought and action.

For the literature and philosophy of classical Greece were not lost or forgotten. In centres of learning, Athens and particularly Alexandria and Pergamum, they were diligently studied throughout the centuries succeeding the great age of Greece. Learned commentaries were written, anthologies compiled, 'source'-books put together; minor problems left over by Plato and Aristotle were taken up by lesser philosophers. If anything new was written, it tended to be the product of the library and the study, artificial and self-conscious, backward-looking and rarely in touch with the present scene, or inspired by contemporary life. Yet, however much smothered by learning and indeed pedantry, the original spirit of Greek literature was not quenched; there were men who read it for itself, not seeking a field in which to exercise and display learning or the dexterities of verbal criticism, but convinced that in the great works of classical Greek literature there were perennial springs at which humanity could satisfy their thirsty souls. Plutarch was one of such men, and that is the kind of language which he used.

It is not too much to say that Plutarch had at his command Hellenic and Hellenistic thought and literature. Yet with those resources at his disposal he originated nothing. His mind was not adventurous; it did not use its accumulated knowledge as a springboard to make a leap; it may have lacked imagination. Yet in one particular realm Plutarch was a man of genius. For he had a supreme gift of sensitiveness to religious and moral values which was acutely alive to inconsistency and was profoundly disturbed by it. It would be wrong to say that this sensitiveness issued in a passion for truth; for 'truth' is apt to be lifted to a metaphysical plane. Plutarch's mind moved on lower levels. It would be better therefore to say that he had a passion for sincerity, and was able to discriminate values with precision and delicacy. With this he combined deep insight into human character and he read therein what man had it in him to be.

There is no need to describe again the spiritual ferment of the Greco-Roman world at this time. Ideas crowded upon men's minds, some from the past inherited from the Greeks of the mainland and of Asia Minor, many from the greater Greece of contemporary times, some from Rome and Italy, from Africa and the provinces of the west, and some from outside the Empire from the furthest east. Never were there so many religions, so many rival systems and so much proliferation of philosophical beliefs with their varying views of life and politics and morals. Of these Plutarch was aware, and no doubt there were other men of learning who were equally aware. But Plutarch viewed this vast panorama of human experience with a reverence which was unique; for, though he was thoroughly alive to the evil in it, he was convinced of the overwhelming preponderance of the good and the valuable. Unworthy symbol and crude imagery might overlay values of supreme importance, but, if a means were found to strip things down to their essentials, good would be found, and, when found, would be seen to be of a piece with good elsewhere. Everywhere there was confusion and chaos; what was needed was a principle with which to sort things out, a principle of order. And to him order meant not merely the sorting out of the pieces of a jig-saw puzzle so that they make a logical whole, but also the creation of an ascending scale of values against which what was good would be seen to be good, and what was evil would be seen to be evil. He believed that the accumulated experience of the Greeks in particular was of pre-eminent use to the men of his time; but he was prepared, in the interests of sincerity and honesty, to submit that experience to a process of sifting, of evaluation.

Most conveniently he gives us in a few words, which have deservedly been often quoted, a definition of the principle by which he proposes to bring order out of chaos and to establish a hierarchy of values. 'Reason,' he says, 'is the mystagogue to Theology.'[1] These three terms need a little enlargement. Reason is not to be written with a capital letter; in this passage it does not mean the Reason that is the supreme ruling principle of the universe, as *e.g.* in Stoicism; nor does it mean some highly developed method of logical analysis. It means the procedures of thought employed by an intelligent man, who, for example, is able to note relationships, to detect similarity and dissimilarity, to draw inferences and to be consistent. Reason of this kind is to work at the accumulated knowledge and experience of men and to sort it out into order. The definition seems to determine in advance the direction in which Reason will move – to Theology. Reason therefore cannot help establishing an order or scale of values in which goodness or God is the highest term; that is to say, the good is rational. By Theology Plutarch means the highest conceptions of which man is capable about the nature of goodness, or, as he says, of God and his activities in the universe; and from the human point of view the most important part of his nature and activity is his dealings with man and man's relation to him.

The third term is 'mystagogue', a technical word borrowed from the Mystery Religions. An aspirant to initiation was placed under the care of a guide and teacher, whose function it was to prepare him for the supreme moment of full initiation; this he did by instruction, by prescribed courses of training, by preliminary rites of purification. Through these stages of progressive education he led his pupil, disclosing more and more of the inner meaning of the cult; just before the last stage he left him; the rest – the moment of revelation when the initiate would see the beatific vision – this he left to the God himself. Plutarch could not have chosen a better word; for he means that Reason, working on the accumulated knowledge and experience of men, will conduct a seeker up the steps towards an understanding of God and his Goodness; from that point Reason can take him no further; direct knowledge of God and communion with his spirit is for God and the soul.

It must not be supposed that we are here considering a theoretical formula; on the contrary, it is a practical plan applied by Plutarch himself and evident to anyone who reads him. Simply put, in his own studies and in his teaching he tested, by means of ordinary commonsense and against a criterion of the highest religious and moral ideals of which his sensitive nature was capable, all the mythologies and religions and practices and creeds and doctrines and habits and codes which had come down to him in the literature and philosophy and social life of his beloved Greece, and anything else which might reach him from the east or the west through his travels and his friends. Through this vast field of knowledge he moves with reverence, one of the great marks of his character; for he believes that no manifestation of the human spirit and its workings is without significance.

It may be said that what Plutarch was attempting was doomed to failure; he was anxious to save the glory of Greece, but he did not realise that traditional Greek religion and Greek mythology were so woven into Greek literature that their removal would leave nothing left. In any case, it may be urged, Plutarch was so in love with the past that he could not be radical or drastic enough in his efforts of rehabilitation; what he failed to do time did for him. This line of argument is not quite fair; it is true that in the past there had been criticism of the morality of the myths and the cults; but Plutarch was attempting to criticise systematically, and it must have cost a considerable reorientation of mind in this man who was brought up under the shadow of Delphi. Secondly, Plutarch's aim was not to remove elements from the tradition but to see historical and contemporary significance in things which could no longer be taken at their face value. If he could look back from to-day, he might well say that history had justified him, for the history of religion is largely a history of reinterpretation and restatement.

Plutarch was a teacher, not a constructive thinker; he created no new system. Few teachers do; they may have at the back of their minds guiding principles, but they do not readily build theoretical constructions but rather make practical application. They are bound to be opportunists, availing themselves of the openings furnished by their pupils, responding to questions in answers adapted to the intelligence and experience of the questioner and then abandoned till some later time. As a teacher Plutarch believed that example and practical application were of more value than precept, that all teaching must be instinct with sincerity and honesty and offered with modesty. Of three well-tried methods of teaching he rejected one and adopted the others. In no uncertain terms he expressed his detestation of the 'epideixis',[2] the 'brilliant' lecture which was meant to dazzle the audience by a pyrotechnic display of learning, or wit or rhetoric or ingenuity; its aim was the applause of the audience for the cleverness of the lecturer. The second method was the sober lecture of the academic lecture-room; when reduced to writing for permanent keeping, the lecture might be addressed to a friend or a group of friends and its form would be revised and perhaps embellished. The third method was the typically Greek method of dialogue or discussion; conversation between men who have some familiarity with the subject to be discussed, and time to pursue it some distance–features not always prominent in modern practice. From such real conversations the literary dialogue had developed; when Plutarch employed the dialogue, no doubt he was glad to follow in the steps of his master Plato, but chiefly he was putting on paper the substance and manner of the conversations, *i.e.* teaching, which made up his life. In Plutarch's hands the literary dialogue stands as regards form midway between Plato and Aristotle. In the Platonic dialogues of the early and middle period question and answer come briskly–in fact, Socrates more than once protests against long speeches. Aristotle, as far as the remaining fragments allow an opinion, seems sometimes to have used the Socratic method but also the method by which the participants set out their views in a continuous statement, the leader, Aristotle, summing up at the end. This was the method used by Cicero.

Plutarch revived the literary form of the dialogue which, as far as we know, had fallen into disuse. That he approached anywhere near the measure of Plato, no one could maintain. But his writing has an attractiveness of its own. The characters are clearly enough drawn for us to know their qualities of mind and disposition. The scene is often graphically set, as in the Pythian dialogues in which we move with the company visiting the treasures of Delphi.* The members, who are often well known to each other, treat each other with great consideration, indeed with sympathy and, when needed, with tolerance. There are often touches of humour which is never malicious, and is the more effective for being quiet and restrained. Plutarch himself often remains rather in the background, but he intervenes effectively and pulls the threads of the argument together; he shows great feeling for the younger members of the group. The depth of thought, the insistent tenacity, the proving of each separate step in the argument, the dramatic quality of a Platonic dialogue may be missing; but a dialogue of Plutarch has a warm humanity which is very agreeable.

ii RECONCILIATION

To see Plutarch's principle of criticism and reconciliation at work, it is fitting to examine first his treatise *How the young should read poetry*. The reasons are three; first, since the principle is a principle of education, Plutarch as a good teacher would wish us to begin with the early stages; secondly, as applied to literature, it is seen at its simplest; and, last, the study of literature will predispose the pupil, in Plutarch's view, to the study of philosophy, and philosophy, of course, is the crown of all studies.

The treatise is addressed to Marcus Sedatius of whom nothing is known, though a man of this name was consul suffectus in the reign of Antoninus Pius, and two men of the name appear in a guild list of A.D. 152 found at Ostia: Plutarch's friend may have been a connexion.[1] A pleasant touch occurs in the opening passage; Plutarch says that the reading of poetry may do a young man much harm besides much good; yet 'it is not possible nor desirable to fence off from poetry a man of the age of my Soclarus and your Cleander'. So the two fathers are to take counsel together how they should read poetry with their young sons.

Poetry is a dangerous mixture; it contains much that gives pleasure and is suitable food for a growing mind; it contains

* See page 33.

much that is disturbing and unbalancing, unless its study is entrusted to a wise guidance. All the same we must not prune the vine so as to kill it. Where there is mere sensationalism, we must be drastic; where poetry takes its themes from philosophy and treats them with imagination, we must use it to the full. Poetry always involves an element of 'myth-making' or fiction, and to that extent it tells lies. The student should realise what is fiction and treat it as such; it will then do no harm. The poets knew they were fabricating, but they were not deceiving. The young must be told that poetry represents life, as does painting – not the beautiful in life but the reality of life, with its beauty and its ugliness.

The style or language of a poet is insidious; to praise does not necessarily mean praise for the substance of a poem. The poet often shows his disapproval of a theme by the way he treats it. He often condemns later a point of view which he has earlier applauded; to interpret him we must try to get a whole view and must not pin him to texts. For instance against Euripides' 'By trickery in many shapes the Gods mislead us', we must set the same author's 'But if the Gods do evil, then they are not gods'.

A passage should be read carefully. When Homer says, 'This is the lot of miserable mortals, to tear their hair in mourning, and to wet their cheeks with tears', we must stress 'miserable', that is, 'miserable' through their own folly; Homer is not condemning life in general. Often the poets loosely attribute to the gods qualities and actions which strictly they should not, just as we say that a human action or even a speech is 'divine'; we realise that this is not accurate use of words; so too we should allow only descriptions of gods which are fitting.

If he is to be truthful, the poet must portray life as it is, with tension between good and evil, with passions in conflict, with change from success to failure or the reverse; the emotional, the unexpected, the irrational startles, even frightens, but it gives pleasure. And, when the poet brings the gods into the human scene, he does not present them as emotionless and sinless; life is made up of risk and opposition, and the gods must feel and

sin as much as anyone else if there is not to be a failure to excite
the reader and throw him into a turmoil.

The young man must realise that life contains good and evil
and that poetry represents both. He will then be armed against
the spell which heroic names exert; to imitate the bad deeds of a
hero and to believe that you are therefore a hero is like imitating
the stammer of Aristotle. The student must be trained to be on
his guard. Just as Cato when a boy did what his tutor told him
to do but also demanded the cause and the reason, so we should
not obey poets as we do tutors or legislators, unless the subject-
matter has reason on its side; if it has reason, it will be good: if
not, it will be revealed as empty and futile. Every passage of
literature is to be put to the question. If this critical spirit is
maintained, good can be got from many unpromising passages
which, if taken uncritically, would be harmful.

In all poetry there is 'philosophy'; the reading of poetry
gently prepares a young student for its serious study. He will
hear at home much that he should not—from his mother or
nurse, from his father or tutor; he will hear that wealth gives
happiness, that virtue is of no account unless you are well off,
that you should avoid hard work and should fear death. Philosophers, of course, have other values than these; and when the
young man who has been properly trained to read literature
hears the views of philosophers, he will get less of a shock; he will
have been progressively prepared for them. In short, 'the young
man needs good guidance in his reading, so that, instead of being prejudiced against philosophy, he may be prepared in advance for it; he will be well-disposed to it and friendly to it and
at home with it, and thus poetry will escort him to philosophy'.

All this counsel is illustrated by more than two hundred quotations from the poets; the upshot of it all is that Cleander's
tutor is to help him to understand that the truths of philosophy,
which is concerned with life in all its aspects, are to be seen in
elementary form in poetry, which with the aid of imagination
presents life as it is; the criticism of reason sifts the good and the
true from the bad and the false; so he will regard poetry as an
introduction to philosophy.

To Plutarch philosophy meant what it had always meant to the people who created it–the criticism of every field of human experience; when the ground had thus been cleared by reason, philosophy was free to erect whatever it liked–cosmological theories, metaphysical hypotheses, ideal states, ideal men. But since Aristotle there had been a marked shift of emphasis. Philosophy had always regarded itself as concerned with a theoretical science of life and as a practical art of living. Now the stress was on this latter aspect; for now 'the many' clamoured for the services of philosophy when before it had been the interest of the few; and the many meant the Greco-Roman world, loud in its clamour for a practical guide to daily life–what to believe and how to behave. Not that Plutarch was not thoroughly at ease on the abstract levels of philosophy, for he was very thoroughly read in the works of all schools; but his great interest was humanity and his mission was to help men to live better lives.

This universal demand had another effect on philosophy; the edges tended to be worn off the various systems; the more controversial elements were allowed to fall into the background, and the elements held in common received more attention, for they were of more general appeal.[2] Thus, Stoicism as adopted by the Romans from the Greeks shed much of its speculative nature; it became in Roman hands a way of life rather than a set of beliefs. Plutarch seems not to have been aware of this change in Stoicism, for his treatise *On the Contradictions of the Stoics* harks back to their original writings and is therefore out of touch with Stoicism, at any rate as it was professed in the west.

'What to believe, and how to behave.' And so from poetry we pass to religion and morals. Of the universality of religion Plutarch is convinced.

If you go through the cities of the world, you will find cities without walls, without learning or kings or houses or riches, without currency or theatres or gymnasia; but no one has ever seen or will see a city without temples or gods; which does not pray to the gods or swear by them or use oracles or sacrifice to obtain benefits or perform rites to avert evil. A city could better do without the soil on which to found it than without religion: take away belief in the gods and it would never begin, and certainly could not continue, to cohere.

So he has deliberately enlarged the scope of his survey beyond Greek religion. In fact, the most comprehensive and revealing announcement of his programme is to be found in his treatise *On Isis and Osiris*, Egyptian gods whose cult was spread widely over the Empire, with a shrine and priestess actually in the heart of Hellenism, Delphi.

God is not a thing without a mind and without a soul, subject to men. We have believed that those who have dealings with men and give us gifts, continuously and perpetually, are gods. There are not different gods for different peoples, not Greek gods and non-Greek gods, not northern and southern gods. The sun and moon and sky and earth and sea are the same for all, but different peoples call them by different names. In the same way, though different methods of worship and different forms of address are determined by law and custom, there is one Logos which orders the universe and one Providence which takes it under its care and there are assistant powers appointed to cover every aspect of it. Worshippers use different sacred symbols, some obscure, some clearer, by which they lead the mind along the path to divine things. But there is danger; some stumble and slip into superstition; others avoid the slough of superstition but, before they know it, fall over the precipice of atheism. And so we must take the Reason of philosophy as our mystagogue and we must reverently scrutinise every detail of doctrine and ritual. . . . We must beware of falling into error from misinterpreting the excellent ordinances laid down by Law concerning sacrifice and festival.

Before proceeding further, we may dispose of two extreme views with which Plutarch will have nothing to do. First, he will not follow those who 'transfer the great names from heaven to earth', who 'destroy the faith implanted in practically all men from the earliest creation', who 'open the gates to a godless mob which humanises divine things' – in short, Euhemerus the Messenian 'is spreading atheism throughout the inhabited world' by teaching that the gods are memories of foregone kings and generals, a doctrine which he bases on some tablets 'written in gold on the isle of Panchon' which 'no barbarian, no Greek, only Euhemerus himself' has seen.[3] Secondly, he will not allow the identification of the gods with natural processes or products; Persephone is not wheat or the harvest, nor Dionysus wine. It would be just as sensible to say the cables of a ship were the steersman, or a needle and thread the tailor. He is a little uncertain about Apollo and the sun; the matter is left without full discussion, but not before he suggests that the belief is creditable to its holders; for they link up their conception of the god with the thing they most value and so gain a spiritual ideal through an image of sense; they should be encouraged to mount higher and see the god in his own being.[4]

Thus, in face of the stubborn fact of the universality of religion, there are limits to rationalism. But there is ample field left for it. God has to break through the barrier of nature and matter in order to speak to men, and men in attempting to hear God's message are liable to be misled by their senses and their intellects and so to misinterpret whatever they receive. Moreover, there are spiritual forces which deliberately cheat men. Revelation then is bound to be blurred or even spurious; and the function of philosophy is to detect when it is untrue. Plutarch is at pains to give a practical demonstration in his treatment of one means by which the will of God is revealed, the Delphic Oracle.

Why the Priestess does not now give oracles in verse need not detain us long. Some of the arguments are reminiscent of modern pleas for 'a simplified form of service expressed in the vernacular'; but for the present purpose its interest lies in its admission that the priestess is a very imperfect vehicle for a divine message. The human soul is an instrument used by God; the soul uses the body; the body of the uneducated peasant girl chosen as priestess is agitated and excited during the trance. When the god of poetry and music uses an instrument of this nature, is it surprising that the message is expressed in unmusical and unmetrical and obscure language? On the other hand *On the failure of the oracles* has much that is relevant. In this lively dialogue very differing views are expressed. Didymus the Cynic fires his ill-humoured shot, 'It is not surprising if the gods have packed up long ago when people put such trivial and foolish questions to them.' He did not stay for the discussion. All kinds of reason are discussed for the disappearance of oracles in Greece, and especially in Boeotia—the decrease of population, the scarcity of important political problems on which to consult the god, the resistance of Nature and Matter, the failure of the vapours or gases which sent the priestess into a trance; finally a reconciliation of these causes is made in a summary offered by Lamprias. He thinks that the human mind has a feeble prophetic power, feeble because it is dimmed by being in a body: it is analogous to memory which in itself is no less wonderful than prophecy, but it looks backwards instead of forwards. Under certain natural conditions of the body which do not occur often, and in places where an exhalation of natural gas helps to put the body into the right state, the prophetic power of the mind is given freedom to operate. At this point Philippus, the historian, breaks in; history shows that Delphi has been of great service to the Greek states in every kind of contingency; and now we are told that Delphi is to be explained in terms of chance and natural causes, and not ascribed to God and Providence. Lamprias admits that he has put the matter onesidedly; but it must be understood that the soul and the natural causes owe their origin to God; or, as he puts it, we must bear in mind both 'the person through whom and the agent by whom' as well as 'the things from which and the means through which'. And so the dialogue leaves us in a middle position, which is neither naturalism nor a belief in the direct operation of the god; it is a compromise between the two. This is exactly Plutarch's role; in the light of reason he reconciles modern theory with ancient belief.

But one supremely important point has been omitted from this brief summary. Early in the dialogue Lamprias had asserted the agency of God in the activity of oracles, but explained their decay by the opposition which Nature or Matter may exert; no one supposes that gods creep into the bodies of prophets; they operate indirectly through natural media. At this point Cleombrotus points out that Nature is here brought in as a kind of middle term between the agent and the finished act. It was Plato, he said, who introduced Nature in this way and he thus relieved philosophers of many difficulties. But more difficulties

still are cleared away if you insert not Nature but daemons between gods and men; daemons knit together the two orders into
a kind of fellowship. In a long speech Cleombrotus demon-
strates his point; for example, many of the repulsive rites and
sacrifices associated with some cults, the unworthy stories about
gods and goddesses, may be inspired by daemons, or indeed be
accounts of their own doings; the oracles themselves may cease
because some capricious daemon withdraws his services. Thus,
by the hypothesis of daemons, religion may be purged, and the
gods may be preserved as good and holy and worthy of worship.
The existence of daemons is accepted by all the company;
whether daemons are immortal, how nearly they approximate to
gods are questions which divide the company. But we must ask
who are these daemons, and if the word conjures up in the mind
of the reader only ideas of devils and imps and even vampires,
he may substitute for it 'spirits' or 'angels'.

iii DAEMONS

Histories of Greek Religion or Philosophy do not usually say
much, if anything, about daemons. Though the idea occurs as
early as Homer, it plays little or no part in recognised cults; for
it had no mythology of its own; rather it attached itself to existing beliefs. In philosophy it lurks in the background from
Thales, to whom 'the universe is alive and full of daemons',[1]
through Heraclitus and Xenophanes, to Plato and his pupil
Xenocrates, who elaborated it in detail. As regards poetry,
Homer uses the word in a vague sense for 'god' or 'divine
agency'; in Hesiod the daemons are the souls of heroes of past
ages and now kindly to men; in Aeschylus the dead become
daemons; in Theognis and Menander the daemon is the guard-
ian angel of the individual man and sometimes of a family.[2] The
most illuminating passage in the literature up to the time of
Plato occurs in the *Symposium*, where it is put into the mouth of
Diotima.

All that is daemonic lies between the mortal and the immortal.
Its functions are to interpret to men communications from the gods

–commandments and favours from the gods in return for men's attentions–and to convey prayers and offerings from men to the gods. Being thus between men and gods the daemon fills up the gap and so acts as a link joining up the whole. Through it as intermediary pass all forms of divination, all the technique of the priests–sacrifices and spells and divination and sorcery. God does not mix with man; the daemonic is the agency through which intercourse and converse take place between men and gods, whether in waking visions or in dreams.[3]

This is a passage which could readily be seized upon by any Platonist anxious to find the authority of his master for a development of a doctrine of daemons; the first, as far as we can tell, to make use of the opportunity now presented was Xenocrates, who had been president of the Academy from 339–314 B.C. and was therefore very acceptable to Plutarch; indeed it is from notices of him by Plutarch and Stobaeus that we know about his views. The world-soul is placed by the Divine Spirit in charge of everything subject to motion and change; it breathes soul into planets and sun and moon which are thus daemonic in nature; at a lower level it occupies the gods of Olympus and the elements; this is the lowest plane on which the Divine Spirit is itself operative. Below this level finite individuals and the individual powers of Nature begin; here good and bad daemons are active, attaching themselves to whatever suits their nature and rendering it happy or unhappy according as they are good or bad; the lower the place in the scale of existence occupied by an individual being, the greater the likelihood that an evil daemon will take up residence in it, for it is so far removed from the Divine Spirit. Whether Plutarch read Xenocrates himself or read some secondary source, for example Poseidonius, is uncertain; but here at least the evil daemon receives the fullest recognition we know before Plutarch.

And so in the good daemon religion was able to find an intermediary between man and the god which philosophy had set beyond the reach of man; in the bad daemon religion found the source of the evil with which man has to contend, and in particular it found a reason for the evil in itself. For, if there was a bad daemon wherever there was evil, it was necessary to suppose that attached to each god was a daemon understudy who familiarised himself with all the good associated with a god in legend and in cult and in rite, and deliberately perverted it. Poor deluded mankind believed that the truth and the perversion of it came from the same divine source; it was the work of reason to sift the one from the other, and so to lead the worshipper towards a real theology. Thus, thought Plutarch, religion and particularly the traditional religion of the Greeks would be saved – and with it Greek literature.

We may now see the daemons at closer quarters, again in *On the failure of the oracles*. Cleombrotus is not sure whether the idea of daemons comes from 'Zoroaster and the Magi', or from 'Thrace and Orpheus', or from Egypt or Phrygia; among the Greeks he points to Homer and particularly to Hesiod, who, he says, holds that there are four classes of reasonable beings, gods, daemons, heroes and men; there can be an upward ascent so that a man can become a hero and then a daemon and then a god; a daemon may however lapse and become a man again; after some period, not clearly defined, a daemon may die. Cleombrotus is cautious about speaking of the 'mysteries', but he is clear that official days of mourning and sacrifice, with their eatings of raw flesh and rendings of live animals, with wailings and self-mutilations and, in extreme cases, human sacrifice, are the work of daemons and not of gods. In the same way the stories about the wandering of gods, their banishment and enslavement and crimes, may be sung in hymns and legend but are the experiences of daemons, not of gods. And he does not spare even Delphi; the story of the struggle between Apollo and the serpent for the possession of the oracle is absurd and unworthy of the god. The main object of his outburst is to urge that oracles and prophecies are in the hands of daemons; when oracles fail, it means that the daemon has deserted the shrine.

At this point Heracleon breaks in. He does not object to the view that oracles should be administered not by gods but by their assistant daemons (for gods might well be released from concern with human affairs), but he does not like the idea of tearing whole armfuls of divine misdemeanours from the pages of Empedocles and attaching them to the daemons who are then to be subject to death like men. Cleombrotus, after enquiring from his neighbour, who is this young man Heracleon? points out that it must be allowed that daemons may be evil and mortal, for otherwise there would be no distinction between them and gods. This reply silences the young man, and Cleombrotus quotes the story of Aemilianus who used to tell how sailors had heard a loud voice from the island of Paxi, off the west coast of Greece, proclaiming that Great Pan was dead; daemons therefore could die. Evidence of daemons in the Western Isles of Scotland was produced by the next speaker Demetrius; Cleombrotus adds to 'the salad-bowl of myths and theories' his account of meeting a hermit near the Red Sea; he too regarded daemons as the source of oracles and he thought that many of the strifes among the gods which occur in the myths were really battles between daemons. From this point the speakers proceed to the problem of the plurality of worlds.

The treatise *On Isis and Osiris* is addressed to Clea, the priestess of Isis at Delphi. Here again Plutarch is anxious to show that Isis and Osiris, whom he describes as daemons, are really the counterparts of other daemons in other countries and that the legends and rites offer nothing specific to themselves. Into the ingenious but far-fetched arguments to demonstrate this thesis we need not go. But the treatise, apart from its significance for the task which Plutarch had undertaken, is important; he realised that the cult of Isis was widely spread over the Empire and he is concerned to show that it was not unique; moreover, though this point would hardly appeal to him, to his descriptions we are indebted for a large part of our knowledge about the rites and legends and doctrines associated with the goddess.[4]

A dialogue entitled *On the daemonic sign of Socrates* must receive only brief mention, since in spite of its name it has little to do with daemons. It is for the most part a graphic account of an historical episode, the return of a party of Theban patriots to Thebes in 379–378 B.C. While they wait they occupy anxious hours by discussing the real meaning of the 'daemonic sign' of Socrates. Many theories are put forward; one of them is that pure souls on occasion can come into contact with spiritual power, can hear a spiritual, but wordless, voice and be guided accordingly. For this spiritual power the word is daemon, but a theory of daemons is not further elaborated.

Enough has been said to indicate the main lines of Plutarch's thought on this topic and to point to its dangers. On the positive side it may be said that Plutarch draws attention to a widespread dissatisfaction with the philosophical conception of a passionless, abstract Deity far removed from the reach of men; moreover he insists that beneath the various forms of cult with its variety of symbols and rites there is a reality which men wherever there are men are passionately striving to apprehend. But to elaborate a system of intermediaries to provide a bridge between God and men may emphasise the gulf still further; in the meantime the intermediaries may usurp a larger place till finally they are identified with the gods. Did Plutarch not pause to think how he was allowing one daemon to usurp the place of Providence, in which he certainly believed, when he said, 'If the daemon which sent down the soul of Alexander had not re-called it so quickly, one law would have looked down upon all men'? The agents become the principals, but still as agents they must be flattered and satisfied, in fact they must be 'worked' by men who are experts in working them.[5] Hence the gate is opened to every kind of magic, and, since the daemons are some good and some bad, the magic may be evil. And so men may be worse off than before; the daemons have become more alive than the gods were and beset every aspect of life and behaviour. In short, in giving a kind of sanction to many superstitions and fancies lurking in the minds of an uncritical multitude, Plutarch was in danger of making worse the chaos and confusion which he sought to set to order and of paralysing the reason which he hoped to use as his instrument.

It must not be thought that when Plutarch invokes the aid of daemons he is borrowing the idea from poets or philosophers. On the contrary he is drawing it from contemporary life. Because the daemons have left few memorials of themselves in architecture and literature, their importance tends to be overlooked. In fact, they are omnipresent and all-powerful, they are embedded deep in the religious memories of the peoples, for they go back to days long before the days of Greek philosophy and religion. The cults of the Greek states, recognised and offi- cially sanctioned, were only one-tenth of the iceberg; the rest, the submerged nine-tenths, were the daemons. They lurk be- hind the Hebrew scriptures in spite of the careful revision in the interests of monotheism, and in the post-exilic literature vague supernatural beings abound. The New Testament is full of them; St. Paul never tires of urging his converts to fight against the powers in the heavenly places. The idols, he says, may be unreal, but the daemons who stand behind the idols are not un- real, 'I am unwilling that you should be partners with dae- mons'.[6] It is the Christian writers, from Justin onwards, who haul the daemons out into the open and battle with them; they leave no doubt about the dimensions of the evil they were com- bating; and they were not fighting with shadows. Two genera- tions after Plutarch's death Clement of Alexandria wrote his *Exhortation to the Greeks*, a document in which he shows himself as learned in Greek religion and literature as Plutarch himself. He is in no doubt about the hold of the daemons upon the minds of the people, and, of course, amid his general derision of Greek cult, he does not fail to demonstrate that the gods are in fact daemons, and the most evil of them. The Christian attack gains in force, till in the *de civitate Dei* of St. Augustine it reaches its climax; he did not minimise the evil; he agreed with Tertullian that the daemons were working for the total overthrow of man.[7]

iv FALSE BELIEF AND UNBELIEF

Contemporary religion, then, Plutarch held, was com- pounded of beliefs which could reasonably be held and beliefs which reason could not tolerate, because they were unworthy of the kind of god which reason demanded. But what were the effects on the individual which followed upon false belief? They are described in an essay which unfortunately goes under the name *On Superstition*.

The title is *Concerning Deisidaimonia*, a word which cannot be rendered as 'superstition' without distorting the meaning. The word is used in a good sense and in a bad sense; it is used by St. Paul in his speech on the Areopagus to mean something praiseworthy, as it is also used by Polybius when he wishes to point to an element of strength in the Roman character.[1] In Plutarch, and elsewhere, it means, as he himself defines it, 'a belief loaded with emotion and a point of view generating a fear which abases a man and crushes him as he supposes that the gods exist but are the causes of trouble and harm to mankind'.

But the title itself is misleading, for the treatise is a comparison of 'superstition' – the word is convenient for brevity's sake – and of atheism. The work is written with rhetorical vehemence and attacks superstition with vigour, giving a certain credit to atheism because it is honest and does not corrupt the character. Some critics have assumed that this piece was one of a pair, corresponding to another treatise, now lost, in which atheism was dealt with equally ruthlessly. The rhetorical element has been taken to indicate a youthful work, a criterion which we have had occasion to observe before; other critics think that the absence of daemons in this essay shows that it was written before *On the failure of the oracles*, that is, before Plutarch had developed his daemonology, and it must be admitted that in an essay on this subject the fear of daemons could well have provided much in the way of illustration, as the very title might have suggested. Yet the absence of any reference to daemons may not really be decisive, for it will be seen later that the essay on Providence[2], which is supposedly written at about the same time as *On the failure of the oracles* makes no reference to them. However, whether youthful or not, the essay has a bearing on the fear of daemons as well as on unworthy conceptions of gods, and is a wonderfully penetrating analysis of the effect of false belief on character. For such descriptions of character Plutarch had precedent in the sketches of different types of man in the *Ethics* of Aristotle and in the *Characters* of Theophrastus, Aristotle's pupil, one of which describes the 'superstitious' man.[3] But Plutarch carries the matter much further.

False judgment, says Plutarch, is a bad thing; add to it emotion and it becomes far worse. You may believe that atoms are the first principle of the universe, but the belief does no moral harm. But if you believe that wealth is the highest god, then, because of the desire attached to the belief, you have not only a false judgment but a judgment which has poison in it, which preys on your soul, drives it frantic, allows it no sleep, infects it with stings of gadflies, pushes it over precipices, strangles it and takes away all frankness of speech. The atheist refuses to acknowledge the gods so that he may not fear them; he is unmoved by any mention of the divine, whereas the superstitious is moved violently and is perverted. The atheist through his ignorance professes disbelief in the power that can help him, superstition adds the belief that the power is harmful to him. Atheism, therefore, is reason falsely guided, superstition is emotion implanted by false reason.

Fear haunts the superstitious when they are awake and asleep; to release themselves from the dreadful things they have imagined or dreamt they resort to quacks and charlatans who prescribe outrageous cures—prostrations, mud-baths and the keeping of Sabbaths. Ritually unblemished victims—whether their tongues be clean and straight, for example—do no good: 'what we demand is that men should worship the gods with a tongue that is righteou. and just.' The superstitious make their own hell for themselves—rivers of fire and darkness haunted by phantoms and wailing voices, chasms and caves crammed with myriads of evil things. The atheist does not torment himself with such horrors, 'but his ignorance is a real calamity, for he deliberately puts out the eye of the mind which affords the clearest and truest vision, the eye which gives him knowledge of God. Atheism is an insensitivity to the divine, which fails to perceive the good, superstition is a highly emotional state which suspects that the good is evil.' When the atheist finds that things unexpectedly go wrong for him, what does he do? If he is a reasonable sort of person, he puts up with the situation in silence, and tries to help himself and comfort himself; if he is impatient and easily vexed, he rails against fortune or luck and cries that nothing goes according to plan or justice. And the superstitious man? At the

slightest misfortune he blames not men nor luck nor himself but
God; every ill that befalls him is a devilish flood of woe poured
over him by God. He gives up hope, brushes off all offers of
help. There is nothing terrifying in an eclipse; but it is terrible
that a man should plunge into the shadow of superstition and
allow the darkness to cloud his reason in matters where reason is
most necessary. When a helmsman is nearly overwhelmed by
storm, he prays to the gods to save him, but he also steers the
ship as skilfully as he can; the farmer prays before he sows or
ploughs but he holds on to the plough-handle as well; this is
Hesiod's advice. To the stout-hearted God is a source of hope,
not an excuse for cowardice. Remember the Jews, who because
it was a Sabbath sat still while the enemy set up ladders and
captured the walls; they were caught in the drag-net of their
own superstition.[4] Watch both these men at a festival; the atheist enjoys it all, he goes into peals of ironic laughter and mutters
asides to his friends, 'how terrified these people are! they are
possessed of the devil to think that all this is done for the gods!'
But that does him no harm. On the other hand the superstitious
man wants to enjoy himself but he cannot; he wears his festival-
crown and grows pale; he sacrifices and quivers; his voice
trembles as he prays and his hands shake as he offers incense;
how absurd Pythagoras is when he says that we are at our best
when we approach the gods! For then the superstitious are at
their wretched worst; to them the temples of the gods are the
dens of wild beasts.

More to the same effect follows; it is summed up at the end
with the exhortation that we must flee from superstition not in
panic but looking where we are going; we must use our reason,
otherwise we shall run down a steep place into atheism; in our
haste we shall leap over what lies in between, namely true reverence for the gods (*eusebeia*).

This is a lively piece of writing—graphic, humorous and pung-
ent. It is more favourable to atheism, because though atheism
may be intellectually misguided it is more honest and more
manly; as a point of view it may be false but it stops there; it
does not seep further and undermine character. It may be blind

and insensitive, but it is not irrational. For Plutarch insists that emotionalism based upon wrong conceptions of the gods destroys the reason which, if it were given encouragement, would release the superstitious from their fetters.

There is no need to point to Bacon's Essay on the same subject; but the Essay of John Smith, the Cambridge Platonist, may be less well-known. The whole work is based largely on Plutarch, whom he frequently quotes verbatim along with other writers, Greek and Latin. One picture quoted from the Neoplatonist Simplicius must be reproduced here, for Plutarch surely, with his love of nautical metaphors, would have approved of it. Repentance, supplication, prayer are like a rope; they ought to draw us nearer to God, not God to us; as in a ship, by fastening a cable to a firm rock, we intend not to draw the rock to the ship but the ship to the rock.[5]

V JUSTICE AND PROVIDENCE

So far we have seen specific attempts by Plutarch to make agreeable to reason, first, Greek literature and then Greek religion; there remains Greek history. Investigations of this matter takes the form of an enquiry into the age-old puzzles why do the wicked flourish, why is justice so long delayed, why do the innocent suffer. Plutarch sees that the questions must be raised in relation to the life of the individual, the history of the group, for example the family, and the history of the city or state. Realising that the problems are in the end insoluble by argument, he concludes the dialogue with a myth, a story which shall place the issue on the level of imagination rather than of reason.

The title of the dialogue is *About those whom the gods delay in punishing*. The speakers are Patrocleas, Plutarch's relation by marriage, Timon his brother and a friend Olympichus and Plutarch himself, who contrary to custom has most to say.[1] The place is Delphi, and the scene is set dramatically. 'That is what Epicurus said and then, before anyone could reply, he was off, leaving us at the end of the colonnade. We stood still without saying anything, amazed at the man's curious behaviour; we looked at each other and then turned back.' Presumably Epicurus was an Epicurean who had fired a Parthian shot of derision against the idea of Providence. The company decides to take up the challenge, and Plutarch asks what had disturbed them most out of the motley collection of missiles with which the man's abusive temper had bombarded Providence.

Patrocleas is badly disturbed; the procrastination of Divine Justice in punishing the wicked shocks him. The delay of the gods is in such open contrast with the speed of wickedness, and it robs the wronged of hope and encourages the wrongdoer to go on to fresh crimes. What good was it punishing Aristocrates for his treachery when the Messenians were already dead? (Two more historical examples follow.)

Slow justice, says Olympichus, makes a mockery of Providence; men do not regard it as punishment, but as a coincidence; and it does no good because it does not encourage repentance. The 'mills of the gods which grind slowly' achieve nothing.

Plutarch who had been 'wrapped up in his thoughts' now takes up the argument at some length. We must not commit the sin of pretending to know more than we do; reverent caution is in the Platonic tradition. A man with no music in him does not venture to describe the intimate thoughts of the composer, nor does the layman ask the surgeon why he does not operate to-day instead of later. The proper time for the curative treatment of punishment is not the same for everyone; justice is an art. And even in human justice there is much unexplained; we do not always know what was in the mind of the legislator. But we must not run away from the issue; so far we are asking for sympathetic understanding. The first consideration is this: God sets himself before us as an example of all that is good and he sets in us virtue which is a kind of likeness of himself, at any rate in those who can follow him. Originally the natural world was unordered and unorganised; it began to change into an ordered system when it modelled itself on, and indeed participated in, God and goodness. There is no method by which man can 'enjoy' God other than by imitating and reaching after all that is beautiful and good in him. And so, when God delays punishment (not through fear of making a mistake or being sorry), he is really giving us a lesson in how to punish, teaching us not to leap hot-blooded on the wrongdoer, but to copy his gentleness and forbearance. We must take Time as our counsellor and then we shall have no cause for regret.

The second point is that human justice is concerned only with retribution; it goes no further than that the wrongdoer must suffer. On the other hand, if God proposes to punish a sick soul, he investigates its passions to see if they can be bent to one side and so a chance of repentance be offered. He knows what a large portion of his goodness souls bring with them into life, how strong it is and how indestructible, how upbringing and bad companionship may corrupt it and yet it can recover and be restored to its proper state. And so he varies his punishments. What is incurable he cuts away, as being injurious to the individual and to others. When sin is due to ignorance rather than to choice, he gives time for reformation; if there is no change of heart, he punishes. History shows how men do in fact change in character (examples are given); and it is in the men of marked personality that the change is most dramatic. A bad farmer may condemn a piece of land covered with thick undergrowth, weeds and marsh; the good farmer sees its possibilities. So strong characters may burst out into strange distorted growths; impatiently we want to lop off all that is prickly; but 'the Judge who is better than we are and sees the promise of what is good and noble waits as time and maturity co-operate with reason and goodness; then nature yields the fruit as it should be.'

Moreover God takes a long view in guiding the course of history. We should not dream of punishing immediately a malefactor who was on the verge of making a new discovery of benefit to us; so God acts in history; if Dionysius had been punished as he deserved at the beginning of his reign, the Carthaginians would have overrun Sicily and no Greek settler would have been left (more examples are given). God acts like the farmer who does not cut down the thistle till he has gathered the asparagus; he refrains from destroying a bad root of a noble race of kings till the due fruit has been borne.

But does Divine Justice really delay? Punishment is contemporary with sin; it grows from the same soil and the same root. Roman law makes the criminal carry out his own cross; sin itself forges its own instruments of punishment—fear, disgrace, foreboding, remorse. So 'if I may be allowed to say so, I think that those who are guilty of unholiness need no God and no man to punish them; their own life is sufficient punishment, a life spoiled by wickedness and confounded.' (This theme is illustrated by historical and mythological allusions and by quotations.)

Timon now takes up the argument with a protest against visiting the sins of the fathers upon the children. The anger of the gods passes underground for some distance, like a river, and then breaks out again and brings ruin to a different set of people.

Plutarch replies that we ought to be consistent; there have been many instances in which the children and descendants of men who had served the state well received privilege and honour. Moreover, we cannot get rid of the continuity, say, of a city; it cannot be divided into many cities according to time. The same is true of a family. Inborn in a man is a part of his parents, active and operative. Justice is not concerned with the immediate injury; the schoolmaster who canes one boy teaches a lesson to many. Soul acts on soul for better or for worse.

Olympichus now interposes that the permanence of the soul seems to have been assumed, just because the gods survey and administer all human affairs according to desert. Ironically Pluarch replies that God is such a bungler that he takes infinite care of men who then wither away like leaves, souls of a day! He is convinced of the continued life of the soul; it is bound up with the idea of Providence. During life the soul is an athlete, engaged in a contest; it may well receive prize and punishment hereafter. Before he tells a myth to sum up the matter, he is anxious to make one more point; man's nature is infected by 'an inborn stain of evil'; it is there from the first, and the wicked man allows it to influence his actions. On the other hand there is also the training given by laws and rules and customs, so effective that the inborn stain can be effaced. Now God can see the soul;

he knows its predispositions; he often chastises a man for a tendency rather than an act, and so he prevents the act and destroys wickedness before it takes control. It is possible for a bad father to have a good son, for the son is released from the penalty of his descent and is 'adopted out of wickedness' into goodness. Then follows the myth.

This dialogue has been summarised with the omission of all the historical and literary allusions with which it is enriched. Perhaps thus condensed the teaching stands out more clearly. It may be regarded as a theodicy, a justification of the ways of God to man, and no doubt many gaps may be found. But it is better to regard it as an expression of the personal faith of a thoughtful and reverent man. If Plutarch's critical method oɪ evaluating Greek literature, Greek religion and Greek history led to a faith of this kind, it cannot be said that the method has wholly failed.

The many ideas which this dialogue touches on are familiar to us – the care of a personal God for the salvation of each soul, the self-made hell of the sinner, repentance, the reformatory function of punishment, inherited dispositions. Some critics have therefore held that Plutarch knew something of Christianity. They support their belief by pointing to some of the phrases – life as an athletic contest, the thistles and the asparagus, the inborn stain, adoption from sin into righteousness – and they argue that, if Plutarch knew about Jews and their customs, he may well have known about Christians. After all he was familiar with the reign of Nero and must have heard about the scapegoats for the fire at Rome; the inquisitive mind which had probed into so many cults would not have allowed him to remain ignorant of yet another.

Against this view, no passage anywhere else contains a direct or indirect reference to Christianity. Moreover, it is possible to find somewhere in ancient literature all the ideas and phrases briefly cited above. The supreme interest of the dialogue lies in this, that these ideas are gathered together and wrought into the working faith of a very earnest man.

The idea of appending a myth to a dialogue is borrowed from

Plato, and the intention is to drive home the moral of the dialogue by an imaginative and almost pictorial illustration. Aridaeus, of Soli, a kinsman of Protogenes, who takes part in three
Table Talks,[2] was a notorious profligate, who none the less made
himself a handsome fortune. He fell from a height, hurt his
head, lay as dead for three days, and at the time of his funeral
recovered. The change in his life was incredible; among the
Cilicians there was no one more honest in business and more
religious; besides he was a doughty opponent and a staunch
friend. Naturally he was asked the reason for the change, and
this was his story. When he lost consciousness, his soul seemed to
open as though it was all one eye, and he gazed upon constella-
tions which sent out rays of light of such power that the soul rode
upon the light, travelling everywhere as though on a calm sea.
He saw much but could describe only a little. First, he saw the
souls of the dead rise up in a bubble of fire; the air parts and the
bubble bursts and the dead step out in human form. At first
they are confused, moving about at great speed in their bewil-
derment. At the edge of the firmament he saw souls who had
become accustomed to their new environment and were kindly.
Among them he saw the soul of a kinsman; it drew near and
addressed him, 'Hullo! Thespesius!' This surprised him and he
replied that his name was Aridaeus. He was then told that
henceforth he was Thespesius (*i.e.* 'blessed'), because by some
divine dispensation he had gone to the after-world with part of
himself, the rest being left on earth as a kind of anchor. And
then he began to describe what he had seen; first, Adrasteia,
daughter of Zeus and Necessity, ensures that no one shall escape
punishment, then the right punishment is assessed, chosen from
three modes, each in the charge of a daemon; if a man has suffered on earth, his retribution is lighter; Justice deals with the
next grade, and, if she finds any incurable, they are hounded by
Furies to a place which it is impossible to look upon or to
describe.

It is not necessary to follow Thespesius further as he sees the
punishments reserved for every form of wickedness, or to re-
produce the pictures of daemons picking up with tongs the souls

of the seekers after riches and plunging them into lakes of molten metal. The story is told with a wealth of imagination, less delicate than in Plato's myths. Anyhow, Thespesius was caught up 'in a sudden jet of wind, as from a pipe, and was hurled back into his body, and opened his eyes at the very edge of his tomb', a reformed man.

A modern reader who has read with some admiration the earlier part of this dialogue with its conception of God as an infinitely patient and sympathetic healer of souls and its conviction that sin is its own punishment, will find the concluding myth to be a crude anticlimax, however well narrated. The only defence can be that it was in the Platonic tradition, and it must be understood so. There was an element of paradox in the use of myth; in the Republic Plato banned poets from his ideal state, yet he finished the dialogue with a poetic fantasy, the myth of Er, who also visited the after-world. Plutarch thinks of sin as its own punishment, yet the representation of torture in his myth might have inspired many a later artist.[3] Plato may say, or make Socrates say, at the end of the Judgment myth in the *Gorgias* that he is persuaded by the story, but he means that he is convinced of the final triumph of Justice. In the same way Plutarch must be taken to mean that he believes, but cannot prove, the certainty of Judgment and the sure opportunity given to all men to be restored to health of soul.[4]

Before we leave the ideas of superstition and of Providence a passage from another treatise[5] deserves to be quoted. For it clearly reproduces something of what religion meant to Plutarch. He has been inveighing against the Epicurean doctrine of a 'passionless' god. Feelings of anger and pleasure cannot be removed from God, he says, without removing religion altogether. It is far better to leave in religion a mixed attitude of fear and awe towards God, since, if we do not, we deprive ourselves of hope and confidence and a refuge from evil. It is true that we should try to get rid of superstition, as we get rid of a stye in the eye, but not at the cost of removing the eye of faith itself. Belief in Providence is not the same thing as a fear of a bogey. The religion of most men contains an element of 'trembling and awe', from which 'superstition' derives its name; but it is accompanied by an overwhelming feeling of joy and hopefulness, of which the signs are many. No gladness is comparable with the gladness we get from spending time in a temple, or keeping a religious festival or witnessing ceremonies or taking part in processions, sacrifice or rite. If God were a harsh tyrant intent on punishment, we should be miserable on such occasions; on the contrary when we become aware of the presence of God, every care and every fear is cast aside; we give ourselves up to joy, transported, even intoxicated, with happiness and laughter. The old, the young, rich and poor, the girl grinding at her mill, the yokel in the fields – all are lifted up in transports of delight. The banquets of kings are as nothing compared with the banquets spread before us as in our hearts we feel ourselves touch the divine. What gladdens us in our festivals is our good hope, our belief that the god is present with us in kindliness of spirit and that he is pleased with what we do. In this happiness no man can share who has renounced belief in Providence.

vi MORAL PROGRESS, AND STOICISM MISUNDERSTOOD

As a teacher of 'the good life' Plutarch believed that religion and ethics were bound up together. His strength lay in his teachings about day-to-day conduct rather than about abstruse philosophical questions, though his interest in them was unflagging.

A teacher takes it for granted when he begins to teach that his subject can be taught and that pupils can make progress in it and can be conscious of their progress. The postulates which a teacher makes at the start of his work sometimes receive no further examination; they are taken more and more for granted and fade further into the back of the mind. But sometimes experience forces them into the open, and then a valuable process of re-appraisal begins, not to prove them wrong but to discover in what senses they are true. No ready-made theory in advance of experience is a substitute for this process.

If the teacher is a preacher of the good life, he is likely to be thrown back upon his postulates more often and more violently than, say, a teacher of a craft. He works by faith; he is not cheered by high percentages of marks scored by his pupils nor by the encouraging report of an external examiner. But his faith is such that it will react with vigour against any attempt to undermine its very foundations; and attack more often strengthens it than causes it to totter.

Some such experience may have been the origin of the writing of the treatise with the title *How a man would be conscious of making progress in virtue*, (which will be shortened to *On progress*). It is an essay addressed to Sosius Senecio; there is, however, no indication to show whether he had posed some problem to Plutarch or whether Plutarch wrote it unasked and sent it to him because he thought it would be of interest.

How on earth, he asks in the first chapter, is the earnest seeker after a better life going to have any sense of progress, and so to be encouraged, if he is told that progress will not lessen his 'folly', that all sins count the same, that unless he is the complete saint he is the complete sinner, that the achievement of goodness is not a matter of toiling step by step along a road or of adding small improvement to improvements already won, but is a change or conversion happening suddenly, almost overnight? These opinions are culled from the Stoic 'paradoxes'; they might well seem discouraging to the moral teacher and Plutarch rebuts them by saying that they are untrue to the facts, or to his experience of the facts.

Perhaps the greatest price which Plutarch paid for his staunch defence of Hellenism was his failure to understand Stoicism, and in particular contemporary Stoicism, and this too though he had Roman friends to expound it to him. The pity of it is made more poignant when it is realised that Stoic teachers and Plutarch were engaged in much the same task, with the same ends in view, and that the teaching of both had largely common ground. Plutarch's somewhat literal mind failed to understand the intention of the Stoic 'paradoxes' and from this failure stemmed his professed antipathy. And yet most of his teaching any Stoic would have accepted, and indeed he ends this treatise

by virtually conceding, unwittingly, some of the Stoic positions
which he impugns.

Stoicism was in its origin the impact of Eastern thought on
Greek thought, and the impact transmitted influences into the
West, into Christianity and into European civilisation, influences not yet exhausted. Whatever else it derived from the East,
it certainly borrowed its form of expression. Reasonable propositions were stated in terse aphorisms so exaggerated as to
appear, if taken literally, quite unreasonable. They summed up
in startling terms whole attitudes of mind; they were meant to
jolt the hearer into thought, and thought sees the truth behind
the exaggeration. From the Old and New Testaments we have
become accustomed to them; to Plutarch they are an offence.
He agreed, of course, with the Stoic principle that 'virtue can be
taught', and he would teach it by precept and example, by
training, including reformative punishment, by selecting the
right literature and by the lives of great men. But he jibs at 'He
who is not wise is a fool', 'He who has one vice has all', 'All sins
are equal', and thinks the whole idea of moral progress is invali-
dated by the doctrine of sudden conversion.

The Stoic would not set up a scale of sins; if a thing was
wrong, it was wrong; to steal two pounds was essentially the
same as stealing two thousand; to weigh sins against each other
was to take the meaning out of morality. And all sins are essentially of the same character, and to commit one kind means that
you have it in you to commit another kind, for all sin proceeds
from the same root, an attitude of mind and will. The 'wise man'
is the Stoic's term for 'saint'; hence, if a man is not a saint, he is
a sinner, and, if wisdom means goodness, he is ignorant or foolish. As for conversion, the Stoic regards 'wisdom', or goodness,
as the supreme state of man; and to him 'wisdom' means insight
into the nature of the good. No argument will convince a man
of the value of the good, no training can lead him right to it. He
may live an exemplary life in his limited and uniform environment, living by rule or code or habit and indeed living better
daily. Confront him with an unprecedented situation, over-
whelm him with calamity, or success, and his nicely calculated

scale of sins and his book of rules will fail him. But there may come to a man, on whatever step of the ladder of moral endeavour he may be, a moment of insight; he has seen the good for what it really is; he has therefore seen his duty. Henceforth he needs no scales and no codes. He has seen the light and can walk by it, and to that extent he is 'self-sufficient'.

If Plutarch had condescended to look into Latin philosophical works, he would have discovered Cicero expounding the paradoxes in a special treatise, and in *de finibus*; and he would have been helped even more if he had read Seneca, who interprets them with much insight: 'I will give my assent to the Stoic paradoxes none of which seem to be untrue or as surprising as appears prima facie.' Of course, it was easy to turn the paradoxes into ridicule, as indeed Cicero did in the law-court when it suited his case, but Plutarch would not joke about a matter pertaining to morals. All the same he missed the point of the paradoxes and he failed to realise that Stoicism did in fact believe in moral progress.[1]

The same inability to understand Stoicism is manifest in the treatise *On the self-contradictions of the Stoics*. It begins with the heart-felt plea that the doctrines of philosophers should be consistent with their lives; for a philosopher's doctrine is a self-imposed law and must be applied to himself, for philosophy is a very serious undertaking. In the Stoic philosophers he finds a lack of correspondence between life and teaching and goes on to detect inconsistencies in their utterances. The work is a most valuable storehouse of quotations from Stoic writers, chiefly Chrysippus whose works are not extant, and is valuable for this alone. But as a criticism of Stoicism it is almost useless, for again many of the interpretations are misunderstood by an obtuse literalness and an inability to do justice to thought towards which Plutarch clearly felt much antipathy.

To return to *On progress*. After the preliminary indignant fulminations against Stoicism Plutarch leaves it alone and proceeds to a description of the signs by which progress reveals itself.

We can be as conscious of progress as we are conscious of movement when we are travelling. There can also be regress, but there can be no standing still; moral effort cannot be suspended; we must fight day and night; we can make no truce with sloth or pleasure. Once this is understood, we can move ahead with confidence and enthusiasm.

Throughout the treatise Plutarch uses the word 'philosophy'. By it he does not mean a theoretical ethical system which at its worst might be only a set of rules applied without reflection. He means the term to include moral endeavour, goodness in practice; the conduct which results is aware of the principles by which it is guided; effort of understanding and effort of will combine to issue in a thoughtful and reflective moral endeavour which shall control and inspire a man's life. This is the sense in which the word philosophy will be used in the paragraphs which follow.

At first progress may be slow, and lapses will occur. Progress in the later stages may be faster, for it means that pleasures have been 'squeezed out'. Too enthusiastic a start may lead to despair later. If we relax effort because we are occupied for the moment with the press of other matters, it will be a good sign if we feel a 'hunger and thirst'. If we have really gained from philosophy, the more sensitive we shall be to our deficiencies. Progress should be smooth, for our training of ourselves should have levelled the path. Often there will be perplexities, as with sailors who have lost sight of the land they have left and see no land in front of them. When men become philosophers, they leave their accustomed ways and do not yet see their goal. When they feel no regret for what they have given up, they may take it as a sign that progress is surely established.

Friends' advice and ridicule sometimes make the philosopher turn back; indifference to them is a sign of progress; if you are unaffected by the success of friends, or their political ambitions, or their brilliant marriages, you are on the road; for you can resist admiring what the crowd admires if you have a deeper admiration for goodness. And don't let fine language mislead you; look at the facts and the situation.

Growth in humility is another sign. If you do a service, do not talk about it; if you have resisted a temptation, say nothing. If progress is real, bombast and vainglory will be laid aside, and will be replaced by silence, the quiet eye, the gentle expression and the desire to listen rather than to utter. 'As people who are being initiated (in the mysteries) at first crowd together jostling and shouting and then, when they have witnessed and performed the sacred rites, watch in silent awe', so at the early stages of philosophy you will see men crowding and talking and swaggering and violently pushing each other, like a crowd of yokels, in their pursuit of fame. But 'he who has gone inside and seen a great light, as though doors were being flung open, takes on a different bearing; he is silent and amazed; with humility and self-restraint he follows the teaching[2] as though it were a god.' Humility, too, implies patience under criticism and willingness to criticise oneself. He who grapples with his faults and inflicts a penance on himself or, if he cannot do that, offers himself to another to counsel and punish him is really demonstrating his hatred of wickedness.

It is a sign, too, if we seek to imitate the actions of people we admire and go on to admire the character inspiring the actions and try to become like it. To help us in all our undertakings we should 'put before our eyes living and past examples of good men and consider what Plato would have done in this situation, what Epaminondas would have said'. We must 'set ourselves to rights as though we were in front of a mirror'.

The philosopher will not regard any sin as trifling; he will attend to all. Nothing will escape him. He has laid a golden foundation for his life, like the foundation of a temple or a palace. He accepts no element of current practice without scrutiny; he tests everything by the rational standard of his philosophy.

This treatise is no textbook piece. Similar sentiments may be found in Plato and Aristotle, to say nothing of less known men, and in Cicero; the major part could come from Seneca, for in spite of Plutarch's strictures it is all good contemporary Stoicism. But what is felt, certainly in a reading of the full text, is that here we have a man who is speaking from his own experience; he has lived through the stages which he describes so sensitively, and he has reflected upon his successes and failures and has seen others succeed and fail. The influence of such a man on his friends must have been very great. But it is of no less interest to us that there were other men to whom moral endeavour was of supreme importance. This is the kind of evidence, which could be multiplied a thousand times, to support the belief that this was an age of great spiritual regeneration.

vii 'JOY, PEACE, LONG-SUFFERING'

Near the beginning of his treatise *On tranquillity of mind* Seneca discusses the meaning of the Greek word *euthumia*.

> This steady stance of the mind the Greeks call euthumia, on which subject Democritus wrote an outstanding work; I call it *tranquillitas* ... Our question, then, is how is the mind to be equable, travelling on a smooth course, being on good terms with itself, looking round on its experiences with contentment, allowing no interruption to its pleasure, but remaining on an even keel, never exalted and never depressed.

About the time that Seneca wrote this definition, St. Paul used the same word when he encouraged the crew of his boat in the face of a storm–'Be of good cheer', just as he had also used it when he stood before Festus–'I do cheerfully make my defence.' And the same word is used by St. James–'Is any among you suffering? Let him pray. Is any cheerful? Let him sing praise.'[1]

Plutarch also wrote a treatise on *euthumia*. Thus Democritus (460–370 B.C.) wrote on the subject, though what he wrote is not extant, and so did Seneca and Plutarch. Seneca had read Democritus, Plutarch quotes Democritus (probably) and no doubt had read him either completely or in extracts, but nowhere does Plutarch show any knowledge of Seneca's philosophical works. Now Cicero knew something of Democritus, who, he says, wished his enquiries into the natural order to leave the reader in a state of 'being of good cheer'. 'He thought the highest good was freedom from fear, which he called *euthumia* and often "the state of mind which is not startled by anything".'[2]

If the clue given by Cicero is correct, it appears that Democritus meant by *euthumia* an imperturbability unaffected by mis-

fortune, at most a passive contentment. This, too, is the suggestion of *tranquillitas*. On the other hand in Plutarch the word
seems to include the ability to meet misfortune with equanimity,
but also to add the more active idea of cheerfulness and even
joy. He is at pains in several passages to add to the word the
strongest Greek words denoting radiant cheerfulness.[3] The New
Testament passages, too, though they refer to occasions of disaster—a storm and a trial—imply much more than an attitude of
uncomplaining resignation. It may well be therefore that in the
four or five hundred years after Democritus the word took on a
more positive meaning and that, when Plutarch adds words
denoting joy, he is not adding a new idea but is underlining an
idea already inherent in the word; he is anxious that it should
not be missed.[4]

Another word, too, claims brief attention. Plutarch addresses
the treatise to Paccius, heading it with the form of greeting usual
in a letter. He says:

> Your letter in which you asked that something on *euthumia*
> should be written for you was late. And now our friend Eros has to
> hurry back to Rome after receiving a letter telling him to hurry.
> And so I have not the time to give to the matter which I should
> have liked, yet I cannot let him leave with empty hands. Accordingly
> I have gathered together some thoughts on *euthumia* from the notes
> which I have in fact made for myself. I take it that you do not
> want a bit of fine writing to please your ears but something for
> practical use in your daily life.

What are these 'notes'?[5] The word is used for notes or memoranda of all kinds, business-men's and bankers' records, minutes
of public bodies, memoranda of writers. What did Plutarch
mean by the word? This question has been variously answered.
Some think it means a single source, perhaps Democritus himself, some a ready-made collection of 'sayings' gathered from
philosophical works, some a collection of such 'sayings' made by
Plutarch, some a commonplace book compiled by Plutarch
from his reading of philosophers together with his own additions which would take the form of apposite quotations from the
poets, illustrative anecdotes and his own reflections. The last

interpretation is the most likely. For, if Plutarch had merely summarised Democritus, he might have saved himself the trouble by referring Paccius to the original. Moreover, he was a practical teacher who taught because he wished to teach; he could hardly not make notes from his reading and annotate those notes by observations of his own. Most readers of the treatise will take the introduction at its face value and believe that Paccius really did write for help and that Plutarch did hurriedly consult his notebooks and put together an answer.[6]

As usual the treatise is full of quotations, sayings and historical allusions to illustrate or to introduce the points of the argument, of which the following is a brief summary.

It is of no use to look to wealth to provide peace of mind.[7] The possession of riches is irrelevant to this enquiry; it cannot heal a man's gout and certainly cannot give peace of mind. Xenophon said we should remember the gods chiefly when things went well for us; and so we ought then to strengthen ourselves with all the reflections which will brace us in advance against misfortune.

Democritus said that to secure peace of mind a man should not engage in public or private affairs. This advice makes peace of mind somewhat expensive! Neither a sheltered life nor a life of ease will shield a man from worry and every violent emotion. Epicurus advised participation in public affairs, but he advised it for the wrong reason, namely to satisfy an ambition which will cause worry if it is not satisfied. This is absurd, for it is not mere activity that gives peace of mind, but activity consisting of good actions; goodness must be active; the omission of good deeds is as disturbing to peace of mind as is the performance of bad deeds.

Particular kinds of lives have been praised as being free from anxiety—farmers, celibates, kings—but there is no truth in this belief, and change of occupation makes no difference. The common element in all lives is inexperience of affairs, failure to think, inability to use the present properly; thus peace of mind is destroyed. The only way to obtain peace of mind is to use one's head; habit cannot take the place of sheer common sense. 'We must cleanse the fountain of peace of mind.' Good sense will enable us to make right use of external goods, to accept what comes to us, to assign each thing to the place where it will do most good. Whoever acts in this way will extract good from evil, as a bee gets honey from a bitter plant.

To help you to gain peace of mind study great men. Learn from others; we shall cease to blame circumstances if we see how others meet trouble 'without pain and indeed with joy'. We should see the good and the beautiful in events as well as the bad and the ugly, and should blunt the edge of the bad by dwelling on the good.

It is absurd to cry like children over things we have lost and not to rejoice in what we have. And what have we not? Do not overlook the blessings common to all; we should rejoice that we are alive, that we are well, that there is a peace and freedom to till our land and sail the seas, to speak and not to speak, to work or to be idle. 'Imagine the opposite of these and you will see what blessings they are. We should enjoy what we have to the full and get the utmost happiness and pleasure from it. Most people desire what others possess and envy destroys peace of mind.'

It is important to keep your ambition within your powers. Strive hard within your own limitations; cultivate your own plot, and don't become disgruntled because you can't become something which you do not have it in your power to become. The treasuries of peace are within you. You can have no peace if you are waiting on tomorrow instead of being thankful for to-day and for yesterday's blessings. Sorrow and pain do not really affect us, that is, the better part of us which cannot really be spoilt by anything external. If your beliefs are founded on reason, you are proof against the future; you must never distrust them and then you will not feel despair but will always be ready to admire, eager and indeed exalted in spirit.

This world is a most sacred temple worthy of the gods; into it a man is introduced at birth to be a witness not of things made with hands but of all the things that the divine intelligence makes manifest to him; they are copies of 'ideas', as Plato said, with the principles of life and motion inherent in them – the sun, the moon and stars, rivers forever gushing with new water, the earth offering sustenance to plants and animals. 'Life is a kind of initiation and is a most complete and perfect religious experience, and so it ought to be full of peace and joy.' Our own festivals some men abuse, treating them as occasions for riotous hilarity; but 'we sit silent and composed; no one mourns during the rite of initiation'. Again, some people rightly enjoy music and the song of birds; they like to watch animals at play and hate to see them in distress; but their own lives they allow to be crushed by ceaseless worry and anxiety; they do not help themselves to obtain any respite and they do not even accept the counsel of their friends to aid them 'to bear the present without complaint and to be thankful for the past and to face the future in cheerful and radiant hope and so to live their lives free from fear and suspicion.'[8]

If there is a certain lack of order in this summary, it is not entirely its fault, for the original treatise, and indeed the nature of the subject, do not favour continuous and logical development. But Plutarch's work is far less disjointed than Seneca's essay which, from Chapter Three onwards, seems to follow no plan. Naturally some of the themes are common to both, but there is much also that is specific to each; it is impossible to detect that they owed anything to any common source.[9]

viii ANIMALS

That Plutarch takes more sympathetic note of the animal creation than any other Greek writer, except the naturalists, would be a thesis no doubt impossible to prove. Yet, for what it is worth, the impression remains. The references to animals, if only in similes, are very frequent, and there are two dialogues which are devoted to 'beast-psychology'.

The full title of the first is *Whether land animals or sea animals are more intelligent*; the treatise falls into two parts—first, a discussion of the premise underlying the title, that animals do in fact possess intelligence, secondly, a comparison of land and sea animals in this respect.

Autobulus begins the discussion by asking whether the essay

in praise of hunting which the company had heard read the day before might not encourage young men to give far too much time to this pursuit.

Soclarus agrees that the writer of the essay—and Plutarch himself is probably meant—had perhaps gone too far; he gave the impression of reviving his memories after a lapse of years, of letting himself go in an exaggerated style to please the younger members of the audience, in fact, of 'joining the boys in the spring of their years'. All the same it was true that hunting did divert the natural blood-lust into a harmless channel.

On the contrary, replies Autobulus; the blood-lust originated from the moment when men first ate the flesh of a hunted animal; they have never lost their pleasure in killing and as a result all feelings of humanity have been blunted. The Pythagoreans take the opposite line and teach kindness to animals; habit becomes established little by little, but it has far-reaching effects upon character. But we have touched on what was inherent in yesterday's conversation, namely the comparative intelligence of land and sea animals and we had better continue it.

But Soclarus asks for delay; for, he says, there is a prior consideration. The Stoics maintain that every state or condition is matched by its opposite; 'mortal' implies 'immortal', and so 'possessed of intelligence' implies 'devoid of intelligence', and this latter state, when used of living things, means 'brute' beasts. Thereupon in a long speech Autobulus explains that the senses imply intelligence. If you assume the animals have no ability to expect or remember, to plan or prepare, to fear or desire, then eyes and ears and touch are meaningless; the senses serve the intelligence of the animal. Hence the dictum that there is no intelligence without sensation, that sensation implies intelligence. Preparation, e.g. of a nest, presupposes a knowledge of an end, and an understanding of the means necessary to achieve it. Moreover, we behave to animals in such a way as to show that we believe in their intelligence; we entice them and train them and punish them. And it is no good saying that they behave as if they remember or plan; you might just as reasonably say that they behave as if they see or indeed as if they were alive.

Soclarus now objects that rationality and morality are bound up together; reason has the good as its end; but no one can say that animals strive after goodness; therefore they do not possess reason.

It is all a matter of degree, replies Autobulus; men vary in respect of reason and morality. So also animals vary; they show differing degrees of social or anti-social behaviour, just as men do. Nor can it be said that men excel in prudence or shrewdness or justice or a sense of fellowship; again it is a matter of degree. Indeed we popularly concede the case for reason in animals when we speak of a mad dog or a mad elephant.

Soclarus weakens somewhat. It appears then, he says, that the Stoics and Peripatetics are faced with a choice of two propositions: (a) animals are not rational, (b) rational beings should be treated with justice. If animals are rational, they should not be eaten nor worked in the service of man. Of these alternatives they choose the first, because they do not wish to accept the consequences of the second.

Exactly, says Autobulus; but this short cut will not do for the philosopher. We must give due consideration to the animals and due consideration to ourselves and our needs. Bion was right when he told some boys that they might be stoning frogs for fun, but the frogs were serious enough when they died, and the same thought could be applied to all blood sports. The only way left is to treat animals with justice; we must not harm them or despise them or be cruel to them.

At this point the two men are joined by some young and some older men; one or two are well known as enjoying hunting, others are islanders or coast dwellers, coming from Euboea and Megara. Autobulus makes one of the newcomers, probably older than the rest, sit by his side as the expert referee 'and then we won't have to bother the volumes of Aristotle'.

The rest of the dialogue—except for a brief conclusion—is left to two young men who have been waiting to take up a discussion left over from the day before—indeed it seems that they have done some homework overnight. And so Aristotimus in a long speech expounds with ample equipment of legend and

natural history the merits of land animals; he is followed by
Phaedimus in an equally long speech in favour of sea animals.
Clearly these last contributions are part of a contest; and it has
been suggested that we are to suppose that two of Plutarch's
young pupils are engaged in a competition, with the older men
as adjudicators. They must surely have been disappointed when
Soclarus in a sententious quotation from Sophocles observes that
the debate has been a good one, that extremes meet in the
middle and that, if the young men combined forces, they would
be a match for anyone who denies intelligence to animals.

This dull summary spoils the dialogue which is full of good
natural history and equally good stories–of the crows which
dropped stones into the jar of water to raise the level so that they
might drink, the bees which carry stones to ballast themselves in
high winds, the geese which hold a stone in their mouths as they
fly over the Caucasus so that they shall not honk and so attract
the eagles which live there, the sentry stork which holds a stone
in one foot so that if he should fall asleep the dropping of the
stone will wake the rest. An account is given of the social life of
ants, whose nests the speaker does not wish to be disturbed by
mere curiosity; he then passes to elephants so that it may be
clear that mind resides equally in the smallest and the largest
animals. We learn about the training of elephants, and especially about one member of a performing troup which was not as
clever as the rest and was often punished; one night it was seen
all by itself practising its acts in the light of the moon. A story is
told of a fox which clearly could argue to itself syllogistically, of
a mule which repeatedly had to carry jars of salt across a river
and discovered that if it got the salt wet it melted and the load
was lightened; the animal was cured by no less a man than
Thales himself, who suggested filling the jars with sponges and
wool. A certain jay could imitate any sound with great skill; one
day a brass band (or its equivalent) passed by; the jay was reduced to silence; for days it said nothing; at last it gave a full
rendering of the band; it had been mentally rehearsing till it was
perfect. We hear of fish that come when called by name, of croc-
odiles that like to have their teeth cleaned with a handkerchief,

of elephants which fill up the ditch into which one of their
number has fallen and make a ramp for its escape. The account
given of the cunning of fish in eluding the hook and the net reads
as though it were written by someone who had practical experience and to a fisherman is of great interest.[1] The long section
given to the dolphin as the most intelligent of animals (the only
animal which takes the initiative in becoming friendly with
man) anticipates in small compass what is now being written
about this animal.

There is no need to go into the question of the sources of this
medley of fact and fiction. Aelian and Plutarch seem to have
derived much from the same writers, especially from Aristotle.[2]

The second dialogue about animals is very different from the
dialogue on the intelligence of animals—indeed in form it is
unique in the whole corpus of Plutarch's works.[3] The characters
are Circe, Odysseus and one of the pigs into whose shape she
had transformed a visitor to her island; for the purpose of the
dialogue she endows the animal with a human voice and allows
Odysseus to question it. For he had learned from her that she
had on her island many Greeks whom she had turned into
wolves and lions and swine, and demanded that she should turn
them back into human form and release them. 'But, by Hecate,'
says Circe, 'it is not as simple as all that . . . first of all you must
ask them if they want to be turned back. If they say no, you must
persuade them by argument; if you lose the argument and they
win, they you will have to be satisfied that your judgment
about your condition and about theirs is all wrong.' And so
Gryllus—for that is the name of the pig, grunter—argues that
animals have virtues which are genuine and sincere since they
are implanted by nature herself, whereas man's virtues, if they
can be so called, are the product of convention and self-interest;
nor are beasts guilty of such bestiality as men are. Odysseus is
driven back to his last position, that animals have no idea of
God; and there the dialogue breaks off.

Once again Plutarch opposes the Stoic point of view about
animals; the arguments are amusing and interesting. The pig
knows his Greek mythology well enough and he makes refer-

ences to well-known beasts which had some connexion with Boeotia. It has therefore been pointed out that he is probably Boeotian in origin, and thus we have a 'Boeotian swine', a proverbial phrase for a fool, overcoming in debate Odysseus, proverbially the wiliest of Greeks; indeed Odysseus himself admits that the pig is something of a sophist.[4]

As regards the form of the dialogue, critics have regarded it as Cynic in character. By this they mean that Menippus, the slave philosopher of Gadara who, when freed, lived at Thebes early in the third century B.C., used dialogue for his own satiric purposes and was ready to make gods, heroes, animals and indeed anyone take part in conversations to discredit all the established institutions of men. We know little about him at first hand; but Lucian, of whom this dialogue may well remind us, was indebted to him and indirectly tells us a good deal.[5] The most notable contribution of Cynicism to Greek literature was its stress on 'the serio-comic',[6] a moral lesson wrapped up in an amusing or satiric form. Moreover long before the Cynics animals had been made to speak and to convey moral teaching; Hesiod* perhaps gives the earliest example, but he is followed by Archilochus and of course by Aesop; shortly before Plutarch was born Phaedrus had said that 'A double use in pretty fable lies; it makes the reader laugh, it makes him wise'. Perhaps most readers will enjoy this dialogue without enquiring too much into its possible sources, and will even allow Plutarch a little inventiveness of his own.

A sample of the best of Plutarch's *Moralia* has been given in summary form in the foregoing pages. There remains much else. There are scientific works like the *Natural Questions*, or *On the face on the moon*. There are essays dealing with questions of morals and behaviour, like *On garrulity* or *On meddlesomeness* and collections of sayings and stories like the *Spartan sayings*. But after making acquaintance with some of the better dialogues or essays a reader must not expect too much from some of those that remain unnoticed here. Some of the extant works may be nothing more

* *Op.* 202.

than Plutarch's notebooks; some lack beginning or end or both; some may be merely drafts; several may not have been intended for publication. They all contain much of interest, but Plutarch should not be judged by them. Some readers will find him, even at his best, a little tedious; to some he will appear rather obvious and trite and verbose and to others his quotations will be wearisome. If it is permissible to infer a man's conversational habits from his style of writing, we might guess that as a talker he could be attractive, and yet we may also ask whether he knew when to stop. But, if a man is really likeable and we have some affection for him, we can tolerate his prosiness, and sometimes that is what we must do with Plutarch. At the same time one of his great attractions is that the reader never knows what is coming next.[7] A series of somewhat platitudinous remarks is suddenly relieved by a sentence attesting keen observation and shrewd judgment of human nature, or by a story which aptly sums up, or by a startling metaphor which makes the matter come alive, or by a digression which holds the attention. Plutarch can be dull, but not for long.

CHAPTER 10

Plutarch and the Roman Empire

i CHANCE OR CHARACTER OR PROVIDENCE?

ANY writer is likely to use the words 'fortune', 'luck', 'chance' and the like very often, and in many passages there is no need to press him for his precise meaning. On the other hand, there may be passages in which it is important that we should know what are the implications of his terms.

Plutarch, like everyone else, ascribes to chance or fortune an event for which he is not concerned or would not be able, if asked, to discover a logical connexion with any other event or sequence of events; as he puts it 'chance is a thing which cannot be discerned and is beyond the grasp of reasoning'.[1] Chance then, means a sequence of which the ground is only partially known or wholly unknown. But to Plutarch this vacuum is unsatisfactory; he fills the gap in knowledge by postulating a power which directs events, or some events, so that what might loosely be ascribed to chance is now related to the will of a supreme deity or a lesser divinity; he relates chance in the sense of 'so it happened' to religion in some form.

Examples will illustrate. Brutus did not know of his victory till twenty days after it occurred; the cause was 'chance' or, less probably, the malice of his commanders. 'Chance' here means 'it just happened so, and I do not know why it so happened'. When Camillus departed from Rome he called down curses on an ungrateful city. Vengeance did indeed pursue the Romans, for disaster succeeded disaster, 'whether chance so befell or whether it was the work of some god to see that ingratitude to virtue does not go unnoticed'. Here 'chance' means that there was no connexion between the curses and the disasters—or perhaps Nemesis was the connexion. In another passage chance and Nemesis are virtually equated. As for Aemilius, 'chance postponed till a later occasion the punishment for his success, but at the moment gave him a pleasure in his victory which was fully satisfying'.[2]

So far, then, we have 'the occurrence of events for which a reason cannot be given' and 'a power which determines (some) events in order to vindicate a moral standard'.

But this is not enough for Plutarch the moralist. Where does man come in? or his will? or his moral aspirations? In the comparison between Theseus and Romulus Plutarch says 'If (as I think) we ought not to regard the misfortunes of men as entirely due to chance[3] but must look for their cause in the moral and emotional differences between individuals'; we must confess that both Romulus and Theseus were guilty of unreasonable anger, but that Romulus' anger made him commit an action which resulted in a series of disasters, while Theseus' anger expressed itself only in words and stopped short there; the misfortunes which he suffered were due to chance, *i.e.* bad luck.

In this passage Plutarch leaves room for the moral and emotional characteristics of men to influence, at least in part, the course of events. In another passage[4] he implies that men could influence events more than they do by a greater sense of moral responsibility; it is worth quoting for it summarises much of Plutarch's beliefs.

The divine, with which we are most anxious to bind ourselves in kinship and in likeness, has three characteristics, indestructibility, power and goodness. Indestructibility belongs to the elements and to the void; earthquakes and thunders, hurricanes and torrents have power; but in justice and right nothing has a share unless by intelligence and by taking the divine into account. The feelings towards the gods which most people have are three, envy, fear and honour; they envy them and count them blessed for their indestructibility and eternity, they fear and dread them for their sovereignty and power, they love and honour and worship them for their righteousness. Such is men's attitude; yet they desire immortality, of which their nature does not admit, they desire power which for the most part lies in the lap of fortune, but goodness, the only one of the divine attributes which is within their reach, they put in the last place–and most foolishly, for the life of those who possess power, good fortune and high office is made a thing divine by righteousness, by wickedness a bestial thing.

The theme that men by their moral reaction to events can modify the course of subsequent events is well illustrated in *On the Fortune of Alexander*. This is a youthful rhetorical work; it deals with the question whether Alexander's achievements were due more to good fortune or to his own character. This topic had been discussed soon after his death and had continued into Roman times and was indeed still a stock subject for disputation.[5] Plutarch's exercise–for such it is–falls into two parts, the second somewhat untidy in form and argument; they are a reply to a previous thesis which had maintained that good luck had been responsible. In the first part Alexander is proclaimed as a philosopher. In person he protests that he was no spoilt child of fortune, but at the cost of ceaseless hardships and many wounds he had enlarged his empire. It was, continues Plutarch, only his high qualities of mind and soul that brought him through triumphant, and they were the gifts of philosophy. True philosophy consists not in theory but in action. With more far-reaching success than Plato and Socrates he had taught the barbarians Hellenic culture; he had given effective expression to the Stoic ideal of the unity of mankind. The second part is loosely attached to the first; 'we forgot to say yesterday' that chance may put power into the hands of a man, but few can use it, and only those of high moral character; Alexander's successors inherited power, but failed through lack of the necessary qualities. Chance had exposed him to hardship and danger; virtue had rescued him. In virtue he surpassed every hero of history or mythology. And there the treatise breaks off.

It is a florid piece of writing. But the moral stands out; a man is able by his character to influence the course of events.

The next steps are easy. If there is a power which vindicates goodness against the evil-doer, the well-doer may be under the protection of a power which will influence events in his favour.[6] And what applies to the individual well-doer may apply to a nation of well-doers. And so chance, or fortune, becomes

Providence, a process which we may now watch in some detail in *On the fortune of the Romans.*

Of this work it can be said at once that it is incomplete and unrevised; it is rhetorical in style. In all probability rival contestants were deputed to deliver speeches on the theme, 'Did the Romans owe more to fortune or to Arete?' and Arete means 'high qualities, character, and especially the moral qualities of a good soldier'. To Plutarch it fell to elaborate the cause of fortune; perhaps on another similar occasion he had to argue on the Arete of the Romans. The thesis on the other side does not survive; and it may be that this fragment was not published by him but preserved to us by his family. That it is unrevised is shown by the pointless double reference in chapters 5 and 10 to the temple of Fortuna at Rome.

The style of this document, after the initial chapters, is exuberant and lively. It contains many quotations and allusions, as do all Plutarch's writings; it cites episodes from Greek history as well as from Roman, and makes reference to more than forty names of mythological and historical Romans.

In the following summary it is important to watch the constant change in the meaning of Fortune.

The first two chapters are judicial in tone. This is the greatest battle Arete and Fortune have ever waged: it will bring no little renown to whichever wins, and victory will dispose of criticism. For Arete is accused of being beautiful but useless, Fortune of being good but unstable. Nobody will be able to deny that, if Roman success is assigned to Arete, she will be proved to have been most useful, for she has brought good things to good men; if Fortune wins, she will be proved to be stable, for she has preserved the gifts she has given. Ion remarked that Fortune and Wisdom, though apparently dissimilar, often bring about similar results. Both may lead to distinction, power, rule. It is the same all-productive Nature which some call wisdom, some fortune. It will reflect glory on Rome if we ask the same question about her as we ask about Nature—is fortune or Providence responsible?

For my part I think that Fortune and Arete made peace and

combined to bring about so great a welding-together of government and power; by combining them they created one of the fairest of all the works of men. Plato says that fire and earth joined to produce the Universe; in the same way Time in co-operation with God laid the foundations of Rome mixing or yoking together Fortune and Arete; their purpose was to take the specific qualities of each and to perfect for all men a central hearth, truly sacred and lavish of all good gifts–a hawser immovable, a prime substance abiding for ever, an anchorage amid the waves and the flux, as Democritus says, for a world tossed in turmoil. Again, the scientists say (here follows an outline of the atomic theory) . . . so in the same way great empires and powers were tossed about by fortune and collided because no one controlled them, though everyone wished they were under control; everywhere there was hopeless drift and movement and change, until Rome took the power and increased and bound within herself nations and peoples and the realms of kings beyond the sea; and then all that was greatest found a sure resting-place; then was peace and order and one immovable encircling ring-fence of government; in the minds of those who wrought all this there dwelt all Arete, though in much Fortune was partner. This will be shown as my theme progresses.

But I think I see, as though from a watch-tower, Arete and Fortune approaching for the contest. Arete comes with smooth walk and steadfast eyes; she hurries in, a long way behind, flushed with eagerness for the battle. She is accompanied by a bodyguard of warriors showing scars, dripping with sweat and blood. Who are they? Of course, the Fabricii, Camilli, Cincinnati, Maximi Fabii, the Claudii, Marcelli, Scipios.

I can see Gaius Marius showing his anger with Fortune; Mucius Scaevola holds up his burning hand and cries, 'Do you think this is a gift from Fortune?' And Horatius, dragging his lame leg from the flood, cries, 'And was it Fortune that crippled me?'

Fortune had a quick step, a saucy look and an arrogant confidence. She outstripped Arete; she was not poised on light wings nor did she tread on tiptoe her slippery ball, but she approached with deceptive step and now she sped away leaving behind disappointment. She had deserted Persia and Assyria, flown lightly over Macedonia, quickly shaken off Alexander, ranged through Egypt and Syria and made a path through their kingdoms; with many a quick turn she had uplifted the Carthaginians; she then crossed the Tiber and approached the Palatine. There she laid aside her wings, put off her sandals, and put away that slippery and deceitful ball. That is how she came to Rome, as one who intended to stay, and that is how she came to the contest.

She is not untrustworthy, as Pindar says she is; Alcman says more justly that she is the sister of Eunomia and Persuasion and is the daughter of Prometheia. She has in her hand the famous cornucopia, abundantly full of all that is provided by the earth, sea, rivers, mines, harbour – all in lavish profusion. She is accompanied by many distinguished people – twelve names follow, some well-known, Numa, Aemilius Paulus, Sulla, some less known, Caius Caprarius, and most are briefly designated in a sentence each. Sulla, in a quotation from Sophocles, acknowledged his debt to Fortune, and was called Felix. Trophies at Chaeronea show him described as Epaphroditus, and Fortune (not Night, as Menander says) has the biggest part in Aphrodite.

Let us then start from here and cite the Romans themselves to bear witness that they owe more to Fortune than to Arete. The rest of this chapter is given to a review of the building of temples at Rome, with the names of the generals who dedicated them. The temple to Fortune was dedicated by Ancus Martius; the various Virtues received their temples much later, and some went without.

Chapter 6 lists the kind of occasions when Caesar had relied on Fortune and she had not failed him; she went with him as he sailed, travelled abroad, went on active service, conducted campaigns; she ruled the sea, turned winter into summer, gave speed to the sluggard and courage to the faltering. Most incredible of all, she turned Pompey to flight and moved Ptolemy to slay his guest so that Pompey might fall but Caesar be not polluted.

In the same way (ch. 7) Augustus confessed his debt to Fortune who aided him not least in making others work for him. For him Cicero was statesman, for him Lepidus fought campaigns, Pansa won victories and Antony gave himself up to excesses. Indeed Cleopatra was no small part of the fortune of Augustus; it was for her that Antony suffered the shipwreck of his life and so left Augustus supreme. The advice offered to Antony by one of his friends sums up the matter.

Why do you have any dealings with that young man? Avoid him: you are his superior in fame, in years: you command more troops, you have fought wars, you outstrip him in experience. But your genius is afraid of his genius; your fortune by itself is great, but it is subservient to his, and, if you do not keep apart from him, it will cross over to him and be gone.

Such is the sure evidence (ch. 8) that these witnesses give. But we must cite evidence also from the facts of history, and for these we must go back to the beginnings of Rome. As regards the birth and upbringing of Romulus, we may say that Fortune laid the foundation and Arete built the edifice. Then follows the story, complete with Mars, Silvia, the wolf, the woodpecker, an anecdote about Themistocles which prompts Fortune to address Romulus, pointing out to him the fortune which had attended him at every stage; finally Plutarch sums up. 'It was Arete that made Romulus great, it was Fortune that watched over him till he became great.'

The next two chapters (9 and 10) explain in detail how Numa's efforts for peace succeeded only because fortune helped him and how Servius dedicated temples to fortune (here much of chapter 5 is repeated).

In chapter 11 Plutarch pulls himself up with the reminder that he must not take evidence only from ancient times, but must forsake the kings and pass on to the well-known events of Roman history. It is true, he says, that war requires courage; but the smooth flow of Roman success, the impetus which carried Rome to power, demonstrate that her Empire was due not to human judgments; rather was she wafted to her destiny by the divinely guided breeze of fortune. And so triumph followed upon triumph; kingdoms and races, islands and continents were added to her realm. And then follows a summary which embraces the acquisition of the early provinces, Hannibal, the Cimbri and Teutones, Antiochus and Mithridates. That mighty 'genius' of the Romans did not blow fitfully nor prosper only briefly; it began with the young Republic and grew and was as potent on sea as on land, in peace as in war, against barbarians as against Greeks.

The catastrophe, which nearly overwhelmed Rome when the city was besieged by the Gauls, was averted only by a series of interventions on the part of fortune; these are enumerated in detail in chapter 12.

Again (ch. 13) these early times do not satisfy Plutarch. For, as Livy says, the records were destroyed by the Gauls. Later times demonstrate even more clearly the kindliness of fortune. I myself think the death of Alexander was part of her kindliness. He had won resounding successes; he was elated and confident; like a star he had sped from East to West; already he was focusing the rays from his arms upon Italy. The struggle would have been against all mankind; for his ambition urged him to go beyond the limits reached by Bacchus and Heracles. He had heard of the might of Rome set across his path like the blade of a sword. The glorious name of the Romans had reached him; they were as athletes trained in a thousand combats. And, when invincible arms wielded by pride which could never give way came into conflict, 'methinks they will not be sundered without the shedding of blood' (a most appropriate quotation, for the words are uttered by the disguised Odysseus, foreshadowing the battle between himself and the suitors; either side, Alexander or Rome, could claim to be battling with 'suitors' to world-power).[7]

And there the document ends; presumably later times were reviewed in the same vein, and perhaps the case for Arete was elaborated. At the end there was probably a truce between the contestants and the contribution of each was duly recognised.

In this fragment there are several puzzling questions. In the early chapters Fortune is set in contrast with Providence: she is the Goddess of Chance, equipped with wings and poised upon a ball; she is fickle and capricious. Soon she becomes the daemon, the genius, the protecting power which attends men from their birth; later she becomes the divine purpose which intervenes to save a people from disaster and to guide it to its high destiny. Starting as fortune, she becomes good fortune; consistent good fortune implies divine ordering, in short Providence. Was Plutarch aware that he had altered the meaning of Fortune as he moved on from the earliest events of Roman history? And was the change intentional? Does he mean that what at first might be regarded as a series of chance happenings is seen upon a wider survey to be no accident but the working out of a purpose and a destiny?

Again, though admittedly the thirteen chapters are a hurried sketch drawn with a special intention, it is noteworthy that, as far as men themselves are concerned, events just happen; there is no indication that on the human plane they might be related, that there might be causes and effects, that the actions of men might influence the actions of men. It is true that such a view of history could not receive much emphasis in an essay whose theme is fortune; but its absence is worth noting, for it will be discussed more fully later.

It has been held that this document is an early rhetorical exercise undertaken by Plutarch when he was a young man; and the question has been seriously asked whether it was written by him before or after he became the pupil of Ammonius, that is when he was about nineteen years old. In the last resort the matter must be decided on internal evidence; while impressions about style will no doubt weigh, the following facts must also be explained.

In the frequent references to literature the poets Homer, Alcman, Pindar, Aeschylus, Sophocles, Timotheus, Menander, are drawn upon; among philosophers Democritus, Plato, Ion; among historians Polybius, who himself had much to say about the fortune of Rome, Valerius Antias who in his Latin history dealt in some detail with the early period of Roman history and was one of Livy's sources; in chapter 10 Plutarch rejects the version of 'those who follow Antias', so that he clearly had access to some other authority. It may have been Livy, to whom he refers in chapter 13. The detailed information which Plutarch furnishes in his account of the course of Roman history as far as he treats it is very striking. Indeed some of it does not occur in the *Lives*, as, *e.g.* the record of the eclipse of the sun which occurred at the birth of Romulus. That as a young man of nineteen Plutarch would know something of the Greek poets is intelligible enough, for his early education would be largely concerned with them. But it is not easy to determine how he could have acquired a knowledge of Roman history and mythology; there is no warrant to think that they formed part of the curriculum; and, though in his father's household, to which Romans were welcome, he might have picked up something, it could not have been systematic enough to provide the data for this essay. The *Roman History* of Dionysius of Halicarnassus he might have read, though it should be remembered that Dionysius takes a point of view contrary to this essay; he considers that the Romans owed their success not to fortune, but to their qualities. Polybius, too, he might have read. But, if it is true, as has been seen, that he came to Latin literature late in life, he did not read Antias and Livy in the original. Did he read some epitome of Livy in Greek, or an anthology of Roman authors in a Greek version? Of this we know nothing; but it seems incredible that a boy of nineteen could have mastered all that the fragment contains, and have expressed it in a style which is imaginative and colourful, with periods carefully framed and sometimes of great length, but clear and easy to read, and with words so arranged as to avoid hiatus, a test of Plutarch's style, and running with characteristic rhythm. At the same time it is difficult to imagine the situation for which a more mature Plutarch would have composed so lively and so learned a document.[8] The puzzle remains.

That Providence may interfere in the history of nations is a belief retained by Plutarch in the writings which can certainly be assigned to his old age.[9] Of his own beloved Greece he says that there seems to have been at that moment some divinely ordered fortune in the revolution of things, putting an end to the freedom of Greece and 'resisting all that men were doing and giving many indications of what was to come'. The first of the Roman lives begins with the words, 'the great name of Rome which in fame has spread through all mankind', and later he explains that we cannot doubt a supernatural origin for Rome 'when we consider of what works fortune is the creator and when we reflect upon the history of Rome—how she could not have reached such a height of power if she had not sprung from a divine origin and been attended by mighty and startling events'. In the same way, after describing a portent, he adds that it may or may not be believed, but;

> Those who assert and defend this marvel have a powerful advocate on their side in the fortune of the city; it is impossible to conceive a city rising to such a height of fame and power from a small and contemptible beginning if God had not on each and several occasions been present with it in many striking manifestations.[10]

But to leave the realm of myth and marvel, there is a significant passage in which Plutarch goes out of his way to offer a general judgment. After the battle of Pharsalus Pompey turned to Cratippus the philosopher and argued with him about Providence. Cratippus declined argument, for it is possible he might have defended the actions of Providence and shown that misgovernment compelled the change from republic to monarchy; he could have asked, 'What evidence can you offer, Pompey, that if you had won the battle you would have used your fortune better than Caesar? We must let the business of the gods go on as it does.'

In all this there was nothing very new. Aristotle had claimed to be the first to discuss the nature of chance; his own conclusion was that chance is the name men give to the unforeseen meeting of two chains of causation. 'Fortune' became a powerful idea in Hellenistic thought and religion. It is not difficult to see how sides were taken; 'unforeseen' may mean 'unforeseeable' by anyone because, there being no connexion, foresight is an irrelevant notion; on the other hand, 'unforeseen' may mean unforeseen by man but foreseen, because intended, by

Providence. So the philosophers differed, while the man in the market place was ready to worship both Chance and Providence at the same time. And people were only too ready to ascribe defeat by Philip, the rise of Alexander, the break-up of his Empire and the emergence of Rome to a blind chance, and so excused themselves.

Already in Polybius Plutarch had an example of an historian of Rome who denied that the Roman achievement which he greatly admired was due to fortune. At the beginning of his history[11] he says that fortune had never brought about such a miracle, or enacted so wonderful a drama as when she established the Roman Empire; yet in fact the Romans deserved their success, for they had accumulated the resources of character and institutions with which to bring it about. They were not Fortune's children. In a later chapter[12] he insists that it is not true, as some Greeks think, that Rome's success was due to chance and just occurred of itself; on the contrary, it was abundantly justified, for she had trained herself in exacting affairs and then had made a determined effort to win universal sovereignty and power, and indeed had carried her undertaking through to fulfilment.

In all that Polybius and Plutarch said about the fortune of Rome there was nothing unfamiliar to the Romans. They had long believed that as a people they were under the care of the gods because from earliest days they had obeyed them. 'Because you bear yourselves as less than the gods you rule the world,' was the text of Horace which summed up the Roman experience of the centuries before him; it became the text on which countless exhortations were later to be based.

On this topic no more must be said here.[13] But it is not irrelevant to add one further point. On the whole the Romans were more inclined to attribute their success to gods than to Fortune; Polybius himself in a famous passage agrees that what held the Commonwealth together was its 'respect for the gods'. It is true that the Romans had a goddess Fortune and dedicated temples to her, as Plutarch himself records. But Fortune, in the strictly Roman sense, is not the 'Chance' of Hellenistic Greece;

she 'brings' (*ferre*) things, indeed she 'brings' things 'forth'. Some of her cult-titles make it clear that in some of her aspects at least she is concerned with fertility and increase. One or two of these titles Plutarch quotes in the *Roman Questions* without realising their significance,[14] Of course, Fortuna is regularly applied by Romans to the destiny of Rome, of cities and of individuals; but there seems to be something positive and constructive in her. She is Good or Favourable Fortune, Fortune who knows what she is about, while Tyche or Chance is, in comparison, neutral and indifferent.

ii ADVICE TO THE GREEKS

When Plutarch wrote, Greece had been part of the Roman Empire for about 250 years. How did this Greek of Greeks view the condition of his native land?

In a passage often quoted Plutarch alludes to the depopulation of Greece in his time. He makes Ammonius say in the course of a discussion On *On the failure of the oracles* that as a result of wars and revolutions of preceding centuries the whole world had been depopulated, but no country more than Greece; it could hardly provide a force of 3,000 heavy infantry,[1] if required, though the small state of Megara alone had sent that number to the battle of Plataea. This is no doubt an exaggeration, whether by Ammonius or by Plutarch. For Plutarch's own account of his life and friendships in Chaeronea and its neighbourhood suggests that Greece supported many families like his own, living a comfortable life on their estates which needed management and cultivation. No doubt industry had suffered severely, for Greek craftsmen were spread over the Mediterranean lands and every province had its own industries. Greece had never been an agricultural land, for its soil was too poor. Plutarch, if the statement is his, was looking back, as he always did, to the days of Pericles or rather Epaminondas, and by comparison towns were less flourishing. Depopulation had already been discussed by Polybius over 200 years before Plutarch wrote; his conclusion was that sheer selfishness was the cause. Plutarch offers no reason. Indeed he tells us nothing about the economic state of Greece, about taxation, about provincial government and administration. He took the Empire, and the place of Greece within it, for granted. He shows no interest in its working or its success, still less in its justification or its destiny. He praises little, he condemns little; he appears hardly to notice what lay round him, and he acquiesced in what he found.

His acquiescence is easily demonstrated.

Perhaps about A.D. 100 a young man who contemplated taking up public life in Sardes wrote to Plutarch for help; he would have liked to come and see Plutarch carry out his public duties in Boeotia, but he had not time. Would Plutarch therefore be good enough to write his advice in a treatise and send it to him? The treatise was written and called *Precepts of government.* It is concerned mainly with the qualities of mind and character desirable in the public man, and naturally it is well furnished with historical examples. But in the middle chapters it is concerned with the relations which should obtain between the leading men of a Greek city and the Roman Government. Here is a summary.[2]

The public man rules the city like a queen bee. He must take the helm in his hands.* He should not be too desirous of office, nor desire it too often. At the same time the wishes of the people should not be rejected; offices should be accepted even if they seem a little below one's dignity; a spirit of co-operation should be shown. It is only fair when you have been honoured with high office to honour in turn some lower office. In the more burdensome offices, like the Boeotarchy with us, a man should behave with moderation and remit a little of their majesty; to the minor offices he should try to add lustre. Thus we (note the 'we') shall avoid being despised for holding the minor offices and jealously envied for holding the major. When a man enters office, it is useless for him to have ready to hand the considerations of which Pericles frequently reminded himself–'You are ruling men who are free, Greeks, Athenian Citizens'. No: he should say to himself 'Though you rule, you are yourself ruled; your city is subject to proconsuls and procurators of the Em-

* Sudden change of metaphor does not worry Plutarch.

peror; this is no ancient Sardes or Lydian Empire. You must have little trust in the crown when you see the shoes above your head. Like an actor you must keep within the role allotted to you by your managers. It is dangerous to go beyond it. We are amused when children try on their father's shoes; it is not amusing when public men imitate acts of their forbears which are unsuited to the times. There is much in Greek history which we can still imitate, but not Plataea or Marathon; these are best left to the rhetorical schools.

Local magistrates and public men should present themselves and their city blameless in the eyes of their rulers; but they should go further and make friends with those in power as a firm support for their city. It is characteristic of the Romans to back up their friends in all political matters. It is right to turn friendship with governors to profit; this is what Polybius and Panaetius did who brought great benefit to their cities through their good relations with Scipio. When Augustus entered Alexandria, he was seen conversing only with Arius among those of his retinue; he soothed all fears by saying that he spared the city because it was great, because it was founded by Alexander, because he wished to please Arius. Arius' service to his city rendered at home was far better than search for profitable administrative posts which involve a life-time abroad waiting at other people's doors. Euripides should be rewritten and made to say that if a palace is to be frequented no dishonour is implied if one's country benefits; apart from this all friendships should be made on a basis of justice and equality.

Even though a country has to be obedient to rulers, there is no need for it to grovel and, because its leg is tied, to offer its neck. Those who defer in small and great matters reduce their city to a state of abject slavery, or rather they destroy it, so paralysing it with fright that it controls nothing. If you invite the decision of your rulers in everything, you compel them to be more despotic than they wish. Avarice, jealousy and uncompromising rivalry ask for the intervention of the superior power, and then the local senate, courts, people lose authority. A

politician should treat the masses as equals, smooth down the
powerful and keep all trouble within the state.'

This advice was addressed to the Greek cities, especially, it
may be presumed, to the Greek cities of Asia Minor, though
Plutarch must have drawn on his own experience which was
gained chiefly in Boeotia and Attica. It points clearly to the
prevailing conditions, and, if it is turned inside out, it may be
interpreted as follows. There was a feverish anxiety to hold
office, and for the wrong reasons. Not only was local office
sought after, but also Roman rank; in another significant passage.[3] Plutarch refers with some irony to the man who is
discontented because he does not wear the shoes of a senator,
then because he does not become praetor and later consul, then
because he was not the first consul of his year to be returned.
The cities were restive, ready on any excuse to antagonise the
ruling power and to waste the good will extended to them. On
the other hand, some sections of the populace refused co-operation with any authority, even their own local magistrates; they
were dissatisfied with the treatment of their own officials; there
was hard feeling between rich and poor, and the rich were
grasping and quarrelsome among themselves.

Plutarch's advice was sound enough. The clock could not be
put back, and the more sensible the Greeks were in recognising
it, the better for them. They would be wise to co-operate with
their rulers. There is a graphic passage in the life of Flamininus[4]
which may be held to reflect Plutarch's views on the fortunes of
Greece. Flamininus has announced to a great assembly at the
Isthmian Games the Freedom of Hellas (196 B.C.) Plutarch
attempts to imagine the thoughts of the people who heard him.

No doubt, as their joy increased, it occurred to them to reckon
up in their own minds and to discuss with each other the state of
Greece—what wars she had undertaken to defend her liberty, yet
she had never gained a more secure and pleasant liberty than this,
won for her by others; almost without bloodshed or casualties she
had gained a prize which was most glorious of all and most worth
fighting for. Courage and wisdom are scarce among men, scarcest
of all goods is a good man. Men like Agesilaus, Lysander, Nicias,
Alcibiades, could manage a war and win land and sea-battles when

they were in command, but to use their successes for generous and noble purposes was beyond them. Omit Marathon, Salamis . . . and you will find that Greece fought all her battles to enslave herself. Every monument she erected recorded her own disasters and dishonours, and she was ruined almost entirely by the evil designs and ambitions of her own leaders. And now foreign men, who appear to retain the faintest spark, the slenderest relic, of the kinship which in ancient times they shared with us Greeks, have rescued us, with great danger and trouble to themselves, from cruel masters and tyrants, and have restored our freedom to us; anyone might well be surprised that from any word or thought of theirs any advantage could possibly result to Greece.

But Plutarch has not finished yet. In a passage of extreme interest he reveals for a moment of unusual candour his opinion of Greece under the Empire, and rounds it off with more advice.

The greatest blessings cities can enjoy are peace, liberty, good seasons, a good supply of men and concord. Now as regards peace the peoples have no demand to press upon their political leaders in the present era; wars against Greeks and against foreigners have taken their leave of us and have completely disappeared. We have as much freedom as our rulers give us and perhaps more freedom would not do us more good. As for abundant crops, and a kindly blending of seasons, and births of children 'like their parents' and the welfare of those children–these the wise man will ask the gods to give to his fellow-citizens. For the public man there only remains, out of the tasks usually assumed to be his, the duty of implanting in the minds of the community lasting concord and friendship, and there is no greater blessing than these.

Then follows an elaboration of this idea of concord; he goes on:

After this he will explain to individuals and to the citizens collectively how weak is the situation of the Greeks, which never-the-less sensible men will prefer to enjoy, living out their lives in quietness and concord, since fortune has left them no possibility of resistance. The survivors of a struggle could win no supremacy, no glory. Get some unimportant decree of a proconsul cancelled or altered; nothing worth while will be achieved, even if it were permanent.[5]

So the Greeks enjoyed peace: they could make representa-tion to the governor; they could get a proconsular ordinance altered. But they would not know how to use the concession. 'Perhaps more freedom would not do us more good.'

No one knew better than Plutarch how Greece had abused her freedom; petty jealousies, insane rivalries, sheer selfishness and the fatal legacy of a famous past inherited by inferior men had caused her downfall. And now he sees the same symptoms manifest in the Greek cities of his day and offers his warning to the young friend who consulted him.

But his advice was not as direct or forthcoming as the indictment voiced by his contemporary, Dio Chrysostom of Prusa in Bithynia. Where Plutarch hints, Dio describes in plain terms and he follows description with a merciless condemnation of the behaviour of Alexandria and the Greek cities of Asia Minor.

The two men were like and unlike. Both were devoted to Greek culture, literature and ideals. Both were absorbed by an intense interest in a practical morality which would give men standards of private and public behaviour. Plutarch was content to give his life to his native city 'that it might not grow less'; Dio was anxious to serve his birthplace if only his fellow-citizens would allow him. Tradition said that Plutarch had known Trajan; Dio was certainly the close friend of Nerva and Trajan; Dio was known to Pliny; there is no evidence that Plutarch was.[6] They were also very unlike. Plutarch was a landed gentleman with an established home; he moved in cultivated circles, addressing select audiences in his own and his friends' houses, lecturing to groups of students and men of letters. Dio was an itinerant preacher, exiled from his home, as ready in the spirit of an evangelist to talk to gatherings of strangers at the street-corners of a remote frontier-town as to address popular assemblies in the squares of ancient Greek cities, such as Nicomedia, Tarsus, even Alexandria itself. Like Plutarch he did not spare the literary or historical allusion, but his style is easy, Attic, persuasive and earnest, and for sheer plain-speaking his public orations have no parallel in Greek literature.[7]

The burden of the indictment is the same; inveterate disputes between cities about trifles, wrangling over empty honours and titles, insatiable appetite for positions and magistracies which carried little more than a meaningless dignity and a feeling of ascendancy over rivals, pursuit of pleasure with all the accompaniments of mass-hysteria, pride in material things and the neglect of all of real value in life. Compared with Dio's lengthy diatribes Plutarch's few words are restrained and gentle, even tactful; but they offer more serious advice about relations with the Romans. Dio is absorbed by his concern that the Greek cities should live in harmony with each other; Plutarch extends the idea to include the co-operation of Greeks and Romans. This is an important idea which is further considered on a later page.

iii AN IMPERIAL IDEAL

Plutarch has little to say about the Emperors; he refers to them all incidentally, but the allusions are not worth collecting here. The loss of the Lives of Augustus, Tiberius, Gaius, Claudius, Nero and Vitellius is serious; we should not expect them to offer very penetrating analyses of imperial policy, but they might well have preserved points unrecorded elsewhere, and it would be interesting to know what his sources were. But he makes a small contribution to the bulky literature which reflected on the nature of kingship. Before this contribution is considered a word or two about this literature may be in place.

The Greeks had always been interested in the idea of kingship. The earliest age of which we know had been an age of kings; in Homer they are taken for granted, and in a few places kingship lived on even after 'aristocracies' or 'democracies' had taken their place; Sparta had its kings even under the Roman occupation. From time to time 'tyrants' had asserted themselves in some of the Greek states, and the prosperity brought about by a strong government of one man had caused many reflective men to think again about the comparative merits of the rule of one and the rule of many. Philosophy took up the matter; the advantages and disadvantages of the 'pure' and the 'mixed' constitution, the nature of sovereignty, the rights of the individual were discussed with an insight and a thoroughness which have left their mark on political thinking ever since.

But it was Alexander, and Alexander's Empire under the rule of the Diadochi, which gave a new impetus to thought about kingship. The benefits which the rule of one man, even though he died young, had brought had changed the Eastern Mediterranean almost past recognition; it had brought about benefits which had scarcely been dreamed of. Philosophers learned in the ideas of Plato and Aristotle were startled by this unique and unexpected event; even the most democratic among them were given pause when the 'voice of the people', wherein, they thought, lay sovereignty, acclaimed the ruler as 'Benefactor' and 'Saviour' and to these titles was ready to add divine honours. Could the undoubted practical merits of the rule of one be justified theoretically? What distinctive features of kingship earned it the right to be regarded as meritorious? Or, to put the same matter differently, what ought a king to be like to be justified in being a king? From theory thought moved to practice, and the pamphlets, as we should call them, offered practical advice to rulers, advising them about the attitudes they should adopt to subjects, to courtiers and flatterers, and offering hints about behaviour in a variety of situations. Into the details of this literature in Hellenistic times it is unnecessary to enter; but it extended into the first and second centuries of the Empire, the ruler now being the Roman Emperor, and from Rome it passed to Europe and took shape in many varieties of 'Mirror of Princes'.

In the lifetime of Plutarch three writers wrote such works. Seneca, by birth a Spaniard, addressed his treatise *On Clemency* to Nero soon after his accession; from it some of the ideas in Portia's great speech were derived. Pliny on his appointment as consul suffectus spoke the usual laudatory address to Trajan and enlarged it into his *Panegyricus*, which is extant. Both these works repel a modern reader by their flattery; it must be remembered, however, that both are highly rhetorical and in this style of writing exaggeration is usual and pardonable; moreover both contain much serious advice carefully thought out and are clearly meant to be in line with the earlier philosophical reflections on kingship. The third writer is Dio Chrysostom who was a close friend of Trajan and wrote four treatises on kingship for his edification. These treatises probably reflect more clearly than those of Seneca and Pliny the thoughts of Hellenistic philosophical writings on this theme.

Plutarch's contribution is contained in a short tract entitled 'To an untrained ruler'.[1] It is short, clearly a fragment or a draft, and it is not likely that it was intended for publication; the date is unknown. A summary follows.

The piece begins with a quotation from Plato, who replied to the Cyrenians, when they invited him to legislate for them, that it was difficult to write laws for a people as prosperous as them. In the same way, continues Plutarch, it is difficult to advise rulers about the nature of government; they are fearful of any restraint upon themselves, for restraint would mean loss of power. They do not understand how wise was Theopompus, King of Sparta, in diverting some of his power into others' hands; the Reason which he derived from philosophy 'sat by his chair as he ruled' and took away the dangerous elements of power and left him all that was sound and healthy.

The moment a ruler acquires power he must be concerned with himself, guiding his own soul, establishing his own character and then he should bring about unity and concord among his subjects. A man who is falling cannot hold others up; you cannot teach if you are ignorant, or set things in order or arrange them if you do not know the meaning of the words in yourself, or govern if you are not governed. . . .

Who then is to rule the ruler? The answer is 'Law, the king of mortals and immortals' according to Pindar–not the law which can be outwardly written in books or tablets, but that Reason (Logos) which is alive within him, always dwelling with him and always on the alert, never leaving him free of control. . . . Rulers are the servants of God charged with the care of men and their well-being; they are responsible for all the good and noble gifts of God to men; some they distribute, some they conserve. It is impossible to enjoy or to make right use of the countless and munificent gifts and blessings bestowed by the gods without Law and Justice and a Ruler. Justice is the purpose and fulfilment of Law; Law is the work of a Ruler; a Ruler is the image of God Almighty; he needs no sculptor to mould him:

by his own efforts he is wrought into the likeness of God, by his own virtue; in himself he creates the fairest of figures that can be beheld and the most God-like. Just as God set the sun and the moon in the sky to be a splendid likeness of himself, so in the cities of men the Ruler is a copy of him, and a Great Light. . . . He has the Logos of God to guide his purposes; he carries no sceptre, thunderbolt or trident, a pose in which many like to imagine themselves and indeed have themselves represented.

This kind of representation angers God.

But, if men will emulate his goodness and model themselves on standards of nobility and beneficence, then he will gladly aid them and give them a share of the righteousness which encompasses him, and of the justice and truth and gentleness. Nothing is more divine than these—not fire or light or the courses of the sun or the risings and settings of the stars, not endless time, not eternity. It is not length of life that gives God his happiness, but the ruling principle of goodness. This it is that is divine, and what is ruled by it becomes fine and noble.

Plutarch goes on to explain that Justice and Right may be poetically represented as sitting by the side of God; but strictly this picture is wrong, for God is himself Justice and Right and is himself 'the most ancient and the most perfect of Laws.' And he forbids attempts to make God part of Nature or Necessity or Chance; he is above all these. Finally we return to earth and we are told that 'in the cities of men God set the light of righteousness as an image of the Logos which surrounds him; this image the saintly and wise men body forth for us from philosophy according as they model themselves on the most beautiful thing in the universe'.

Now in all this there is nothing new, neither in thought nor expression. The main ideas are: within the ruler dwells the Logos of God; the ruler is the servant of God, and his image; he is charged with the duty of doing good to men; the badge of the Logos is goodness. The ruler as Logos can be traced back to Ecphantus, a Pythagorean philosopher who says that 'God fashioned him (the ruler) after himself as the archetype'; the Logos is incarnate in him and is the source of his power to save men from sin. And centuries afterwards Eusebius brings up the same word in his Oration to Constantine, A.D. 336; he cannot say the ruler is Logos, but he does say 'the Logos of God from whom and through whom the ruler who is the friend of God bears the image of the Kingdom of Heaven and, imitating what is higher, directs and steers all that is on earth'. The idea of the ruler as the benefactor and servant of men is on almost every page of Dio's essays. In fact parallels could be quoted for every sentence of Plutarch, even the figure of the sun and the moon.[2]

Throughout his works Plutarch has many occasions to treat of kings; he does not often reflect on the nature of kingship. In the Life of Demetrius there are several passages which are relevant; but the passage most worth quoting is in the Life of Numa.[3] The Romans beg Numa to accept the office of king, for fear that there would be internal dissensions and civil war. (That is, they want 'concord'.) His father and Marcius then approach him privately, and beg him to accept 'this divine gift' and Plutarch gives us their exact words! He is to believe that 'being king is really the service of God, who raises up and does not allow to remain dormant and idle the great righteousness which resides in you'. Kingship, the exhortation continues, offers a sensible man great scope for good deeds, for the magnificent worship of the gods and for disciplining men in habits of piety, 'since men are most speedily and easily led to adopt new habits by a ruler'. Then more about the fear of war; a king would be a bond of goodwill and friendship.

Auspicious omens followed upon this speech, and Numa accepts kingship as a means to 'fellowship and the mingling of the citizens'. There is no need to point out the repetition of the same ideas—service to man is service to God, the indwelling of righteousness in the ruler, and the desire for concord.

This brief review of Plutarch's attitude to Rome has taken us thus far; in the first part of this chapter it was seen that he expressed his admiration for Roman achievements, and saw in them the guiding hand of Providence; in the second part that he deplored the inability of the Greek cities to live in concord and confessed the advantages of Roman rule; to increase those advantages he advised co-operation between Greeks and Romans. The reader may have felt that this advice was a little grudgingly given. But, whereas in the old days Greeks divided the world into Greeks and barbarians, Greeks of Plutarch's time admitted a tripartite division, Greeks, Romans and the rest, while Romans agreed to accept the division, Romans, Greeks and the rest. However grudging, he realised that it was the right advice. In the third section it has been seen that Plutarch appears to identify himself with ideas about the rule of one man, namely, that it was to the advantage of the ruled provided that behind it lay ideals of service to man and service to God. Living as he did in an age when the world was growing smaller, when one law was spreading over the nations, when men of all races were increasingly living at peace and opportunity was more freely open to all men of ability, when, for example, Gallio a Spaniard could be Roman proconsul in Greek Corinth, when there was a commerce of ideas which was, and perhaps is, without parallel, why did not Plutarch's thought take a further step?

To explain this question we must turn aside and consider the two treatises *On the Fortune of Alexander*. Perhaps no one gave rise to more discussion in antiquity than Alexander – his achievements, his character, his ideas (for he was regarded as a philosopher) and his intentions; he died young; how had he done what he had done? Was he the instrument of Heaven chosen because of his character, or the darling of Fortune and himself responsible for nothing? And would he have conquered the West, and with what purpose? In a highly rhetorical style – a little tedious to us – Plutarch deals with some of these questions; the style suggests that the composition of the two essays is to be placed early in Plutarch's life. They are significant as being a sample of much that was written and is now lost; they are important for two or three passages.

'Few of us read the Laws of Plato; thousands of men lived, and still live, under the Laws of Alexander.'[4]

The political theory of Zeno which is much admired is directed to this one main objective, that we should not live in separate city-states or parishes divided from one another each by its own rights, but that we should regard all men as fellow-members of parish and city-state; that there should be one way of life and one organisation, just as though one flock were grazing together on a common pasture under a common law.[5] Zeno dreamed a dream or drew an imaginary picture of law and government inspired by philosophy; Alexander achieved the practical realisation of Zeno's theory. Aristotle advised him to behave to the Greeks as a leader, and to non-Greeks as a master–to care for the one set of men as though they were friends and kindred, but to treat the other set as though they were plants or animals. He did not follow this advice and so he avoided filling up the days of his rule with wars and banishments and civil disturbances festering below the surface. On the contrary, he thought he was sent by God to reconcile and draw together in concord the nations as a whole. He fused men together not by force of arms but by ideas.[6] From every quarter he brought them together to make a unity; as in a loving-cup he mixed their ways of life and their customs, their marriages and their daily behaviour; he laid down that all men should consider the inhabited world as their country, the army as their citadel and their stronghold, and should think of the good as their kinsmen and the bad as foreigners.

Distinction in dress and similar externals was to mean nothing; 'goodness is the sign of Greek-ness, and badness the sign of non-Greek-ness'.[7] And a little later:

'if the power (daemon) which sent the soul of Alexander into this world had not been in such a hurry to recall it, one law would now be looking down (*like the sun*) upon all men and they would turn their gaze upon one system of justice as though upon a light which all could see, and thus would they be governed. But, as things turned out, part of the world remained unlit by the sun–the part which never saw Alexander.

Who then is to claim credit for this revolutionary idea, Zeno or Alexander? Zeno began to teach in Athens some twenty years after Alexander's death; when years later he wrote his *Politeia*, he 'dreamed' of a common city of gods and men, but not of all men, only of some men. In a famous Raleigh Lecture the late Sir William Tarn elaborated the view which he had already anticipated in the Cambridge Ancient History,[8] that

Alexander 'was the pioneer of one of the supreme revolutions in the world's outlook, the first man who contemplated the brotherhood of man or the unity of mankind'. He does not claim to have given exact proof of this; 'it is one of those difficult borderlands of history where one does not get proofs which could be put to a jury'.

For our immediate purpose the proofs do not matter; the point is that Plutarch believed that the chief of Alexander's ideas was the ideal of the unity of mankind. Yet nowhere does he give any hint that he sees Alexander's ideal gradually being realised by the Roman Empire. He had written the Life of Augustus and must have been aware of the promise of a new age; he had met men of every nation; at Delphi he and a traveller returned from Scotland and another from the Red Sea had met and talked; he may even have handled the coins issued by Trajan which bore the legend *Salus generis humani*, the welfare of the human race.[9] Under the Roman Emperor the unity of civilisation was gradually taking place, and most people knew it. When in A.D. 98 Pliny said that 'the Emperor and God shared the task of reconciling nations at variance and curbing disturbance by reason as much as by rule', that the Emperor was a 'vice-regent of the Father of the Universe in his care for the whole human race'[10] he used ideas, and almost phrases, which we have already seen Plutarch apply to Alexander.

If Plutarch's Hellenism would not let him see, or would not allow him to admit, what was obvious to everyone else, at any rate Aelius Aristides, born in the year of Trajan's death, made amends. He too was a Greek, educated at Pergamum and Athens. In his panegyric on Rome he describes the world as it was a generation after Plutarch's death; but the processes which resulted in the age of Antoninus Pius were at work in Plutarch's life. Panegyric though it may be, the speech contains a penetrating analysis of the Empire as it was seen by his contemporaries; the role of the army as a civilising influence in the Empire is specially well treated. In a series of quick pictures the economic life is described more fully than in any other document. Of Greece he says that cities abound on the coasts and inland; some are newly-founded and some are old foundations made prosperous again. 'The Romans continue to care for the Greeks . . . stretching out a hand to them, raising them when they are fallen, leaving some of their own long established rulers free and independent and leading on the others with all restraint and foresight. The non-Greeks they educate each according to their abilities, gently but firmly.' The saying that earth is the mother of all men and the common fatherland of all you have made true. Greek and non-Greek are free to . . . travel with ease wherever they like, as though from their own country to their own country. 'The inhabited world is one city.' 'Its ruler rules over free men, who gladly recognise him as their ruler; for they want the unity which is now secured; no longer are there Greeks and non-Greeks, natives or foreigners.' And Aristides has a very poor opinion of Alexander and his rule; he says nothing about Alexander's ideal of the unity of mankind, with which Plutarch was familiar. Hellene though he was, he drew his picture of the world as a unity from observation.[11]

On the deification of rulers Plutarch has little to say. Naturally he refers to the divine honours paid to the Greek kings of whom he writes; when he makes any comment it is generally to the effect that divinity resides in goodness of character and not in exploits of war. Honours paid for any other reason are justly suspect to a ruler of sense. But he is willing to accord deification to any good man, whether ruler or not.

We must certainly believe that their virtues and their souls, according to their natures and under divine justice, pass out of men into heroes, out of heroes into daemons, out of daemons (if, that is, they are thoroughly cleansed as by some rite of initiation and are sanctified by leaving behind them all that belongs to mortality and the senses) into gods–and this not by any decree of a city, but in all truth and by the will of right reason; thus they receive as their due their noblest and most blessed consummation.

Whether 'not by any decree of a city' is specially charged with meaning we cannot tell.

Nor has he anything direct to say about the deification of

Roman Emperors. There is, however, one passage that suggests a kind of divinity that dwelt in the Emperor even in his lifetime. In an essay *On Exile* he described how people had lived in remote places, on a small piece of land–Alcmon, for example, on a sandbank in the river Achelous–in their desire to get away from anxieties. 'Tiberius Caesar lived for the seven years before his death in Capreae and all that time *the sacred principle of imperial power which governs the inhabited world* was concentrated in his heart and never changed its location. Upon him the cares of imperial rule poured in, borne from every quarter of the world' and spoiled the tranquillity of his island retreat. 'If a man who has gone off to a small island can't get rid of merely small worries, then indeed he is unhappy.' What precisely Plutarch meant by the phrase in italics is difficult to say. It would be interesting to hear comments on the passage by Tacitus.[13]

iv PLUTARCH'S SILENCE

As has been seen, Plutarch makes very few allusions to contemporary events and conditions. There is to be found in his writings no description of the Roman world of his day such as Aristides gives in his highly appreciative assessment of the Roman achievement in the provinces. It is disappointing that a man with so wide a circle of friends, who had travelled in the Eastern Mediterranean, visited Rome more than once and journeyed to north Italy, who wrote so much should have left so little for us to glean about the world as it was in his time. Is it right to blame him? His silence must be explained by the nature of the man himself, by the nature of the times and by the reaction of such a man to such times.

Plutarch lived in the past. His mind ranges freely over Greek mythology, religion, literature and history. If he reflects upon these, he reflects upon people and motives, rather than upon movement and development of ideas and thought. Philosophical matters he approaches from the standpoint of Platonism as it was understood in Hellenistic times, though he was acquainted with teachings of Epicureanism and especially

Stoicism, which he had to some extent unconsciously appropriated. In politics he is bounded by the limits of the Greek city-state; in terms of it he thinks of society, government and administration. It is true that he is conversant with Hellenistic thought about the nature of the ideal ruler, but, like Dio Chrysostom, he is concerned with moral qualities; it would have been beyond him, it may be feared, to analyse the nature of the Augustan principate as Polybius had analysed the nature of the Roman constitution. The lives of Galba and Otho offer us nothing upon the causes of the troubles; he remarks that nothing is worse than a military force moving about the empire uncontrolled; the disasters that befell the Roman Empire after the fall of Nero may be likened to the attacks of the Giants upon Olympus; an unrestrained soldiery drove out one commander after another, 'like one nail driven on top of another'. But there is no reflection upon the reasons for this indiscipline, no suggestion that Nero's downfall and its consequences were due to the Emperor's failure to keep in touch with the army.

To look back to the past need not necessarily imply blindness to the present. Yet Plutarch gives little evidence that he grasped the significance of anything that he saw in his travels or in his reading of history. He draws almost never on his experiences abroad. He may have been singularly unobservant, he may have looked through the present scene and contemplated only its past, he may have had no interest, feeling that what lay before him lay also before his readers, for whom he could at any rate recreate the past. No one can maintain that he had a first-rate mind; but it was a mind essentially kindly, unwilling to think ill of anyone, tolerant, though shrewd in the judgment of character; it may be that such a man accepts things as they seem to be and takes them for granted. Nor was he as conscious of writing for posterity as, say, Thucydides; but posterity has acclaimed him for what he is, and, though much tempted, has no right to complain that he did not do something which he had not the disposition, and perhaps not the ability, to do for them.

There was nothing in the nature of the times to account for

Plutarch's silence, though there is much to explain it. Admittedly, he lived through the reign of Domitian and would have avoided criticism of contemporary events, supposing he had been inclined to make it; but there is no evidence that he was expelled with other philosophers from Italy by Vespasian (indeed he was at Rome when Vespasian was an old man) or by Domitian some years later. In point of fact it is hard to see how Plutarch's lectures could give offence. Under Nerva and Trajan there was no fear of imperial disfavour, and, if tradition is to be believed, Plutarch was at least known to Trajan. And, as most of his writings are to be dated to Trajan's reign, there was no reason why they should not have alluded to contemporary conditions. And, if the Lamprias Catalogue is to be believed, Plutarch did in fact write lives of the Emperors.

At the same time there are features of the age which help to explain Plutarch's apparent reticence. Certainly after the accession of Trajan events in the capital affected very little the provinces in general; men lived in their towns and villages and were scarcely aware that they were subject to Roman rule. Local politics, trade, education, social life went on undisturbed, and over all there was a sense of security and well-being which had resulted increasingly as the Roman peace was consolidated. The present seemed to be firmly established; Rome had come to distant lands and the benefits she conferred would last. There was no need to look to the future; it would not be very different; after much striving men had now reached the plateau of existence where with the accumulated knowledge of Greco-Roman civilisation they would continue to live, for nothing else could be contemplated.

For a man of Plutarch's disposition this was a congenial attitude of mind. We think of our age as one of profound and rapid change; the period of Plutarch's life and the half century that followed his death were scarcely conscious of change. If Plutarch wrote biographies for posterity, he wrote them because he thought that posterity should have moral examples in front of it; it would never have occurred to him that an account of existing conditions could be of any benefit to them. After all, later generations would live in much the same environment as his generation: they would know for themselves. The present was taken for granted: the future would be like the present. People did not look forward to a succeeding age when things might be different. No one seriously thought of a Utopia; there were no 'causes' to support, no reform movements which would turn men's thoughts to a future. Plutarch and his contemporaries must not be blamed for not doing what it could not possibly occur to them to do. Rather, we should be grateful for what it did occur to them to do, and especially to Plutarch for this abundance which he has set before us.

CHAPTER 11

Plutarch's Knowledge of Latin; the Sources of the *Lives*, Roman and Greek

ALL Plutarch's works are written in Greek. Yet he lived in a Roman world in which he himself says Latin was spread throughout; he had Roman friends and wrote the lives of Romans, for which the sources were partly in Greek and mainly in Latin. How well did he know Latin?

When I visited Rome and other parts of Italy I had not leisure to gain practice in the Latin language because of the public business which I had undertaken and the number of people who thronged to be taught philosophy. It was late therefore, when I was well into middle age, that I began to read the Latin authors. My experience may seem strange but it is none the less true; I did not gain the knowledge of things through the words; rather I was able somehow or other as a result of my experience of things to follow the words. The beauty of Latin narrative and its speed, the figures and harmony and the rest in which the language takes pleasure we do think elegant and agreeable. But the practice and application required to this end are no easy matters: they are for those who have more leisure than I, as well as the gifts of youth, to satisfy such ambitions.[1]

This is a most important passage; it means that Plutarch did what so many others have done after him; he picked up the language as he pursued his way in a limited field of studies. The subject-matter (the 'things') were already half-known; he knew the kind of thing he was likely to find; and he could move fairly freely within a chosen area, and, as he moved, he became more proficient.

Elsewhere he remarks that Latin, the language which practically everyone uses, dispenses largely with prepositions and does not have an article; it uses its words 'without tassels'. In quoting *veni vidi vici* he says that, in Latin, words ending in the same sound 'give a terse form of expression which is very telling'. Indeed, he often ventures into derivations of Latin words, not very successfully, though his explanation of *fetialis* (=*fecialis*) is now regarded as possible; and in one of the *Table Talks* Lamprias, his brother, embarks upon a series of humorous derivations.[2]

Much misplaced fun has been made of Plutarch for his mistakes in Latin. In fact, they amount to little. He writes *patrōnas* for *patronos;* inscriptions now show that a Greek form *patrōn* came to be established alongside *patronus*. It is true that elsewhere he constructs *sine* with a genitive to translate the Greek *aneu* with a genitive; of the two correct meanings of *vicus* he chooses 'villages' (*kōmas*) rather than 'streets'. In another passage he translates *prosecuisset* as though it were the pluperfect subjunctive of *prosequor*—no doubt a howler; but who, having learnt German as Plutarch learnt his Latin, that is, by reading for the subject-matter of a special field, is likely to be sound on all his strong verbs, or even to be guiltless of a slip in reading?[3] Since these are virtually the only charges, the case surely must be dismissed. What is undoubtedly proved is that Plutarch did consult Latin sources, for the mistakes in translation are of his own making.

To what use, then, did Plutarch put his knowledge of Latin? What Latin writers did he consult? Whole sections of Latin literature may be written off at once; he shows no knowledge of Latin drama, or of poetry, except for two quotations from Horace, or of philosophy, except an anecdote about Seneca, which he need not have obtained from Seneca himself. Clearly Plutarch had no interest in Latin literature as such; the poets would be too difficult, the philosophers had nothing to teach him; and, as his interest was in real people, he confined himself virtually to the historians. He refers to Varro, Cato, Cicero, Livy, Caesar, Sallust, Augustus; less well-known are Nigidius Figulus, Fenestella, Lutatius Catulus, Cluvius Rufus, the Gracchi; there are also about twenty others. The *Memoirs* of Sulla were probably in Greek, and he clearly had read these.

The difficulty is to know what his references mean. Had he

consulted these works himself, or is he content to take it on the authority of one writer that another writer had made such and such a statement? The probability is that he adopted both practices; but it is often impossible to know when he is relying on his own reading and when on second-hand statements.

That Plutarch did not underestimate the importance of books is shown by an interesting passage which immediately precedes his statement that he came late to the study of Latin authors.

Suppose that someone has undertaken to write a history which involves gathering together material from sources which are not ready to hand and written in his own language, but which are numerous, written in a foreign language and scattered in the writings of others. He needs first of all as a starting point to live in a city of reputation, of fair size and devoted to the arts. There he will have books of all kinds in abundance; moreover, all that has escaped the writers of books but has been stored away in people's memories and thus is conspicuously entitled to belief he will pick up by hearsay and will make further enquiries. In this way he will see to it that he does not render his work deficient in many things essential to it.

And then Plutarch explains that he lived in a small city, and was devoted to it 'lest it should become smaller', and that, while he was in Italy, he had been very busy and had therefore come late to the study of Latin writers.

The tremendous range of learning shown in Plutarch's own writings compels us to believe that he followed his own advice. Wherever he went he must have consulted books, at Athens and at Rome notably; and at home he must have had a good library collected by his father, his brother and, no doubt chiefly, by himself. A catalogue of his library would be well worth one of his less interesting essays in exchange. But also he probably laid his Roman friends under contribution, drawing heavily on their resources and their kindness. From *On Tranquillity* we know that friends in Rome wrote to him when he was in Chaeronea and it may well be that he consulted them by letter; still more would he profit from talk with them in Italy or in Greece.

Indeed it is from this treatise that we learn something of his method of working. He was asked to send hurriedly to a friend some counsel which would comfort and strengthen him. He immediately consulted his notebooks, and the essay starts with a quotation and as it progresses makes use of many more. We must believe that Plutarch's notebooks were very considerable in bulk; as he read, he must have noted what interested him, and presumably reduced this accumulation of material to some kind of system. It is true that the memory of students in those days must have been, by modern standards, remarkable; but such are Plutarch's resources of detailed and exact knowledge, so accurate are his thousands of references, when they can be checked, and so wide the range of his reading that he must have relied on more than memory. Moreover, it is difficult for modern readers to appreciate the difficulty of running down a particular passage when there were no standard codes of reference, pages, chapters, lines, indices. Scholars probably made their own private methods of reference, and, while a few epitomes of long works survive, many more must have been made for individual use, and been employed very much as the analyses which precede the chapters in some modern works. In that case Plutarch's notebooks contained not only quotations which seemed to him of appeal or of use, no doubt classified, but also summaries and abstracts, some at length, some little more than main headings, and no doubt the innumerable miscellaneous jottings which so assiduous a collector could not resist.

Speaking generally, an ancient historian based his narrative mainly on a single source; he was prepared to take over a very great deal and to let it stand without acknowledgment. When he diverged from his main authorities, or added an alternative version, he tended to name the source. Or he might name his main authority when he wished to assert its superior credibility as against other versions, named or implied. Plutarch at any rate seems often to follow this practice, though there are never-the-less many passages where he names his authority merely to authenticate his statement. Thus, if a writer incorporated a good deal of material derived from previous writers, his main claim to originality lay in the manner in which he presented it, and on that he was content to let his reputation depend.

A brief illustration may be offered. For great sections of the *Histories* of Tacitus there is no indication of the source. Put alongside these sections the corresponding passages of Plutarch (in the lives of Galba and Otho for example) and it is strikingly clear that there is a common origin; for it is unthinkable that Tacitus borrowed from Plutarch, and almost as unthinkable that Plutarch relied on Tacitus. But the resemblance is so great that both authors must have used material practically as it stood in the original; they appropriated what they found (probably in Pliny the Elder) yet the styles of Plutarch and Tacitus invite no comparison; each writer's manner is his own.

During the last one hundred and fifty years much work has been done on Plutarch's sources. No indication can be given here of its thoroughness; sometimes its conclusions seem somewhat speculative, often they are convincing. Even slight knowledge of it will induce the belief that Plutarch was tolerably well equipped and that he did read Latin authors. Yet a tradition seems to have grown up among critics that he had hardly any Latin, and that what he had was ludicrously unsound; therefore, it is said, he must have derived much from epitomes of Roman authors in Greek and collections of passages from Latin writers obligingly put into Greek by compilers and translators of whom we know next to nothing.

Reference is made to Livy nearly twenty times. Often the phrase is simply 'Livy says that . . .' or 'as Livy says' or 'as Livy says in his history'. But sometimes it is fuller; for example, 'this is the account given by Cornelius Nepos, and those who follow him, and by Valerius Maximus, but Livy and Caesar Augustus say . . .', and the passage refers to Hannibal's treatment of Marcellus when he was killed in battle. We do not know what were the versions of Nepos and Caesar Augustus: but, when the accounts of Livy, Valerius Maximus and Plutarch are compared, Plutarch's is the most interesting and circumstantial.[4]

Plutarch refers to the Letters of Cicero ten times, nine times in the *Lives* and once in the *Moralia*; these references include at least one to a letter which we do not possess, but which may well have been written. But it is very difficult to know what degree of firsthand knowledge the references imply. For the writing of history on any scale letters must be read in bulk, though information on some individual point could be obtained by consulting one letter. Did Plutarch really read the letters? For instance in the *Life of Cicero* he quotes from a letter written by Cicero, in which he writes that he is in a state of indecision: to which side should he turn since Pompey has a justifiable case for going to war, while Caesar deals with events more practically and looks after his friends; he knows whom he should fly from but not whom he should fly to. We have the letter, though in fact Cicero says he has someone to fly from but no one to follow. In the next sentence Plutarch says that Trebatius wrote to Cicero saying that Caesar urged Cicero to join his party and share in his hopes, but that, if he felt he was too old to do this, he should stay neutral in Greece. To this Cicero wrote an angry answer, saying that he would do nothing that did not become his past life. The letters sound plausible, but we have not got them; Plutarch sums up the paragraph by saying, 'Such is the record in Cicero's letters'.[5]

Again Plutarch says that Cicero himself admits that 'the best of the measures which he took when he restored the state in his consulship were thought out with the help of Publius Nigidius the philosopher'. To this point there is a reference in a letter to Nigidius which survives 'I am without the friends whose goodwill my defence of the state, carried through with your aid, won for me in days gone by'. If Plutarch picked up this point direct from the letter, he must have read Cicero's letters with some care. That he should have read Cicero's Greek letters, which we do not possess, is more likely, and indeed he appears to know them well – well enough to say that two particular letters, which he indicates, are 'the only two Greek letters to be written in anger'. But it is possible that Plutarch was able to extract much detail from the Life of Cicero written by Tiro, just as he probably copied from the same author's book of Ciceronian jests.[6]

When we pass to the sources for the Greek *Lives*, we are confronted by the same difficulties in an even more aggravated form. For naturally Plutarch was more fully acquainted with Greek historians than with Roman historians, and he refers to far more 'authorities' for the Greek *Lives* than for the Roman. And, as most of these authorities are not extant, it is more difficult for us to know to what extent Plutarch relies on them. Had he read them in extenso? Had he consulted them only on the topic about which he was writing? Is he therefore ignorant about their views on other matters? Does he rely on summaries of them, or is he quoting what he had been told by his friends about their views? And so on.

It might naturally be expected that Plutarch would have a good knowledge of the Greek historians Herodotus, Thucydides and Xenophon. With a good index to the text it is possible to establish how often a writer is quoted by Plutarch and in which works. Here we must allude to a certain rough and ready rule which has come to be adopted in Plutarchean criticism; it is used in default of a better. In the *Moralia* a citation, direct or indirect, is made very often for the purpose of illustration; it is not vital to the argument; it could be omitted. Such citations occur only to a mind familiar with the work from which citation is made, and, if references are made over the whole range of the work, it is a reasonable conclusion that the whole work has been read and is well known. But when a historian consults a source to establish a particular point, *e.g.* if he is writing a 'life' and consults a fairly comprehensive historical work, he may not have read outside the field he is concerned with; no inference can be drawn that the whole work is known to him and forms part of his stock in trade. Now Herodotus, Thucydides and Xenophon are all quoted more often in the *Moralia* than in the *Lives*, while of the separate works of Xenophon the *Cyropaedeia*, the *Memorabilia*, the *Oeconomicus* and the *Cynegetica* are quoted only in the *Moralia*, as indeed might be expected.

How well Plutarch knew Herodotus may be learnt from a special tract which he wrote about him. It bears the title *On Herodotus' Spite*, and has been called the 'first instance in literature of the slashing review'; the book under review really had been read. And it is true that, though Greek and Latin writers attack each other often enough, in this pamphlet there is a systematic survey of Herodotus, book by book, with the offending passages quoted in full and the critic's outraged and often sarcastic comments following. Plutarch begins by laying down in general terms methods of creating prejudice in a reader, and accuses Herodotus of employing all of them. They are familiar enough to us; a writer may use harsher terms than he need; he can drag in faults when they are irrelevant or he can damn with faint praise; if there are two accounts of an episode, he can choose the more discreditable; he can spoil a fine action by imputing a mean motive or assign a bad reason when a better one is equally likely. He can malign by insinuation and cover himself by saying that he does not believe what, of course, he wants his reader to believe. Or he may exaggerate a man's faults and immediately add a virtue or two, and hope to obtain belief in both by a show of impartiality. Briefly, Plutarch cannot endure that there should be any criticism of the states who saved Greece from the Persian, and in particular he is concerned to defend the conduct of the Boeotians. There is no doubt that he does in fact score some points against Herodotus. For example, Herodotus allows that Thebes sent 400 men to Thermopylae, but he says that they stayed under compulsion and surrendered at the first opportunity, whereupon they were branded as slaves by the Persians. Sarcastically Plutarch objects that this was a curious way of encouraging Greeks to favour the cause of Persia, and, if Herodotus does not see it, he must be blinded by spite. In the same way Plutarch will not accept any criticism of the behaviour of Sparta or Argos in the wars.[7] He carries his patriotism too far. Herodotus may have relied on tendentious sources, but, taken as a whole, his account reveals him as free from a personal partiality as Plutarch is fanatically biased in favour of the Greek cities; they can do no wrong.

But for Thucydides Plutarch felt great admiration and expressed it generously in the *Life of Nicias*. He does not want to be misunderstood when he undertakes the life of this man; it is in treating of this period, he says, that Thucydides has outshone even himself in feeling, in vividness, in lively and varied presentation. 'I do not wish to be thought to be competing with him.' And so he proposes to give a summary, especially of Nicias' actions which reveal his character; as for other matters not generally known, he will gather them up with care from scattered remarks in historians, or in dedicatory inscriptions and decrees; and he will not amass useless information but will hand on material by which the reader can grasp the qualities and the character of the man. He is equally generous to Xenophon. 'Many people,' he says 'have described this battle'–the battle of Cunaxa: and who were these historians and had Plutarch himself read their accounts?–'but Xenophon puts it before our eyes and dwells on the events as though they were actually happening at the moment instead of being past and over; he makes the reader feel what those engaged actually felt and makes him share in the dangers; so vivid is his description'. Plutarch refers to Xenophon several times in this Life; in one passage he finds him at variance with the historian Ctesias, and judicially sums up that each side has something to be said for it. But later he detects Ctesias telling a glaring lie and proves Xenophon to be right. Since Ctesias, who was a doctor at the Persian court and helped Artaxerxes at the battle, wrote a History of Persia in twenty-three books, he may well be one of the sources whom Plutarch consulted for a special purpose only, namely this Life, since he is cited only in it–except for one passage which must not be missed. Plutarch is explaining that animals have been known to count, and, on Ctesias' authority, he tells the story of the oxen at Susae which carried buckets of water to irrigate the King's garden; the ration was one hundred buckets per day for each animal. When the hundredth bucket had been carried, the oxen refused to carry more, and nothing would induce them, not even violence, to carry a hundred and one[8]

Greek historians whom Plutarch had probably read in extenso are Ephorus, Timaeus (a main source for the Life of Timoleon), Theopompus and the important but elusive Poseidonius. It would be tedious to note the use of these made in the *Lives*; but the risk must be run with one of them, Ephorus, for purposes of illustration. 'Ephorus, Dinon, Clitarchus, Heraclides and several others say . . . ; Thucydides and Charon of Lampsacus say. . . . The opinion of Thucydides fits the dates better.' In the *Life of Camillus* we learn that Ephorus, Callisthenes, Demetrius and Phylarchus knew the date of the fall of Troy; it was the 24th May; the year is not stated! Elsewhere Plutarch notes that a particular point is mentioned neither in Theopompus nor in Ephorus nor in Xenophon; Ephorus, Callisthenes, Polybius disagree with one another about the number of men in a Spartan *mora*. In the *Life of Lysander* Plutarch tells a long story about Lysander tampering with the Delphic oracle; it was clearly not in the main authority which he was following, for he says 'we shall narrate it taking Ephorus, who was a historian and a philosopher, for our guide'. In the essay on Herodotus he notes that Ephorus made a derogatory statement about Themistocles (he quotes it), but Thucydides says nothing on the point.[9]

It will be seen, therefore, that we do not owe much positive information to Plutarch's references to Ephorus. But it is valuable to know that he was used, even though we cannot say precisely how much he was used in the narrative when no acknowledgment is made to him. For apart from Xenophon, Ephorus was the most important Greek historian of the fourth century (*c*. 405–330 B.C.); his history stretched from the earliest times to 341 B.C. so that for part of it he was a contemporary writer. Not many fragments survive, but Diodorus virtually summarised much of his work, and it is possible to gather his point of view and to know something of his sources. In one respect his history was unique, for it treated the history of the Greek peninsula as one unit.

In the third and second centuries a 'school' of historiography was developed which laid stress on the characters of history, collecting stories and anecdotes and so adding some qualities of the historical novel. The purpose was to entertain and even to excite. To Plutarch, always interested in the characters of men, this type of writing may have offered some attraction; at any rate in the *Lives* he quotes Duris (*c.* 340–260 B.C.) who, besides being tyrant of Samos, wrote a good deal of history and criticism. Another writer of the same type was Phylarchus; he appears to have written a fairly detailed history of the period 270–220 B.C.; it was not however planned on chronological lines, and may well have laid stress on personalities; at any rate Plutarch drew extensively from it for his *Lives of Agis* and *Cleomenes*.

To come to later historians who wrote in Greek, Polybius was used by Plutarch, who clearly was under a great debt to his biography of Philopoemen, which is not extant. He is cited also in the *Lives of Aratus, Agis* and *Cleomenes*. But he owed a greater debt to the *Universal History* which extends from 220 B.C. to 144 B.C. From this Plutarch derived a good deal for his *Lives of Aemilius, Cato Major, the Gracchi,* and also for the early treatise *On the fortune of the Romans.* Polybius was also a source used by Livy, and by Diodorus; but there is no evidence that Plutarch used Diodorus, though he must surely have known of him. Nor does he cite the *Geographica* of Strabo, but he uses Strabo's history which has not come down to us.[10]

Besides the Greek writers already mentioned Plutarch cites dozens more, but their works are not extant. It stands out quite clearly that he read or consulted a great number of writers, gathering information here, collecting judgments there and noting variations from the usually accepted tradition. But most of the names mean little to us, and modern critics often appear to be moving about in a mist searching for unsubstantial figures in the hope that they will whisper something of value. This work of investigating the sources of individual *Lives* was perhaps begun in 1820 by A. H. L. Heeren in his *de fontibus et auctoritate vitarum parallelarum*, published in Göttingen. But critical method had not advanced very far; the more rigorous methods of modern enquiry have done something to give the shadowy figures more substance and to trace lines of historical traditions, with their prejudices and exaggerations.

The result has been a clearer understanding of Plutarch's method of working and of the kind of source he worked on.

Sometimes he himself might be disappointed by the findings of criticism. For example, in the *Life of Alexander* he quotes thirty times from the letters of Alexander. He does not conceal his delight in using them, as though claiming to be the first historian to do so. Heeren takes him at his word and treats the letters as the most important document. But modern criticism now regards these letters as forgeries–inventions fabricated round one or two genuine letters, for which there is independent testimony, and gathered into a collection. So whole sections of this *Life* are discredited; a pity! On the other hand our knowledge of Solon was dependent mainly on the remains of his poems, and on the *Life* by Plutarch until Aristotle's *Athenaion Politeia* was discovered in 1890. Plutarch is now seen to have embodied in his *Life* a great deal of good material.[11]

CHAPTER 12

Amyot and English Translations of the *Lives*

In the fifteenth century the *Lives* were turned into Latin by Guarinus and others and a century later by Budé. They soon passed into modern European languages – turned into Italian by B. Jaconello in 1482, into Spanish by Alfonso de Palencia in 1491, into German by H. Boner in 1541. In the early middle years of the sixteenth century George de Sélve and others translated selections into French.

The *Moralia*, too, were translated. For example, Sir Thomas Elyot undertook a spurious work *On educating children*, Sir Thomas Wyatt (1503–42) rendered Budé's Latin version of *On tranquillity*; Erasmus turned *Precepts on health* into Latin which was put into English by Wyer, the well-known printer of his time. The whole of the *Moralia* appeared in Germany in the sixteenth century, the most notable version being by W. Xylander, in Latin.

But the translator who made Plutarch well known to Europe was Jacques Amyot. Through him Plutarch's influence penetrated widely and deeply into French and English thought; it was presented in a form at once attractive and accessible and was taken up into literature, politics, historiography and philosophy. As is well known, Montaigne owed a great deal to Plutarch; Rousseau began to read the *Lives* at the age of six and his writings are permeated by ideas taken from them; through him the life and institutions of France were profoundly changed and so the life of Europe. This subject has been treated in many monographs; the intention of this chapter is to provide a few notes on Amyot and the English translators who followed him.

Of his life it is enough to say that he was born in 1513 at Melun; his parents were French and they were poor. Never-the-less he was educated in Paris and later in Bourges where through the influence of Marguerita de Valois he became Professor of French and Latin. By Francis I he was given the Abbey of Bellozane, and later he was made Bishop of Auxerre by Pope Pius IV. Here he remained for many years till he died in 1593.

His interest in Plutarch began early in his life and it remained with him. It is true that he did translations also of some books of Diodorus and also the Tale of Daphnis and Chloe, but his amazing industry was given chiefly to Plutarch.

His two main objectives were to establish a good text for his author and to translate it in such a way that the public of his time, who were not equipped with a knowledge of classical history and institutions, would read with ease and pleasure a version so phrased as to carry its own explanations.

And so he paid many visits to Italy to examine and compare Latin and French manuscripts, and he was specially indebted to the Latin translation of Guarinus, published at Brescia in 1488; indeed he appears sometimes to have translated the Latin version rather than the Greek original. Sometimes when he was not satisfied with the existing texts he resorted to conjecture.

His own translations he revised constantly, taking enormous pains to obtain clarity and ease and at the same time faithfulness to the original. The result is that critics who are competent to judge say that his language achieves simplicity and purity and his version reads like an original work. Often, however, he must have found it difficult to reconcile his desire to be accurate and his determination to be understood. It was the technical terms that worried him. To make them carry meaning he resorted to methods which we to-day should call, at the least, misleading; but in his defence it must be said that his public had not the knowledge nor the experience possessed by the reader of an English translation of Plutarch nowadays.

It was reasonable, for example, to translate σημειόγραφοι (shorthand-writers) by 'notaires, ç'est à dire, d'escrivains qui par notes de lettres abregées figurent toute une sentence ou tout un mot'; it is a long gloss but it is not misleading. In the same way ῥαβδοῦχος (lictor) appears as 'massier' or 'sergent' and sometimes more fully, as 'massier portant les haches'. But it is not easy to guess what Amyot's readers made of the Acropolis and the Capitol when they were described as a 'chasteau'. It is when he comes to the words of religion that he is most daring. In his time 'le temple' did not mean a religious building, and so he does not scruple to render ἱερόν (temple) by 'église' or 'chapelle'. He does not call priests 'évéques', as his predecessor Seyssel had done, but he does translate ἱεροσύνη (office of priest) as 'prélature'. And what was his Christian public to make of a priestess? Seyssel had rendered it by 'abbesse', Calvin by 'nonnain de payens'; Amyot is content with 'réligieuse'. But, having gone so far, he could not draw back, and when he has to translate ἐναγής (under a curse) he is not content with 'maudit' but adds 'et excommunié'. As for γυναικωνῖτις (the women's quarters of the house) what could be further from Athenian society and nearer to the sixteenth century than 'les cabinets des dames'?

But Amyot was also a priest and bishop, and so he adopts a practice of which we cannot say Plutarch would have disapproved, if we remember how he proclaims a motive of morality for writing the *Lives*. In the margins Amyot gives a very brief summary of the contents of a chapter; in the same place he is liable to insert what a later translator called 'idle declamations on trite morals and obvious sentiments'. For example, his marginal comment on *Sulla* 27 is 'Le diable pousse tousjours à la roue et selon que Dieu luy permet n'a pas faute d'illusions pour encourager ses misérables esclaves'. Two prodigies had occurred, not very striking, which seemed to foretell Sulla's success. Again, on *Coriolanus* 24 he remarks 'Satan se fourre à la traverse tant pour atiser le feu de division par des prodiges de mensange que pour établir tant plus ses superstitions et idolatries'. In the Life of Brutus 24, when Brutus has prepared an unusually good banquet, and his supporters were drinking success to his cause, Amyot notes, 'Un bon esprit vaut mieux que plusieurs mains. L'espérance se trouve volontiers ès banquets.' The leaders in the French revolution might have found some of his comments salutary, as, for example, 'La providence divine se rit des conseils que les grands prennent pour troubler le repos de petits; et les fait tellement embrouiller eux mesmes qu'ils deviennent cruels ennemis lors qu'ils semblaioyent avoir contraité amitié inviolable ensemble',[1] or perhaps even more to the point, 'Il n'y a beste cruelle si furieuse qu'une commune mutinée', a comment on the behaviour of the mob after the murder of Caesar.[2]

Plutarch was no less fortunate in his English translator, for, though Thomas North translated Amyot's French version, he presented Plutarch in a form which was destined to have great influence on English literature and on English style. He was the second son of the first Lord North. He was born about 1535 and may have gone to Peterhouse, his father's college. But he was certainly entered at Lincoln's Inn in 1557. It is not clear that he ever carried his legal studies very far, for he published in December of the same year his first translation. This book was called 'The Diale of Princes, compiled by the Reverend father in God, Don Antony Guevara, Bishop of Guadix . . . Englished out of the French by Thomas North, second son of Lord North, right necessarie and pleasaunt to all gentylmen and others which are lovers of vertue.' It was an English version of Guevara's *Libro Aureo*, which was in turn a Spanish version, being freely adapted, of the *Meditations* of Marcus Aurelius.

We do not know what North was engaged with for the next thirteen years or so; he gives no indication of the year in which he started his study of Amyot's Plutarch. But we know that in 1574 he accompanied his elder brother Roger to France. Roger North was sent as Ambassador Extraordinary to congratulate Henry III on his accession. Thomas no doubt went to help his brother, for he was a good linguist. Roger's mission had in view much more than a merely formal visit of courtesy. Contemporary sources give a pretty full account of his mission, of the intrigues with which he was supposed to cope, of his encounters with the Queen Mother, Catherine de Medici, and of Queen Elizabeth's anger at the account which he gave her of the French attitude to her. But for the present purpose it is enough to note that at the French Court he could have met Amyot. There is no evidence that he did; but Amyot was often at Court, for he was Chief Almoner and a Privy Counsellor.

The brothers were home by 1575 and were in attendance on Queen Elizabeth when she paid her famous visit to Kenilworth. It is said that Shakespeare, then a boy of eleven years, was in the crowd that watched the celebrations held there. Thus, Shakespeare might conceivably have set eyes on the translator of Amyot's Plutarch's *Lives*, to whom he was to owe so much, while the year before that translator might have talked to Amyot himself. It is pleasant to imagine that coincidence might have stretched so far.

Thomas was evidently attracted by moralising works, for in 1570 he translated from the Italian 'The Moral Philosophy of Doni. Drawne out of the ancient authors'. This was a collection of Oriental fables, chiefly those of Bidpai (better known as Pilpay), collected by Antonio Francesco Doni, who was born at Florence in 1513. The first edition of the *Lives* appeared in 1579: its title was 'The Lives of the noble Grecians and Romanes, compared together by that grave, learned Philosopher and Historiographer Plutarke of Chaeronea'. Besides a translation of Amyot's very long address to the reader, which occupies six folio pages in North, there are two dedications by North himself, one to the Queen and one to the reader. To the Queen, who is told that she is 'meeter to be the chief storie, than a student therein, and can better understand it in Greeke than any man can make it English', he writes:

How many examples shall your subjects read here, of several persons and whole armyes, of noble and base, of younger and older, that both by sea and lande, at home and abroad, have strayned their wits, not regarded their states, ventured their persons, cast away their lives . . . then well may the readers thinke; if they have done this for heathen Kings, what should we do for Christian Princes? if they have done this for glorye, what should we do for religion? If they have done this without hope of heaven, what should we do that look for immortalitie?

The dedication to the reader is commendably short.

> The profit of stories and the praise of the Author are sufficiently declared by Amiot in his Epistle to the Reader; so that I shall not need to make many words thereof. And indeed if you will supply the defects of this translation, with your own diligence and understanding: you shall not need to trust him. You may prove yourselves, that there is no prophane study better than Plutarch. All other learning is private, fitter for Universities than Cities, fuller of contemplations than experience, more commendable in Students themselves, than profitable unto others. Whereas stories are fit for every place, reach to all persons, serve all times, reach the living, revive the dead, so far excelling all other Books, as it is better to see learning in Noblemens Lives than to read it in Philosophers writings. Now for the Authour, I will not deny that love may deceive me, for I must needs love him with whom I have taken such pain; but I believe I might be held to affirm that he hath written the profitablest Story of all others. For all other were fain to take their matter, as the fortune of the Countries whereof they wrote fall out. But this man being excellent in wit, learning and experience, hath chosen the special Acts of the best persons, of the famousest Nations of the world. But I will leave the judgement to your selves. My only purpose is to desire you to excuse the faults of my translation, with your own gentleness, and with the opinions of my diligence and good intent. And so I wish you all the profit of the book. Fare ye well.

Again Plutarch, it may be guessed, would have thoroughly approved: his works were to be treated as a storehouse of moral wisdom,* and by someone capable of loving their author. Perhaps, too, Plutarch would have liked to know that, in the spirit of some of his favourite Greek heroes, Thomas North raised a band of 300 men of Ely and took command of them when news of the threat of the Armada reached England and that, in 1591, he was knighted by the Queen.

About one hundred years later another translation appeared in consecutive volumes. It appears to owe its existence to the enterprise of a publisher, for it was published in 1683 by Jacob Tonson 'at the sign of the Judge's Head in Chancery Lane, near Fleet Street'. It was entrusted, according to 'The Publisher

---

* North removed Amyot's sententious marginal notes, and added a good summary of his own.

to the Reader', to 'persons equal to the enterprize and not only
Criticks in the Tongue but Men of known fame and Abilities,
for style and ornament, but I shall rather refer you to the learned
and Ingenious Translations of this first part as a specimen of
what you may promise yourself for the rest'. The translators'
names are given; they prove to be almost as numerous as the
Lives themselves; some are Fellows of Oxford and Cambridge
Colleges; one at least is a Doctor of Medicine; but there is no
one of great note. But the translation takes the name of no less
a person than John Dryden, for he wrote the epistle dedicatory
to the Duke of Ormond and he contributed a long introduction
containing a Life of Plutarch; but it is scarcely believable that
he exercised any editorial power to revise and co-ordinate the
efforts of the large team of translators.

Dryden, it is to be feared, had little respect for his predecessor,
North.

As that translation was only from the French, so it suffered this
double disadvantage, first that it was but a copy of a copy and that
too but lamely taken from the Greek original; secondly, that the
English language was then unpolished and far from the perfection
which it has since attained; so that the first version is not only
ungrammatical and ungraceful but in many places almost unintel-
ligible. For which reasons, and lest so useful a piece of history should
be oppressed under the rubbish of Antiquated words, some ingenious
and learned gentlemen have undertaken this task; and what would
have been the labour of one man's life will by the several endeavours
of many be now accomplished in the compass of a year.

This condemnation of his beloved North was unendurable to
George Wyndham, the editor of North's Plutarch in the Tudor
Translations, 1895.

It was a colossal impertinence to put out The Lives among the
greeklings of Grub Street, in order to 'complete the whole in a year'
but it must be noted that this, after North's, is the one version that
can be read without impatience. Dryden's hacks were not artists,
but neither were they prigs; the vocabulary was not yet a charnel
of decayed metaphor, and if they missed the rapture of sixteenth
century stylism, they had not bleached the colour, carded the texture, and ironed the surface of their language to the well-glazed

insignificance of the later eighteenth century. Their Plutarch is no longer arrayed in the royal robes of Amyot and North, but he is spared the cheap though formal tailoring of . . .

We shall see later whom he has in mind.

The publisher of the 1683 edition of Dryden's *Lives* claimed that 'Plutarch's worthies' were 'made yet more famous by a Translator that gives a farther Lustre, even to Plutarch himself'. Yet in 1727 the same firm issued a revised translation, explaining that 'when this work was first undertaken, the gentlemen who generally engaged in it had not their helps and advantages with which the learned work is at present supplied'. The publisher's note goes on to say that the original translators would no doubt 'have succeeded much better' if they could have availed themselves of the work since done in improving the Greek texts. The 'helps and advantages' were chiefly the London edition by Bryanus & Solanus, and Dacier's French translation.[3] And so the 1683 version was altered out of all recognition; the Life by Dryden remained: the translation was revised by the adoption of Dacier's rendering construed into English in passages where revision seemed to be called for, and great quantities of Dacier's notes were added, besides his chronological tables. A special introduction points out the difference between Dryden's *Life of Plutarch* and Dacier's *Life*. Dryden had boasted a little too soon: in his life he had said that 'the same Amiot is tasked for an infinite number of mistakes by his countrymen of the present Age: which is enough to recommend this translation of our Authour into the English toungue, being not from any copy but from the Greek Original'. But now this translation was to be revised and considerably interlarded by passages translated from another French version, and to be accompanied by copious notes derived from the French edition.

However, the publishing firm was not satisfied. It was now J. and R. Tonson and its address was in the Strand. In 1758 it put out another edition with a different attitude in its prefatory note. Mr. Dryden, it is explained, considered speed important, but 'different styles, and different ideas of the duty of a translator, must always render such a performance irregular and unequal and that no author's work can appear to advantage'. So the public is informed that the work was revised 1727, but even so the note candidly continues:

many of the faults were so gross that they were apparent even to those readers who were quite unacquainted with the original. The language in general was mean and often ungrammatical; the mistakes, omissions and unnecessary additions were very numerous; and in those lives where the language was less liable to censure there was frequently an excessive liberty or great carelessness in expressing the meaning of the author.

Then it is promised that the present edition will be more correct since it has been 'diligently compared with the Greek'. There was another revision yet to come!

The quotation from George Wyndham given above may now be completed 'he is spared the cheap though formal tailoring of Dacier and the Langhornes'; for it was the brothers Langhorne who offered the public the next English translation. They had indeed asked for Wyndham's scorn; for in their introduction they had omitted all mention of North's name; their only references to North's translation are 'and from that book (Amiot) it was translated into English in the time of Queen Elizabeth', and 'after the old English translation of Plutarch which was professedly taken from Amiot's French.' Dryden fared rather better, but not the translation; for Dryden the man was given an honourable mention.

That great man, who is never to be mentioned without pity and admiration, was prevailed upon, by his necessities, to head a company of translators and to lend the sanction of his glorious name to a translation of Plutarch, written, as he himself acknowledges, by almost as many hands as there were *Lives*. That this motley work was full of errors, inequalities and inconsistencies, is not in the least to be wondered at. Of such a variety of translators it would have been very singular if some had not failed in learning, and some in language. The truth is that the greatest part of them were deficient in both. . . . Some few blundered at the Greek; some drew from the scholiasts' Latin; and others, more humble, trod scrupulously in the paces of Amiot. Thus copying the idioms of different languages they proceeded like the workmen at Babel and fell into a confusion of tongues while they attempted to speak the same.

The brothers Langhorne were the sons of the Rev. Joseph Langhorne, of Winton in the parish of Kirkby Stephen in Westmorland, a place which in those days must have been remote and isolated. The elder brother was William, born in 1721, the younger was John, born in 1735. John, the more important of the two, went to the village school and later to the school at Appleby. He then became a private tutor, then worked at a school in Wakefield: after another spell of tutoring he went to Clare Hall, Cambridge, but did not take a degree. After being curate at Dagenham, assistant preacher at Lincoln's Inn, he became Rector of Blagdon, in Somerset, in 1766. After the death of his wife he went to live for some long period with his brother, who was perpetual curate of Folkestone. There the brothers worked at their Plutarch and published it in 1770. What attracted them to Plutarch is not clear: for they were poets. John published a great deal of poetry, while William seems to have concentrated on 'practical paraphrases' of Job and parts of Isaiah. About 1772 John married again and returned to Blagdon, where he died in 1779.

In their introduction to the *Lives* the Langhornes complain that Amyot's margins are everywhere covered with 'idle declamations on trite morals and obvious sentiments', for 'in those times they followed the method of the old divines which was to make practical improvements of every matter'. In place of these 'observations' the brothers offer explanatory notes, often useful, which they took from Dacier or composed themselves. They also provided a new Life of Plutarch, to replace that of Dryden. But even they could not avoid a certain tendency to make their own points, as Amyot had made his. For example,

it was a happy circumstance in the discipline of their (*i.e.* the Greeks') schools that the parent only had the power of corporal punishment; the rod and the ferule were snatched from the hand of the petty tyrant: his office alone was to inform the mind: he had no authority to dastardise the spirit: he had no power to extinguish the generous flame of freedom or to break down the noble independency of the soul by the slavish, debasing and degrading application of the rod. This mode of punishment in our public schools is one of the worst remains of barbarism that prevails among us

and so on at some length. And, later, the Greeks

did not, like us, employ their youth in the acquisition of words; they were engaged in pursuits of a higher nature: in acquiring the knowledge of things. They did not, like us, spend seven or ten years of scholastic labour in making a general acquaintance with two dead languages. These years were employed in the study of nature, and in gaining the elements of philosophical knowledge from her original economy and laws.

The Langhornes' translation held the field until a new version appeared. Arthur Hugh Clough, after resigning his Oriel fellowship in 1848 and spending an unhappy three or four years as Head of University College, London, migrated to America and settled at Cambridge, Massachusetts. While he was there, he was approached by an American firm of publishers to undertake a revision of Dryden's *Plutarch*. Nine months later, in 1854, he returned to England to take up an examinership in the Education Office. He continued the work of revision, and eventually the whole was published in 1859–60. It is now the most readily accessible translation of the *Lives*, being reprinted in the Everyman Library, with the short life of Plutarch originally written by Clough. His revision is conscientious and painstaking and gives a much more accurate rendering of the Greek. The special distinctivenesses of the Dryden version are smoothed away. The result is a translation which, if unremarkable, is serviceable, except that the chapters are not numbered.

Epilogue

WRITERS of the generation after Plutarch's death have little to say about him. But his fame grew; for Apuleius, writing in Africa, made the hero of the 'Golden Ass' a descendant of 'the famous Plutarch'.

But at last he was recognised in Rome. Aulus Gellius was a judge in private cases at Rome in the reigns of Hadrian and Antoninus and Marcus Aurelius. He remained in practice to the end of his short life; he was about forty-five years old when he died. As a young man he stayed some time in Athens where Calvisius Taurus was his teacher in philosophy; here too he was the guest of Herodes Atticus. During the winter nights in Athens he collected notes on any topic that interested him, and no doubt by day pursued his enquiries further. Coming back to Rome he wrote up his notes in twenty books; the work he entitled *Noctes Atticae*, a miscellany of interesting topics of all kinds, philological, literary, historical, personal, philosophical.

Whatever further life the gods will for me, whatever spare time I can find after attending to my private affairs and educating my children I shall devote to putting together these miniature discussions as I recollect them. The number of books will go up, the gods aiding me, as my life advances, and I do not want its span to be prolonged unless I remain capable of this kind of writing and reflection.

Here was a man after Plutarch's heart.

Gellius was not content with publishing notes, as others had done. Some of his topics were treated in reports of conversations arising from events which had actually occurred. As Ammonius, Plutarch's teacher, appears in his dialogues, so Calvisius Taurus appears in Gellius, and so do many more of his friends, among whom was Favorinus, Plutarch's young friend. Sometimes Gellius took pains to introduce the scene and to arrange the setting; he seldom took equal pains to finish off. Many of his notes are mere notes, but here is an outline of one of the longer sketches.[1]

Taurus was going from Athens to Delphi to see the Pythian games and to watch the vast concourse of people gathered together from all parts of Greece. He took Gellius with him. When they reached Lebadea in Boeotia, Taurus received news that a philosopher friend of his was ill. He abandoned the journey to Delphi, left the carriages and went on foot to see his friend, who was ill with abdominal pain and fever. He was groaning loudly, but his groans seemed to testify not to the pain but to his battle with the pain. Taurus sent for a doctor, and after doing his best to encourage his friend left him. On the way back to the carriages a discussion took place about the ways in which pain may be borne. One of the philosopher's pupils argues with his teacher till eventually they reach the carriages and the journey is resumed.

The parallelism with Plutarch's dialogues is obvious – the teacher, the pupils, Delphi, the episode which gives rise to the discussion, the topic, the final rounding-off. The queries which suggest themselves cannot be answered. Did Taurus know Plutarch? Certainly he calls him 'our Plutarch, a man learned and wise'. Did Favorinus draw the attention of Gellius to the Boeotian philosopher? Did the journey to Delphi take place, or was it conceived in the spirit of the *Pythian Dialogues*? Gellius tells a story about Plutarch which is recorded nowhere else[2] and quotes passages from the *Moralia*, sometimes in Greek sometimes in Latin translation, and he knows the names of treatises from which he does not quote. The very first word of the work is Plutarch's name, which almost invites us to believe that Gellius was sounding a keynote and asking us to realise that he is a Roman Plutarch. It is all very tantalising; but none the less here is Plutarch recognised at Rome, and imitated.

He was known better in the East than in the West. Clement of Alexandria, John Chrysostom, Eusebius all knew of him, and Basil owed him a great debt. Theodoret believed he had read the Gospels. The Latin fathers on the whole do not know of him, nor does Boethius. The use made of Plutarch by John

EPILOGUE

of Salisbury has already been seen. But from the time of Boethius he virtually goes underground like a river, to use one of his own similes, and reappears a thousand years later, to influence French and later European life and thought and letters in a manner which has few parallels. The history of the influence of Plutarch in Europe through the Renaissance and the French Revolution and beyond has not yet been written. Hirzel has drawn a valuable ground plan; very many monographs have provided material; but no one has erected the building.

The fourteenth and fifteenth centuries, and again the seventeenth and eighteenth centuries, were in search of new ideas, and fresh resources were laid open to them in the new learning, that is to say in classical literature rediscovered. Here was a vast storehouse of human experience. In the early centuries of our era classical learning had been condensed into summaries and handbooks designed to be the elementary textbooks of the new European nations. Now some of these nations were outgrowing their early primers and were ready to read the originals from which the summaries were made. Forgotten and indeed unknown authors were brought to light and eagerly read. Why did Plutarch, an unassuming Greek from an obscure village in Greece, play so great a part in this revival of learning? The answer to this question would be revealed in the comprehensive history of Plutarch's influence which it has been suggested above is overdue. It is possible that part of the reason is as follows.

The French literary critic Brunetière is quoted by Hirzel as saying that what Homer was to the Greek tragedians Plutarch was to the French dramatists. In other words French drama did not derive from a study of the *Poetics* of Aristotle but from the characters and the situations presented to them on a heroic plane in Plutarch's *Lives*. If this analogy is enlarged to cover the fields of politics, government, social life, art and letters, something can be seen of the secret of Plutarch's success. In the *Lives* classical ideas and classical standards of thought and behaviour were embodied in people who had lived those ideas; abstract conceptions were presented in portraits; vivified by the enthusiastic affection of men who felt they had awakened from medieval

175

torpor, those portraits became real men. Here ideas long embodied in classical civilisation but new to their discoverers could be seen in operation in graphic form; peoples had lived by them and could live by them again. And to those portraits was added the self-portrait, unconsciously drawn in the *Lives* and in the *Moralia*, of the good man humbly living according to the highest classical standards, at ease with himself and of benefit to his friends, the ideal of a 'verray parfit' gentleman for which the new Europe was looking. Perhaps no writer's professed purpose has achieved a greater measure of success.

Notes

Chapter 1

[1] *pro Flacco* 16

[2] The full text is in Dessau *I.L.S.* 8794: it was edited by M. Holleaux, *Bull. Corr. Hell.* 12 (1888) p. 570. Neither the exact date nor the name Messalina are certain.

[3] *de ser.* Plutarch is equally enthusiastic about the 'freedom of Hellas' granted by Flamininus in 196 B.C.: he does not understand that it was meaningless: see *Flam.* 12

[4] Cic. *Fam.* 4.5.4. Caesar's restoration Plut. *Caes.* 57

[5] *Ant.* 68

[6] Böckh *C.I.G.* 1625

[7] See further G. F. Hertzberg, *Geschichte Griechenlands unter der Herrschaft der Römer*, Halle 1868, still indispensable; J. P. Mahaffy, *The Greek world under Roman sway*, London 1890; P. Graindor, *Athènes de Tibère à Trajan*, Cairo 1931; Tenney Frank, *Economic survey of Ancient Rome*, vol. iv, Baltimore 1938; J. Day, *An economic history of Athens under Roman domination*, New York 1942; M. Rostovtzeff, *Social and economic history of the Roman Empire*, rev. ed, Oxford 1957

Chapter 2

[1] *C.I.G.* 1713. The statue contains no honorary titles attached to the Emperor's name and may perhaps be dated early.

[2] Ditt. *Syll.*[3] 843

[3] Perhaps twenty years cf. *An Seni* 17

[4] 2.8; 3.8, 9. *Praec. ger.* 20. Plutarch observed his father's advice in his writings and his use of 'we' for 'I' sometimes causes obscurity, *e.g.* in *Amat.* 2 where it might be wrongly inferred that Flavianus was Plutarch's son.

[5] *de soll. animal.* 7

[6] *Cim.* 1; *Ant.* 68.7; 1.5.1; 28.3

[7] Vitruvius 6.7

[8] 1.26

[9] *Quaest. conviv.* 8.1

[10] 48

PLUTARCH AND HIS TIMES

11 The Stoic philosopher Sextus of Chaeronea, who taught Marcus Aurelius Greek literature, was Plutarch's nephew (brother's son) SHA. *Marc. Ant.* 3.2 Eutrop. 8. 12 Suid. Σέξτος. In a curious passage of Apuleius, Lucius, the hero of the 'Golden Ass', claims for himself descent from Plutarch and Sextus 1.2, 2.3; but this is only an ambitious fancy and proves nothing but the fame of Plutarch, certainly not Apuleius' descent. There is good evidence at Eleusis (Ditt. *Syll.*³ 845) for a Nicagoras who flourished under Philip the Arabian and for a Minucianus in the reign of Gallienus as descendants of the family. The Roman Gentile name appears in L. Mestrius Autobulos, 'Platonic philosopher', to whom Flavius Autobulos his grandson dedicated a statue, probably in the third century, at Chaeronea, *Syll.*³ 843. Another inscription, *Syll.*³ 844, records Sextus Claudius Autobulos, 'called after his father, the sixth from Plutarch, who in Greece displayed all virtue in his life and his writings, philosopher'. But the matter can be taken further; for the wife of Himerios the famous sophist, a salaried professor of rhetoric at Athens and for a time the Emperor Julian's secretary, claimed descent from Plutarch through Nicagoras and Minucianus, and, when be besought the Athenians to grant citizenship to his three-year-old son, Rufinus, he put forward the plea of descent from Plutarch 'through whom you educate all men', *Funeral Oration*, 8.21. The boy died young and with him the record ends, but it has taken us well into the fourth century A.D.

12 *Travels in Northern Greece*, London, ii. 112; *Griechische Reiseskizzen*, Braunschweig 1853, p. 296. The chair seems to have survived till 1898, cf. J. G. Frazer, *Pausanias' description of Greece*, Vol. 5, pp. 207–8. *C.I.G.G.S.*, 1.3422 gives the inscription on the base of a head of Plutarch (now lost) at Chaeronea.

Chapter 3

1 1.3; 1.4; 3.1; 7.4

2 8.7; 4.1; 7.4

3 *I.G.* ix. 1.61; ix. 1. 190, 192, 193, 200

4 This story about Cronus is told also in *de fac.* 26

5 For inscription see Dessau *I.L.S.* 8861; the matter has been most recently discussed by I. A. Richmond in *Antiquity* 1940 p. 193: the identification was first made by C. W. King in the *Archaeol. Journ.* xxxix pp. 23–37, 1882. See also Dessau in *Hermes* 46, pp. 156–60, 1911. Richmond suggests that the Ravenna List, and also Ptolemy, were indebted to such explorations as these; *e.g.* the Ravenna List notes that one island was called Minerva, off the north-west of Scotland. Richmond also says that off Lewis is a group of islands called 'Charmed', *i.e.* the 'Sacred' of the Plutarch passage. It should be remarked that, if A.D. 83/84 is right, it is only a

178

year or two before Agricola's fleet rounded Cape Wrath. Perhaps Demetrius helped to find a route.

[6] *Quaest. Conviv.* 9.5, 12, 13; 3.4; *de fac.* 13, 22

[7] 1.9; 9.2; 8.10; 6.9; 5.5

[8] *Quaest. Conviv.* 7.8.4, *Conviv. Sept. Sap.* 13

Chapter 4

[1] Plin. *N.H.* 34.36. The question was trite enough, 'Who were the parents of Homer and where was he born?' The answer was Telemachus and Polycaste, and Ithaca.

[2] *de E.*1; *An seni* 17; ἐπιμελητής see the inscr. cited ch. 2 n. 1; *An seni* 4

[3] *de Pyth. orac.* 29

[4] The word here translated 'management' is from the same verb as the official title which Plutarch held, translated earlier as 'manager'. But other interpreters, *e.g.* R. Flacelière, in *Plutarque sur les oracles de la Pythie*, Le Puy, 1936, think that Plutarch is here putting his own views into the mouth of Theon. 'I', then, is to mean Plutarch, and 'him who has been responsible' is taken to refer to Trajan or Hadrian, whose 'divinity' aided the planning. It is also objected that Theon does not appear in any surviving record of Delphi. This view does not recommend itself; for (*a*) it assumes that Theon is a lay figure; are any of Plutarch's characters merely mouthpieces of himself? (*b*) the suppression of a name is pointless if the Emperor is meant, indeed tactless; if Plutarch is meant, it is entirely in character, (*c*) the play on 'manager' and 'management' is lost, (*d*) Theon may not appear in the records; but Polycrates does not; is he also to be regarded as a figure, though Petraeus does appear? R. Oakesmith thinks a Roman official is meant.

[5] *Charmides* 164e, 165a

[6] Eus. *P.E.* 5.16

[7] The Pythian Dialogues have been separately edited, with text, translation and notes, by R. Flacelière—*Sur les oracles de Pythie*, Le Puy 1936, *Sur l'E de Delphes*, Paris 1941, *Sur le disparition des oracles*, Paris 1947. For Delphi see H. W. Parke and D. E. W. Wormell, *The Delphic Oracle*, 2 vols., Oxford 1956

Chapter 5

[1] *Quaest. Conviv.* 1.10.1

[2] *On whether the affections of the body or the mind are worse.*

[3] *C.I.L.* 3.566

[4] *Dem.* 2.2

[5] *de soll. animal.* 19

[6] *de curios.* 15

[7] *Poplic.* 15.4

[8] He may have been Cn. Cornelius Ti. Pulcher who held several official posts in Achaea. *C.I.G.* 1186

[9] He may have been related to the Sosii who Horace (*Epist.* 1.20.2, 2.3.345) tells us were publishers. But it is pure speculation to suggest, as has been done, that he may have published Plutarch's works.

[10] 2.3, 3.3

[11] By a curious coincidence the seventh book of the *Table Talks* deals with several matters concerned with the right ordering of a dinner party, and Martial's friend, Priscus, wrote a book on the same subject. 'What is the best kind of dinner party Priscus' eloquent pages discuss; much that he says comes from a gentle mind, much from a lofty mind, but all shows learning: what is the best kind of dinner party? Why, one where there is no fluteplayer (Martial 9.77), and one of the *Table Talks* (9.77) discusses the same point as is contained in Martial's last line. Now Martial died about A.D.104; the *Table Talks* were published probably A.D. 100–110; it would be hazardous to propose a connexion between the book written by Martial's friend and Plutarch's own book.

Chapter 6

[1] 4.4

[2] There were other links between Senecio and Pliny. Senecio's daughter, Sosia Polla, married Q. Pompeius Falco, a friend and correspondent of Pliny, and, as one of the letters is concerned to tell him about a young poet whose recitation Pliny had attended, interested in literature. Sosia was also the granddaughter of Sextus Julius Frontinus, who was commissioner of the water supply of Rome in A.D. 97, a writer and governor of Britain about A.D. 74–78. He was also a friend of Pliny. Sosia must have spent much time abroad, for her husband held several provincial governorships (Dess. *I.L.S.* 1036, 1037. See also 8820, 1104.); to her he dedicated an inscription in the Isle of Samos while he was proconsul of Asia *c.* A.D. 107. But in the early nineties she may well have been in Rome. It would seem incredible that through Senecio, his daughter, his son-in-law, his daughter's grandfather, Pliny should not have heard of Plutarch; yet Pliny, who was not averse from claiming acquaintance with well-known people, makes no mention of him.

[3] Suidas means 'Fortress', an 'armoury' of texts and quotations and statements gathered chiefly from abridgments and collections of passages of authors, many of whom have not come down to us. Nevertheless it preserves much that goes back to original authorities.

NOTES

4 The story is rejected at length by O. Gréard.

5 As it stands in a literal English version, this dedication presents some oddities. A collection of *Sayings of kings and generals* can scarcely be called the first-fruits of philosophy. The phrase 'also lives' suggests that the 'collection' contains something more than 'lives', which is impossible if the collection consists of lives. The word for 'collection', σύνταγμα, is generally used for a collection inside a single book or volume; possibly it could be used of a series of volumes. Moreover it is not clear whose collection it is; instead of 'my collection' we have merely 'the collection'. There is no person known to us as Seiramnes. After the anecdote about Seiramnes it is disconcerting to find ourselves back to the *Lives* referred to merely as 'there'. The sayings of distinguished men may perhaps be 'samples' of their lives, but scarcely 'seeds'. In the final sentence but one we should expect the thought to be, 'I do not think the time you spend on them will bore you'; but that would require a most unusual sense of the word καιρός which is here translated 'opportunity' (*i.e.* of reading them); none the less 'time spent' may be the meaning of the writer. Finally, 'briefly' seems to suggest, though perhaps not necessarily, that the *Sayings* are drawn from the *Lives* and so, with respect to the sayings and not the deeds, give a shortened version of the *Lives*. But this is not so; there is a great deal in the *Sayings* that is not in the *Lives* and much in the *Lives* that is not in the *Sayings*. On the other hand it is in Plutarch's manner to make his point with stories to illustrate it, and the general style is not out of keeping. Volkman 1.211 has a long and detailed criticism of the preface and the *Sayings*. His points seem of somewhat unequal value. It may be noted that καιρός in late Greek may mean χρόνος.

6 Plutarch sends greetings to Trajan.

I knew that your modesty did not crave for the Principate, though you studied to deserve it by attractiveness of character. You will be judged to be all the more worthy of it because men think you far removed from any charge of being ambitious of it. I rejoice in your high qualities and in my own good fortune, that is, if you discharge aright the office you have so justly deserved. In any case I have no doubt you will be exposed to danger and I to the talk of critics, since Rome never tolerated cowardice in Emperors and popular chatter always turns back the misdeeds of pupils upon their teachers. Thus Seneca is attacked by critics because of his pupil Nero; the wildness of his pupils is thrown back at Quintilian [the reference to Quintilian should be noted; the name does not occur in Plutarch's works], and Socrates is charged with being too indulgent to his pupil (Alcibiades). Anything at all will go right for you if you remain true to yourself. If first you order yourself, and then order all things with the highest standards in view, everything without exception will go right for you. I have made clear to you the robustness of the political system of your ancestors; if you hold fast to it, your life has Plutarch's support. Indeed I call this letter as my witness, for if you go on to destroy the Empire you will not have Plutarch's support. [John then adds: 'there follow the heads of the political system which I have been at pains to insert in the present work in due measure; at the same time I have followed the trend of Plutarch's views rather than the exact steps of his words'.]

The first essential is that the Emperor should take the measurement of himself as a whole and should take careful note of what is in the whole body of the State, whose representative he is. Now the State is a kind of body (as Plutarch holds) which is endowed with life by the gift of the divine power and is kept going by the will of the supreme justice and is controlled by the regulating principle of reason. Those things which start and give shape to religious observance in us and transmit ceremonies in honour of God (not to say gods, as Plutarch does) fulfil the function of the soul in the body of the State. Those men who have charge of religious observance we must look up to as though they were the soul of the body and pay veneration to them. For who doubts that the servants of holiness are the representatives of God himself? Further, just as the soul exercises primacy over the whole body, so those whom God calls officers set in charge of religion are in charge of the whole body.

Augustus Caesar was subject to the priests right up to the time when he was made Pontifex Maximus so that he might not be subordinate to anyone at all, and a little later he was counted among the gods in his lifetime. The Emperor fulfils the role of the head in the State; he is subject to God only and to those who represent God on Earth, for in the human body too the head is animated and directed by the soul. The Senate takes the place of the heart from which proceed the movements initiating good and bad deeds. Judges and governors of provinces claim for themselves the functions of eyes, ears and tongue; officials and soldiers are equated with the hands, while those who stand close to the Emperor are like the ribs. Quaestors and the secretariate (I do not use this term in the special sense of secretariate concerned with prisons; I mean the private secretariate of the Emperor) suggest comparison with the stomach and bowels; if through greed these have taken in vast quantities of food and hold what they have taken in too long, they cause countless incurable diseases so that the whole body is in danger of collapse from the harm done by them. Workers on the land [It is possible that the Latin word *agricolae* does duty for αὐτουργοί in the original; αὐτουργοί was translated in one of its meanings 'agricultural workers', though its wider meaning, 'men doing the actual manual work', was intended.] are equivalent to the feet which are in perpetual contact with the ground; for the feet the forethought exercised by the head is essential, especially in so far as they discover new paths as they step over the ground in obedience to the body; and the help of boots is given to them as their due, for they hold erect, support and move forward the massive structure of the whole body. Take away from the most sturdy body the supports provided by the feet and it cannot progress through its own strength: it will either creep along in a humiliating, ineffective and awkward manner or it will move as dumb animals do. [John here explains that Plutarch here elaborates his theme at length; but it would be 'a servile interpretation' to give the exact words; moreover there is much relating to pagan religion which Plutarch thought it necessary to emphasise but which is better omitted; he will give briefly the gist of the teaching 'with which Plutarch tried to mould the Emperor and his officials in the cause of the promotion of justice'.]

Chapter 7

1 *Thes.* 1; *Pelop.* 2

2 *Alex.* 1; *Timol. pr.*

3 *Per.* 2

4 *Demetr.* 1

5 *e.g.* by K. Ziegler.

6 *Galb.* 2; *Dem. ad. fin.*; *Cat. min.* 25

7 *Fam.* 1.9.9

8 *Att.* 4.5.1 See also *Q. Fr.* 2.5.3

9 *Caes.* 24; App. *B.C.* 2.17

10

Life of Caesar 21	Life of Pompey 51	Life of Crassus 14
Most of the outstanding and influential men joined him, at Luca,	Used Gallic spoil to send money to praetors, aediles, etc., and their wives. Hence, when he arrived at Luca, crowds of men and women raced to get to him first – Pompey, Crassus, 120 lictors of proconsuls and praetors, 200 senators.	When Caesar came to Luca
Pompey, Crassus, Appius, propraetor of Sardinia and Nepos, proconsul of Spain, 120 lictors,		many people from Rome came, including Pompey and Crassus who met him secretly, and they decided
more than 200 senators.		
	Caesar sent all away with money and high hopes.	to get a firmer grip on affairs and to take all power into their own hands;

Life of Caesar 21	*Life of Pompey 51*	*Life of Crassus 14*
Pompey and Crassus to be consuls in the next year.	Pompey and Crassus should stand for consulship; Caesar would send soldiers to vote for them.	Pompey and Crassus to obtain the consulship in the next year; Caesar to write to his friends and send soldiers to vote.
Money should be provided for Caesar.		
Caesar's command should be prolonged for another 5 years.	Caesar's command should be prolonged for another 5 years.	Caesar to keep his army
	Pompey and Crassus to ensure provinces and an army for themselves.	Pompey and Crassus to obtain new armies and new provinces.
When the Senate voted the money, Cato was not present, for he had been expressly sent to Cyprus: Favorinus protested and left the house, but none listened to his warning; for all wanted to gratify Caesar.	When these arrangements were generally known (ἐπὶ τούτοις ἐξενεχθεῖσιν, perhaps = *quibus elatis* of Plutarch's Latin source) the leading men were indignant; Marcellinus in the popular assembly demanded from both whether they intended to stand for the consulship. And when the people demanded answer Pompey replied that ... and Crassus said ...	When they returned to Rome, they immediately fell under suspicion; there was a strong report that the conference boded no good. In the Senate Marcellinus and Domitius asked Pompey whether he intended to stand for the consulship; he replied ... Crassus said ...

[11] *Alex.* 35 end.

[12] *Aem.* 14; *Flam.* 9

[13] There is an interesting digression on credulity in chapter 38

[14] It should not be inferred that all the *Lives* were written before the *Roman Questions;* the *Questions* are cited in the lives of Romulus and Camillus. We do not know the order in which the lives were written.

Chapter 8

[1] *Rom.* 15. *Cam.* 19 The question is whether αἴτια means all three books, Roman, Greek and Barbarian, or, in the context, the Roman.

[2] Perhaps indirectly through Verrius Flaccus.

[3] Modern philologists regard the connexion of *lictor* with a root lig- as a bit of popular etymology, but can give no better answer. They think *macellum* was borrowed from Greek which borrowed it from a Semitic source. Paulus, Festus, 112. 14 gives the Macellus story, while Varro 1.1. 5.146 preserves the theory of a Greek origin.

NOTES

[4] 1, 15, 18, 22, 28, 35, 45

[5] See P. de Labriolle, *La réaction païenne*, Paris 1942 pp. 489–508. For the *Greek* and *Roman Questions* see H. J. Rose, *The Roman Questions of Plutarch*, Oxford 1924, and W. R. Halliday, *The Greek Questions*, Oxford 1928

Chapter 9

i

[1] *de Is.* 67.

[2] It can be maintained that in his youthful works Plutarch did indulge in a little display, forgivable perhaps in a young man.

ii

[1] See Dess. *I.L.S.* 5423, 6174. The MSS of Plutarch have ὦ Μάρκε Σηδάτε, but Sedatus appears to be a cognomen, while Sedatius is a nomen. Hence Wyttenbach altered the text.

[2] Cf., *e.g.* Sen. *Ep.* 21 'You must not regard these views as the property of Epicurus; they are common property. The practice observed in the Senate should be adopted in philosophy too. When a speaker expresses an opinion which I partly approve, I ask him to split it into parts and then I follow with him (*on the ground common to us*).'

[3] *adv. Col.* 31. *de Is.* 67. *de Is.* 23. Euhemerus, *fl.* 300 B.C., said he had seen some pillars on Panchaia in the Red Sea which contained an account of the (human) exploits of Uranus, Cronus and Zeus. Christian writers, esp. Lactantius, seized on Euhemerism to discredit the Greek gods; see Aug. *de civ. Dei* 6.7

[4] *de E.* 21

iii

[1] Diog. Laert. 1.27

[2] Hom. *Il.* 3.420, Hes. *Op.* 122, Aesch. *Pers.* 628, Theogn. 161, Men. *fr.* 550 Kock.

[3] 202 d.

[4] See 26 and 30 for daemons.

[5] See Lucian *passim*, esp. *de sacrificiis*.

[6] 1 *Cor.* 10. 20

[7] Aug. *de civ. Dei* 8. 14–22 in particular: a long description in Minucius Felix 26, 27; Tert. *Apol.* 22: See further R. H. Barrow, *Introduction to the de civitate Dei of St. Augustine*, London 1950 pp. 210–18

iv

[1] Cf. *e.g.* Xen. *Cyr.* 3.3.58, Ar. *Pol.* 5.11.25

[2] *de sera*

[3] To him superstition is essentially cowardice. The sketch is not one of his best.

⁴ 2 *Macc.* 2.32

⁵ It is not clear whether this analogy is due to Epictetus, on whom Simplicius is commenting, or to Simplicius himself. John Smith's Essay is given in full in Vol. II of A. O. Pritchard's *Select Essays of Plutarch*, Oxford 1918

v

¹ Patrocleas is Plutarch's γαμβρός. We do not know of any daughter of Plutarch except Timoxena who died young nor of any sister, so that we have no reason to translate as son-in-law or as brother-in-law. But he had a θυγατριδῆ (*Consol. ad ux.*, *ad init.*) which can mean niece; so Patrocleas may have been his niece's husband.

² 7.1, 8.4, 9.2, also in *Amat.*

³ As, *e.g.* the artist of the west window of Fairford Church.

⁴ There are two other myths in Plutarch—in *On the Genius of Socrates* and in *On the face on the circle of the moon.*

⁵ *non posse suav.* 20 sq.

vi

¹ Cic. *Paradoxica*; Sen. *Ep.* 87.1; Cic. *pro Mur.* 61; Epictetus perhaps puts the matter shortly—'progress is turning to your own will and exercising it and making it better by effort'. 1.4.18. The idea runs throughout Seneca.

² or faith or reason?

vii

¹ *Acts* 24.10; 27.22, 25, 36; *James* 5.13. The dating of these books, including Seneca's, is not known for certain.

² *de fin.* 5.29. ut esset bono animo; ἀθαμβίαν; animum terrore liberum.

³ ἱλαρός and γῆθος.

⁴ The Latin translation of the title of Plutarch's treatise is *de tranquillitate animi*, borrowed no doubt from Seneca; though it is in fact difficult to find another similar Latin word, it is misleading to English ears.

⁵ ὑπομνήματα.

⁶ The treatise by Seneca is less convincing. Annaeus Serenus expounds his difficulties in the first part and Seneca replies not very appositely in the second part.

⁷ This expression is adopted for brevity's sake, but it should be interpreted in the sense discussed earlier in the text.

⁸ πρὸς τὸ λοιπὸν ἵλεω τὴν ἐλπίδα καὶ φαιδρὰν ἔχοντες

⁹ Parallels may be collected from H. N. Fowler, *Harvard Studies in Classical Philology*, 1890, pp. 139–52, together with discussion of sources. An early Sam Wellerism occurs in chapter 6. Plutarch has been saying that from the most unexpectedly unfortunate occurrences we may derive benefit.

NOTES

' "Not so bad after all" as the man said who threw a stone at a dog, missed it and hit his stepmother.'

viii

1 The lower part of the fishing line should be a hair from a stallion's tail, says Plutarch–advice given a generation ago to the writer by a Yorkshire fisherman who probably had never heard of Izaac Walton. He too insisted on a stallion's tail but gave no reason; Plutarch does.

2 See the ref. given in the Teubner edition vol. vi, and in vol. xii of the Loeb edition.

3 *Brut. animal*. There are also two short essays on vegetarianism *de esu carnium*.

4 According to Pliny *N.H.* 35. 114 gryllus means: (*a*) a specific comic character, presumably human, named Gryllus, (*b*) a comic picture of this character or, more probably, of anyone. When the pig is called Gryllus, perhaps there is a double suggestion of: (*a*) grunter, esp. as Βοιωτία ὗς, (cf. χοιρογρύλλιος of LXX *Ps*. 104. 18), (*b*) the comic character Gryllus. The articles on P. Oxy. 2331 in *Class Rev.* vii. (new series) 3 pp. 189–92 and *Greece and Rome* vol. 5. (new series) 2 pp. 171–3 do not seem to reckon sufficiently with the possibility that γρύλλος may mean the character and not the picture.

5 See D. R. Dudley, *A History of Cynicism*, London 1937. pp. 69–74

6 σπουδαιογέλοιον Diog. Laert. 9.17

7 *E.g.* 'A man plucked a nightingale and found little meat on it. ' "You are a voice and nothing else," he said.' Hence our 'vox et praeterea nihil'. *Apophth. Lacon. varia* 13

Chapter 10

i

1 *Nic.* 11

2 *Brut.* 47; *Cam.* 13; *Aem.* 22

3 Here he uses the word δαίμων which, as the last sentence of the chapter shows, means 'chance' personified.

4 *Arist.* 6

5 See *e.g.* Cic. *fin.* 2.116, and esp. Livy 9. 17–19. Also, contemporary with Plutarch, Dio Chrys. i–iv, lxiv

6 *Numa* 4

7 With this treatment of Rome *v.* Alexander should be compared the well-known digression of Livy in 9. 16–19, where he gives his reason for thinking that Rome would have won.

[8] Volkman i. p. 45 thinks it was a lecture given in Rome.

[9] The *de fortuna* is merely a set of early notes; the *de fato* is probably spurious.

[10] *Dem.* 19; *Rom.* 1, 8; *Cam.* 6

[11] 1.3-4

[12] 1.63.9

[13] For a treatment of this theme see F. Altheim, *A History of Roman Religion,* Eng. trans., London 1938, esp. pp. 411 *sqq.*

[14] 74

ii

[1] This is sometimes interpreted to mean 3,000 fit men, which is absurd; 3,000 trained soldiers is another matter and need have no bearing on population at all.

[2] Chapters 17-19

[3] 11

[4] *De tranq.* 10

[5] *Praec. ger.* 22.7 *sqq.*

[6] Plin. *Ep.* 10.81, 82

[7] The only evidence that Plutarch and Dio were friendly is: (*a*) a notice of an oration πρὸς Δίωνα in the Lamprias Catalogue; πρὸς is ambiguous; (*b*) Dio was the teacher of Favorinus who was a close friend of Plutarch; but this proves nothing.

iii

[1] The Greek is πρὸς ἡγεμόνα ἀπαιδευτόν; the adjective is hard to translate; it probably includes 'uninstructed theoretically' and 'inexperienced'. The Latin title *ineruditum* hardly hits it off.

[2] Briefly, see J. Kaerst, *Geschichte des Hellenismus* ii (2), Leipzig 1917, E. R. Goodenough, *The Political Philosophy of Hellenistic Kingship,* New Haven 1928, W. W. Tarn, *Hellenistic Civilisation,* 3rd ed., London 1952; M. P. Charlesworth, *Harvard Theological Review,* xxviii, 1, pp. 5-44, 1935; for St. Augustine's 'mirror of princes' perhaps reference may be made to the writer's *Introduction to St. Augustine, The City of God,* London 1950, where there is a fuller outline of the theory of kingship than can be given here.

[3] 6

[4] 1.5

[5] There is an elaborate joke here; *cosmos* = 'order', organisation' and so 'the universe'; *nomos* = 'pasture' and 'law'.

[6] The word is Logos, reason, principles, perhaps ideals.

[7] A clumsy translation, but 'Hellenisation' – itself a barbarous word – does not quite express the meaning.

NOTES

[8] *C.A.H.* vi. p. 437

[9] Probably A.D. 103. The phrase is first used on the coinage of Vindex and Galba, A.D. 68, *salus* no doubt bearing a somewhat restricted meaning; under Trajan the meaning was likely to be broader, but on both coins *humani generis* means the same. So, too, *pax orbis terrarum* occurs on coins of Otho, Vespasian and Titus; whereas on Galba's coins *securitas populi Romani* occurs, in A.D. 189 the phrase is *securitas orbis*.

[10] *Pan.* 8.3–5

[11] 96; 100; 24. For a panegyric on Aristides see M. Rostovtzeff *Social and Economic History of the Roman Empire.*

[12] *Arist.* 6; *Demetr.* 30; See also *de se laud.* 12 *ad fin.*

[13] τὸ τῆς οἰκουμένης ἡγεμονικὸν ἱερόν 9. There are inscriptions from Phrygia and Lydia showing that ἱερός =imperial, applied to the fisc and to 'letters' of Caesar; I. G. Rom. 3.727, 4.571. In the East the word, because used freely, became attenuated in meaning; but it is doubtful if Plutarch, the priest of Delphi, would give anything but its original meaning to the word, namely sacred. See K. Scott, *Plutarch and the Ruler Cult,* Transactions of the Philological Assoc. 1929 (pp. 117–35) (though he does not take matters much further).

Chapter 11

[1] *Dem.* 2

[2] *Platon. Quaest.* 10.3; *Caes.* 50; *Quaest. conv.* 6.5; *Num.* 12

[3] πατρῶνας Rom. 13, cf. Dess. 8832, 8833. οἴνε πατρός οἷον ἄνευ πατρός *Quaest. Rom.* 103. οὐίκους *Luc.* 37–prosecuisset Liv. 5.21.8, Plut. *Cam.* 5.6. There is another alleged mistranslation, viz. Caes. 17 compared with Suet. *Jul.* 53 conditum oleum pro viridi appositum. If μύρον is taken as 'scented or spiced wine', and, if Colum. 12.50 and Cato 117 are taken into account, Plutarch's translation becomes reasonable. A misunderstanding is to be seen in *Cic.* 33 where Plutarch has ὥστε εὖ τοῖς νεκροῖς ὡς τεθνηκότα κείμενον διαλαθεῖν for Cic. *Sest.* 76 seque servorum et libertorum corporibus obtexit.

[4]

Livy 27.27, 28	*Val. Max.* 5.1 Ext. 6	*Plut. Marc.* 29, 30
(Authorities differ about the death of Marcellus, but) 'most record that he left the camp to reconnoitre the position and was surrounded by an ambush.' (28. Hannibal moved his position to the rising	'When Marcellus was reconnoitring the Carthaginians' movements with more zeal than discretion, he was killed; Hannibal granted him a proper funeral; he provided a scarlet cloak and a	'Marcellus decided to ride out and reconnoitre' (The account, furnished with a quotation from Pindar, describes the auspices taken by Marcellus, the hill on which the ambush took

PLUTARCH AND HIS TIMES

Livy 27.27,28	Val. Max. 5.1 Ext. 6	Plut. Marc. 29, 30
ground where the ambush had taken place) and 'then he found the body of Marcellus and buried it'.	gold* crown and laid the body on a pyre.' (*v.l. laurea = of laurel leaves.)	place and continues . . .) 'When Hannibal heard that Marcellus had fallen he ran out to the spot and stood by the body for some time admiring its strength and beauty. He uttered no word of triumph and in his face he showed no sign of pleasure at having killed an enterprising and formidable enemy, but expressed surprise at the unexpectedness of his death. He drew the ring from Marcellus' finger, arranged the body suitably and wrapped it round' and so on.

Again, on the question whether Marcellus ever defeated Hannibal, Plutarch says that Polybius takes one view, 'but we believe Livy, Caesar and Nepos, and of the Greek writers King Juba, and we maintain that Hannibal's troops did suffer defeats and reverses at the hands of Marcellus.' Cf. *Pelop. et Marcell.* 1. Plutarch, as far as we can check him, is correct. Polybius does in fact regard Hannibal as never defeated by Marcellus; Livy records several defeats; of Caesar and Nepos and Juba we can say nothing, for Nepos' lives of distinguished Roman generals is lost and nothing relevant survives of Caesar or Juba.

Another pair of passages may be placed in parallel.

Plut. Cam. 38	Livy 6.25
When Camillus approached them, the Tusculans, cleverly setting right their mistake (*i.e.* in preparing for revolt) filled the fields with men working on the land, as though in time of peace, and shepherding flocks. They kept the gates open and the children doing their lessons in the schools; the artisan element of the population were seen in the workshops busy at their crafts, the better class people in the market-place dressed in their usual clothes.	When the Romans entered their territory, there was no movement of people away from the roads; agriculture was not interrupted: the gates were wide open and people went about in their ordinary clothes in close contact with the generals: supplies for the army were being brought into the camp quietly from the city and the countryside. Camillus pitched his camp before the gates, and, anxious to learn whether there was the same appearance of peace in the city as in the fields, went in and saw the house doors wide open, the shops open and their goods displayed: workmen were busy with their jobs: the schools resounded with the children repeating lessons, the streets were full. . . .

190

NOTES

Some of the picturesque details occur in both accounts and it may well be that Plutarch borrowed from Livy. On the other hand in another pair of passages there is an interesting difference.

Plut. Cam. 6	*Livy 5.22.3*
Livy says that Camillus touched the statue of the goddess (Juno) and called upon her in prayer, while some of the bystanders declared that the goddess was signifying her willing agreement to follow him.	then, when someone, whether touched by some divine inspiration or as a youthful joke, said 'Do you want to go to Rome, Juno?' the rest cried out that the goddess nodded in assent.

The idea of 'touching' in both passages may be due to a coincidence, or Plutarch may be drawing on his memory which retained the idea of 'touching' but confused the context.

⁵ *Att.* 8.7.2; Plut. *Cic.* 37. If he is thinking of *Att.* 7.17.3, he is so careless as to be valueless.

⁶ *An seni* 27; Cic. *fam.* 4.13; Plut. *Cic.* 24

⁷ Cf. Plut. 22, 25 with Hdt. 3.47, and 28 with 7.139

⁸ de *soll. anim.* 21

⁹ *Them.* 27; *Cam.* 19; *Alc.* 32; *Pelop.* 17; *Lys.* 25; cf. further *Lys.* 17; *Cim.* 12; *Dio* 35, 36; *Timol.* 4

¹⁰ In *Sull.*, *Luc.* and *Caes.*

¹¹ A reader who wishes to see samples of such criticism in English may refer to *Classical Quarterly* 1940, p. 1 *sqq.* (R. E. Smith on the sources for *Titus, Paullus, Cato Major*), 1939, p. 1 *sqq.* (Westlake on *Pelopidas*); in the *Journal of Hellenic Studies* he can see how far criticism may go (vol. 59, p. 229 *sqq.* article on the sources of *Life of Alexander* by J. E. Powell); here the conclusion is that Plutarch used two books: (*a*) the letters of Alexander, (*b*) a *variorum* Biography of Alexander in which were collected extracts from at least the twenty-four writers whom Plutarch cites in the *Life.* See also p. 200

Chapter 12

¹ *Ant.* 9

² René Sturel, *Jacques Amyot, traducteur des vies parallèles de Plutarque*, Paris 1908; A. Cioranescu, *Vie de Jacques Amyot*, Droz, 1941; E. Huguet, *Les procédés d'adaptation de Jacques Amyot*, in *Revue du seizième siècle*, xii, pp. 44–77 (1925).

³ Dacier did, among other things, an edition of Horace, now undeservedly neglected; he and his remarkable wife Anne Lefèvre are worth acquaintance.

Epilogue

¹ 12.5

² 1.26; see p. 18

Appendix A

THE SO-CALLED LAMPRIAS CATALOGUE

In the lexicon of Suidas there is the following note, 'Lamprias the son of Plutarch, of Chaeronea, wrote a list (πίνακα) of all his father's writings on the whole of Greek and Roman history (ἱστορίας)'.

'History' must here be used in a broad sense, perhaps 'Greek and Roman studies'.

Some of the manuscripts contain this list, others do not. It contains 227 titles; the list is given in Pauly-Wissowa, *Real-encyclopädie, s.v. Plutarch* 61 (Ziegler) and in Bernardakis vii. 473 (Teubner); the surviving works cover only 83 of these titles. On the other hand 18 of the works which we have are absent from the list (notably the *Quaest. Conv.*): also we know indirectly of 15 works which we have not got and which are not included in the Lamprias Catalogue. The only titles expressly relating to Roman things are lives of Scipio, Augustus, Tiberius, Caligula, Claudius, Nero, Vitellius. Clearly Plutarch was a far more voluminous writer than even his extant works suggest.

In some manuscripts the list is preceded by a letter which has no indication of the writer or the person to whom he was writing. In the past it was assumed on the strength of the Suidas passage that the list was the work of Lamprias, son of Plutarch, and that he wrote an introductory letter; for the writer of the letter explains that he sends, at the request of the unknown addressee, a list of his father's works.

But to this view there are objections.

1. There is no evidence that Plutarch had a son called Lamprias; his grandfather and one of his brothers were called Lamprias.

2. The catalogue is very careless. As we have seen, there are important omissions from the list.

3. The letter is stilted in style. Here is a translation.

I have never forgotten the time we spent together in Asia, nor your enthusiasm for learning, nor your devotion to your friends. And so the moment I received your letter I recognised your name and was delighted to learn that you were well and had not forgotten me. In turn I send you greetings; I have despatched the copy (of the list of?) of my father's writings which you wanted. My good wishes for your health.

Ziegler points out that in the oldest manuscript of the Catalogue, of the

twelfth century, (Parisinus gr. 1678) this letter is missing. He thinks therefore that the letter was a forgery of the 13th or 14th century. Moreover he
regards it as certain that the forgery was modelled on a letter of Pliny (3.5)
to Baebius Macer. 'It gives me great pleasure that you read my uncle's
books with such devotion that you want to have them all and ask what is
included in "all". I will act as a guide and I will even let you know in what
order they were written; for to scholars this too is a welcome piece of
information.' And then he gives a list of the works, with notes.

In both these letters a relative of a well-known writer sends a list of his
works in answer to the request of a correspondent. But otherwise there is
no similarity in language or sentiment, and the Greek letter shows imagination in adding a reference to a previous acquaintance in Asia.

The theory, then, is that a medieval forger, finding a list of Plutarch's
works and knowing Suidas' (or some other writer's) notice that Lamprias,
a son of Plutarch, composed such a list, and recollecting Pliny's letter,
concocted a letter which would explain the reason for the list and give it
authenticity.

The most likely conclusions are:

1. That Suidas is mistaken.

2. That the letter is a forgery, as Ziegler suggests.

3. That there is no reason to assume dependence of the Greek letter on
the letter of Pliny.

4. That the list probably records those of Plutarch's works contained in
some (unknown) library, as Max Treu suggests, in *Der Sogenannte Lamprias-
Katalog*, 1873.

Instead of the letter one manuscript (Ven. 248) has the following note in
Greek, apparently composed by the writer of the manuscript, Joannes
Rhosus.

> In addition to all this (presumably the index of the *Lives*, which im-
> mediately precedes) at some date in the past, as was recorded in some
> ancient book, summaries also of the undermentioned treatises were
> discovered, but they have not been preserved to us, or at any rate only
> the titles. I have not yet come across them anywhere. But for the benefit
> of scholars, so that they may know how voluminous were the works of
> this learned man from Chaeronea, I have here set out their titles.

Then follows the heading 'List of Plutarch's works', followed by the list
itself.

Appendix B

TABLE OF TITLES

Moralia

The text of the book refers to the writings of Plutarch by English titles, the notes by abbreviated Latin titles. The following list sets them in parallel. The Greek title is often very cumbrous, the traditional Latin title aims at brevity. The pages in which the work is noticed at some length are cited: incidental references are not listed.

Ad princ(ipem) inerud(itum)
  To an untrained ruler. p. 139
Adv(ersus) Col(oten)
  Against Colotes. p.82
Amat(orius)
  Treatise on love.
An seni (gerenda respublica sit)
  Should an old man engage in politics?
Brut(a) animal(ia ratione uti)
  On reason in animals. p. 23, 116
Coniug(alia) praec(epta)
  Marriage Precepts. p. 20, 29
Consol(atio) ad ux(orem)
  Consolation to his wife. p. 19
Conv(ivium) sept(em) sap(ientium)
  The Table Talk of the Seven wise men.
De adul(atore et amico)
  How to distinguish between flatterer and friend.
De cap(ienda ex inimicis) util(itate)
  On turning the enmity of others to one's own good. p. 40
De def(ectu or(aculorum)
  On the failure of the oracles. p. 84, 88, 92
De E (apud Delphos)
  On the E at Delphi. p. 32, 84
De esu (carnium)
  On the eating of meat.
De exil(io)
  On exile. p. 146

195

De fac(ie in orbe lunae)
   On the face on the circle of the moon.
De fort(una) Alex(andri)
   On the fortune of Alexander. p. 121
De fort(una) Rom(anorum)
   On the fortune of the Romans. p. 122
De gen(io) Socr(atis)
   On the genius of Socrates. p. 89
De Herod(oti) mal(ignitate)
   On Herodotus' spite. p. 156
De Is(ide et Osiride)
   On Isis and Osiris. p. 28, 83, 84, 89
De poet(is) aud(iendis)
   How the young should listen to poetry. p. 79
De profect(ibus in virtute)
   On consciousness of progress in virtue. p. 41, 103, 105
De Pyth(iae) orac(ulis)
   Why the priestess does not now give oracles in verse. p. 33, 84
De sera (numinis vindicta)
   About those whom the gods delay in punishing. p. 92, 95
De soll(ertia) animal(ium)
   On intelligence in animals. p. 112
De Stoic(orum) repugn(antiis)
   On the contradictions of the Stoics. p. 82, 105
De superst(itione)
   On superstition. p. 91
De tranqu(illitate)
   On tranquillity. p. 40, 108, 152
Non posse suav(iter vivi secundum Epicurum)
   You cannot live a happy life if you follow Epicurus.
Platon(icae) quaest(iones)
   Platonic questions.
Praec(epta) ger(endae reipublicae)
   Precepts of government. p. 132
Quaest(iones) conv(ivales)
   Table Talks. p. 13-16, ch. 3
Quaest(iones) Graec(ae)
   Greek questions. ch. 8
Quaest(iones) Rom(anae)
   Roman questions. ch. 8

APPENDIX B

Lives

The numbers show the place of a life in the traditional order and also the pairs.

7 Aem(ilius)	6 Cor(iolanus)	2 Num(a)
16 Ages(ilaus)	4 Crass(us)	Otho
19 Ag(is)	21 Demetr(ius)	8 Pelop(idas)
6 Alci(ibiades)	20 Dem(osthenes)	5 Per(icles)
17 Alex(ander)	23 Dion	10 Philo(poemen)
22 Ant(onius)	15 Eum(enes)	18 Phoc(ion)
Arat(us)	10 Flam(ininus)	16 Pomp(ey)
9 Arist(ides)	Galba	3 Publ(icola)
Art(axerxes)	19 C. Gracch(us)	11 Pyrrh(us)
23 Brut(us)	19 Ti. Gracch(us)	1 Rom(ulus)
17 Caes(ar)	13 Luc(ullus)	15 Sert(orius)
4 Cam(illus)	2 Lyc(urgus)	3 Sol(on)
9 Cat(o)	12 Lys(ander)	12 Sull(a)
18 Cat(o) min(or)	8 Marc(ellus)	4 Them(istocles)
21 Cic(ero)	11 Mar(ius)	1 Thes(eus)
13 Cim(on)	5 Max(imus)	7 Timol(eon)
19 Cleom(enes)	14 Nic(ias)	

Appendix C

SOME BOOKS

The chief general studies of Plutarch are:

R. Volkman, *Leben, Schriften und Philosophie des Plutarch von Chaeronea*, Berlin 1869

Octave Gréard, *De la morale de Plutarque*, 2nd ed., Paris 1874

R. Hirzel, *Der Dialog*, ii, pp. 124–237, Leipzig 1895

—*Plutarch*, Leipsig 1912 (two-thirds of this book is given to an excellent summary of the later history of Plutarch's works and his influence on European thought and literature, see above, p. 175)

J. J. Hartman, *de Plutarchi scriptis et philosophia*, Leiden 1916

K. Ziegler, *Plutarchos von Chaironeia* in Pauly-Wissowa, *Real-Encyclopädie*

and in English

R. C. Trench, *Plutarch*, four lectures, London 1873

J. Oakesmith, *The Religion of Plutarch*, London 1902

S. Dill, *Roman Society from Nero to Marcus Aurelius*, London 1905 (see the index; a very sympathetic study).

J. P. Mahaffy, *The Silver Age of the Greek World*, Chicago, London 1906

T. R. Glover, *The Conflict of Religions in the Early Roman Empire*, London 1909 pp. 75–112

The bibliography of Plutarch is enormous; older works may be found in Ziegler's article. The following may also be noted; books and articles already cited in the notes are not repeated here.

H. von Arnim, *Plutarch uber Dämonen und Mantik*, Amsterdam 1921

G. Soury, *La démonologie de Plutarque*, Paris 1942

J. Defradas, *Septem sapientium convivium*, Paris 1954

R. Westman, *Adversus Coloten*, Helsingfors 1955 (als philosophie-gesichtliche Quelle).

R. Flacelière, *Amatorius*, Paris 1953

P. Raingeard, *Le περὶ τοῦ προσώπου de Plutarque*, Chartres 1934

L. Parmentier, *Recherches sur le traité d'Isis et d'Osiris de Plutarque*, Brussels 1920

T. Hopfner, *Plutarch über Isis und Osiris*, Prague 1940

V. Cilento *De Iside (etc.)*, Florence 1962

PLUTARCH AND HIS TIMES

The following editions of *Lives* generally discuss the sources.

Budé edition, *Vies*, vol. i Theseus to Numa 1957, vol. ii
Solon to Camillus 1961 (with introduction, text and translation)
A. Garzetti, *Caesar*, Florence 1954
E. G. Hardy, *Galba and Otho*, London 1890
H. A. Holden, *Gracchi*, Cambridge 1885
   —*Sulla*, 1886
   —*Timoleon*, 1889
   —*Themistocles*, 1892
E. Manni, *Demetrius Poliorcetes*, Florence 1952
W. H. Porter, *Life of Aratus*, Cork 1937
   —*Life of Dion*, Dublin 1952
G. Underhill, *Gracchi*, Oxford 1885

In the Loeb edition all the *Lives* have been published in 11 volumes, and 11, out of 15, volumes of the *Moralia* have appeared.

The published portions of the new Teubner text include the *Lives* down to Cicero and five parts of the *Moralia*, published in 1959 and 1960. This edition has a valuable apparatus of parallel passages and refers also to books or articles on a life or a treatise.

Index